OTHER WORKS BY VICTOR PERERA

The Conversion (a novel)

The Loch Ness Monster Watchers

The Last Lords of Palenque:
The Lacandon Mayas of the Mexican Rain Forest
(with Robert D. Bruce)

Rites: A Guatemalan Boyhood

Unfinished Conquest: The Guatemalan Tragedy

EDITOR AND TRANSLATOR

Testimony: Death of a Guatemalan Village,
by Victor Montejo

THE CROSS AND THE PEAR TREE

בס"ד

לזכר עולם לל"ל

אני מצוה צוואת בריא ,מעתה ועד עולם

לבני טובים השנים ,אהרן חיים

פירירא ז"ל ויוסף נסים הי"ו שלום

יוכלו לעקור דירתם, ולא ליקח נשיהם

מירושלים עה"ק לעד לעולם ,בכח תורה

בכח מצות כיבור אוא ובכה

ירושלים נ ח ש עה"ק ובכח גזירת

שלא יוכלו לעבור על המצוה הואת

לעד לעולם ואם יצטרכו לאיזה שליחות

מצוה הם לבדם .יוכלו לילך ולחזור לירושתו

עד ששה חודשים ולא עוד ,ואם שמוע

תשמעו,את אשד אנכי מצוה אתכם שלא

לדור בחו"ל לעד לעולם ,תזכו לכל ברכות התורה

ולמען ירבו ימיכם וימי בניכם ויכו

וכבד את אוא למען יאריכון ימיך

כי בי ירבו ימיך ויוסיפו לך שחיים

ותזכו לעושר לכבוד והיים ובחרת בחיים

ממני עבדי צדזק משה פירירא

ובהקיים כל הנו"ל אני מזחל לכם, בעה"ז ובעה"ב מג

Testament of Yitzhak Moshe Perera, ca. 1921,
detailing a "family curse" that would haunt generations of Pereras

THE CROSS AND
THE PEAR TREE
A Sephardic Journey

VICTOR PERERA

UNIVERSITY OF CALIFORNIA PRESS

Berkeley and Los Angeles

University of California Press
Berkeley and Los Angeles, California

First Paperback Printing 1996

Portions of this book have appeared, in somewhat different form,
in *Commentary, The New York Times, Present Tense, Tikkun,
Antioch Review* and the *Melton Journal.*

Library of Congress Cataloging-in-Publication Data

Perera, Victor, 1934–
    The cross and the pear tree : a Sephardic journey / Victor Perera.
    p.   cm.
    Previously published: New York : Knopf, 1995.
    Includes bibliographical references and index.
    ISBN 0-520-20652-5
    1. Sephardim—History.   2. Pereira family.   3. Jews—Genealogy.
I. Title.
DS134.P47   1996
929'.2'089924046—dc20   96-20172
                                                    CIP

Printed in the United States of America
1 2 3 4 5 6 7 8 9

For all the Pere(i)ras

who have given substance to this chronicle,

Jewish and Gentile, living and dead, sung and unsung

If I forget thee, O Jerusalem . . .

CONTENTS

ACKNOWLEDGMENTS

Among the numerous friends and associates who have contributed to this chronicle, two names stand out: my former professor at Brooklyn College, Mair José Benardete, who first placed the seed of this under-taking in my conscience and taught me to take pride in my Sephardic heritage, warts and all; and Eliyahu Eliachar, who laid down the guidelines for this long journey, which has only just begun, and provided the first glimpses of the treasure trove I would find.

A true chronicle of the adventures, misadventures and accomplishments of the Pere(i)ra clan would fill many tomes, and it was never my intention to do a definitive history. In assembling this book, I have taken the storyteller's license above that of the untrained historian's. I have left many stones unturned on the often tortuous but never insignificant trails blazed by my ancestors. Apart from my immediate family and my direct ancestors—those I was able to trace—I have chosen members of the extended Pere(i)ra family whose lives illuminate important facets of the Sephardic experience. I did not have very far to look for illustrious or reprobate representatives of my clan to flesh out this chronicle, as the Pere(i)ra name contains multitudes.

Once again, I wish to thank my agent, Gloria Loomis, for standing by me during the many seasons of travail and joy that have gone into the preparation of this manuscript. I also thank my English publisher, T. G. Rosenthal, and my editor of long standing, Jonathan Segal, for having the patience of Job.

The Cross and the Pear Tree: A Sephardic Journey was completed with the generous assistance of a Lila Wallace–Reader's Digest Fund Writing Award and several residencies at the Virginia Center for the Creative Arts. I also wish to acknowledge the collaboration of Rabbi Marc Angel of Congregation Shearith Israel and Janice Ovadiah of Sephardic House.

V.P.

THE CROSS AND THE PEAR TREE

INTRODUCTION

WHEN I WAS growing up in Guatemala in the 1940s my mother, who spoke seven languages, often lapsed into Ladino—Judeo-Spanish—the tongue of her ancestors. Like any self-respecting Sephardic Jew born and raised in the Middle East, she had a pungent phrase for every occasion. If I balked at finishing my okra or eggplant, detestable vegetables she persisted in foisting on me because they contained iron, she would snap, *"Manga, ishto, deja ya tus desmodres."* ("Eat, animal, enough of your antics.")

I caught on early that Mother's Spanish was considered odd in our adopted country. Bent as I was on mastering the local idiom in order to gain acceptance as "normal," I had scant appreciation for Ladino, which is a living archive of the wisdom and prejudices as well as the fortunes and misfortunes of our tribe. Mother's borrowing from the Italian *mangiare,* for instance, harks back to our ancestors' passage through Leghorn (Livorno) in the eighteenth century, after they took flight from Spain and Portugal. *Desmodres* derives from a medieval Castilian term—long since fallen into disuse in mainstream Spanish—meaning "immoderations" or "bad manners." (*Ishto* is a vulgar Mayan expletive Mother tacked on for effect.)

A second reason for my distaste for Ladino as a child was Mother's frequent use of it to belittle or curse me. I can still feel the sting of each *"pustema!"* (carbuncle), *"pisgado!"* (deadweight) and *"landra!"* (plague) she flung in my face when she found me in bed and late for school, or engaged in mischief. By comparison, the rare occasions when she called me by my Hebrew name, Haim, and stroked the nape of my neck as she intoned *"los oghos de mi cara"* ("the eyes of my face") or *"mi rey que no me manques"* ("my king may you always be") fell like sunshine on a rainy day. Sadly, Mother despised her sojourn in Guatemala, which she considered an undeserved banishment; the earthy Ladino idiom was a balm to lighten her season of discontent.

Although the antecedents of Mother's Ladino can be found in *refraneros* (phrase books) from Morocco, Yugoslavia and Salonika, where our ancestors tarried, Mother was not above coining her own epithets when the spirit moved her. In the early 1940s, she greeted the horrendous news from Europe by slapping her cheek, screwing up her eyebrows and inveighing, *"Adió! Que se muera Hitler meghor!"* ("Lord, better Hitler should die!")

The gesticulations that punctuated Mother's verbal flights were inseparable from their content, and are impossible to reproduce. Regardless of how many dictionaries or phrase books survive the now-departing—and very likely the last—generation of Ladinophones, the body language and vocal inflections that give Judeo-Spanish its histrionic flavor will be buried with the protagonists, never to return.

When Mother responded to one of my tall tales with *"Etcha otro huevo en la olla, este salió caldudo"* ("Toss another egg in the pot, this one came out soupy"), her sidelong glance and lift of the shoulders conveyed the disdain of one of Solomon's concubines for her rivals. Behind the Sancho Panza wit of many of Mother's gems lurked a biblical heft and resonance, enriched by 2,000 years of exile, resourcefulness and travail.

THE ORIGINS OF Ladino, which also goes under the appellation Judezmo, are rooted in Spain's earliest history. Since Jews almost certainly inhabited the Iberian Peninsula before the birth of Christ, their contribution to the Castilian language is incontestable, and yet almost impossible to assess. Modern Spanish abounds with the Greek, Arabic and Hebrew vocables Jews brought with them to the land they called "Sepharad," following the destruction of the First and Second Temples in Jerusalem, as well as in later migrations from the Levant. (The Castilian honorific "Don," according to the nineteenth-century scholar E. H. Lindo, derives from the Hebrew *Adon,* meaning "sire" or "lord.") Although a good measure of my mother's Ladino was forged in the Diaspora after our ancestors were expelled from Spain, its progenitor was spoken in the *aljamas* (Jewish quarters) of Granada, Córdoba, Sevilla and Toledo.

In the 1490s, the Inquisition and the Expulsion impelled a number of Spanish Jews and Jewish converts—*conversos*—to sign on as crew members on Columbus's voyages. (By one of those historic coincidences redolent with symbolism, Columbus set sail to "discover" the New World the day after the Edict of Expulsion went into effect.) It should surprise no one if assiduous researchers confirm the popular belief that the captains' logs on the *Niña* and the *Pinta* were written in a variant of Ladino. Columbus's own journal, quoted in a spate of

Author and mother, 1936

books timed to the five-hundredth anniversary of his 1492 voyage, was composed in an eccentric, Italianate Castilian my mother would have found perfectly congenial.

Today Ladino has a matchless exotic appeal, particularly among scholars and writers. When I met, on separate occasions, with Jorge Luis Borges and Thornton Wilder, their interest was instantly aroused by my mouthing a few Judeo-Spanish proverbs, which they pro-nounced marvelous. Borges was beguiled by the peculiar intimacy of Ladino diminutives, as in *"El amor es un guzanico que entra por el ojico . . ."*: "Love is a little worm that enters through the little eye. . . ." (The saying concludes, "When it reaches the heart, friend, hold on tight!") Wilder was drawn to the intimations of Kabbala—the compendium of Jewish mystical writings—in proverbs like "The living cannot perform the of-fice of the dead." *("Los bivos no pueden fazer el offizio de los muertos.")*

In the academies, the quincentennial commemoration of the Ex-pulsion sparked an explosion of Sephardic studies unequaled since the Middle Ages. Symposia on Ladino and related subjects are held nearly every year in Europe and in Israel, which is now one of the last outposts of Sephardic culture. The books and Ph.D. dissertations appearing in growing numbers in the United States and Europe reveal that every facet of Jewish life in Salonika, Sarajevo, and Izmir was distilled into proverbs, ballads and epigrams.

Salonika, where my mother's and father's forebears lived before emigrating to Palestine, was the crown jewel of Sephardic culture after the Expulsion, and came to be known as the "Jerusalem of the Bal-kans." Jews have lived in Salonika since 316 B.C., when it was founded by Alexander the Great. After Bayezid II welcomed the ex-pelled Jews to the Ottoman Empire, their numbers overwhelmed the Greek-speaking Romaniot Jews who had dwelt in Salonika since the time of Alexander. Perhaps fourteenth-century Spain had more ye-shivas, but at its height toward the end of the nineteenth century, when the Ottoman Turks still ruled the city, more than half of Salonika's population were Sephardic Jews who attended Sabbath services in no less than sixty synagogues. They collected their own taxes and rents, and ran their own fire, police and sanitation departments. Under the Turks, Jews established their own yeshivas and tried civil and religious cases in rabbinical courts.

The Ladino of Salonika conserved the fifteenth-century regional idioms of Cataluña, Asturias, Galicia and other Spanish provinces.

Portuguese usages became common after the arrival of the first emi-grants from Lisbon, Coimbra and Oporto. Fourteen newspapers and hundreds of books were turned out by the Jews' printing presses; these included Talmudic commentaries and scientific texts as well as books of poetry and dozens of *romanzes*, or novels. Theatrical works were per-formed in Ladino, the rudiments of which even Gentiles had to master if they wished to conduct business in Salonika. Ladino was written in *aljamiado*, or Hebrew script, as twelfth-century Spanish was by learned Jews in Granada and Córdoba, and as Yiddish is still written by East-ern European immigrants today. Later on, religious and temporal works were transcribed in "Rashi," a modified Hebrew script. After a Sabbath evening repast which traditionally included spinach *burrecas* washed down with Turkish raki and white wine, a typical Salonika family would gather to read aloud from the *Me'am Lo'ez*, the fifteen-vol-ume Ladino masterwork that was the Sephardic exile's Bible, *Arabian Nights* and *Poor Richard's Almanack* rolled into one.

Salonika's proverbs attest that Sephardim placed a high value on early marriage—"A house without a woman is a rudderless ship"— and on frugality without avarice—"If you hoard overmuch, you eat decay." They counseled honest dealing: "Lean on a good tree, enjoy a good shade." Too many daughters led to bankruptcy, because of multi-ple dowries: "One daughter, a marvel. Two, in good taste. Three, a bad sign. Four daughters and one mother: a pauper's old age for the fa-ther." Gossip was likened to an early death: "Better to fall in a raging river, than in people's tongues"; "The tongue has no bone, but it can break bones." Bodily functions are constantly alluded to for dramatic effect: "If you come for the kisses, you must stay for the farts"; "Lean too far over, expose your asshole"; "With a boutique under the navel, you die of neither cold nor hunger." On the other hand, there is the stern admonition: "Be neither a whore nor a procuress."

The early Ladino ballads sing of El Cid's heroics against the Moors and the romantic imbroglios of the kings of Aragon and Castile; and they are redolent with the attars of the Alhambra and the Moza-rabic lays and legends it inspired. But in matters of the heart and the purse Spanish Jews were more often, like so many La Rochefoucaulds, tart-tongued and purged of illusions: "Fifty percent of troubles resolve themselves, fifty percent never"; "To learn science, you need wealth"; "Marry for love, live in sorrow." Even in prosperous times, a taint of fatalism, or *malocchio*, colored many proverbs: "Five minutes of happiness, a hundred years of grief"; "Speak the truth, lose a friend"; "If you want it all, you lose the little and you lose the all"; "God delays, but does not forget." Insults ("ill-seated ass!"), diseases ("Don't count your daughter a beauty until she is over the measles and smallpox") and thumbnail appraisals ("A wise man and merchant, a prize for the wife") abound in the proverbs and maxims. Iberian Jews carefully weighed the value of everything and everyone they came into contact with: "God save us from a new tradesman and an old whore" (or, alternatively, a doctor and a fortune-teller). In a treacherous world, the fundamentals alone endure: "A mother's love, the rest is air." ("*Amor de madre, lo demás es ayre.*")

At the turn of the twentieth century, when Sephardim entered Italian or French schools such as those of the Alliance Israélite Universelle, these languages replaced Ladino among the educated Jews of Salonika. But those who emigrated to Palestine, including my father's and mother's forebears, spoke Ladino and Hebrew interchangeably, and my Israeli aunts still do so today. My father's ancestors left Salonika for Jerusalem over a century before 1912, when the Greeks expelled the Turks from Salonika and imposed the Greek language and punitive taxes on the Jews. With the end of Ottoman rule, the Salonika Sephardic community fell into decline, and some 30,000 emigrated to Palestine, France and the Americas.

By 1941, when the Nazis entered Salonika, the Jewish community had shrunk to less than a third of the city's population, but it remained a dynamic and culturally distinct presence. The years of Nazi occupation eerily resembled the opening decade of the Inquisition in Spain four and a half centuries earlier. Salonika's 56,000 Jews were herded into ghettos and forced to wear yellow badges. The community's Ashkenazic chief rabbi was sent to a reeducation camp in Vienna after he delivered an anti-Nazi sermon, and he returned a German collaborator. The comportment of Rabbi Zvi Koretz after his return from Vienna inevitably recalls that of Spanish rabbis who, pressed by the Inquisition, converted and turned their learning in Torah and Talmud against their former coreligionists.

To the mystification of his congregation, Rabbi Koretz remained silent when the Nazis desecrated the Jewish cemetery and removed marble tombstones to line the Nazi officers' swimming pool. Among the headstones rifled was that of my distant cousin Cavalier

Enrico Lopes Perera, a Livornese surgeon of high repute who died in 1895. Rabbi Koretz counseled restraint after a German specialist from Frankfurt made off with tens of thousands of irreplaceable books and manuscripts, none of which were seen again.

The Nazis put Rabbi Koretz in charge of inventorying the community's goods and financial assets to expedite their confiscation when another trainload of Jews was rounded up for transport to Auschwitz. (The rabbi assured his congregants they were being sent to labor camps in Cracow.) And it was almost certainly Koretz who drew up the list of one hundred prominent Jews to be held as hostages by the Nazis. Until the end, when he himself was arrested and put on a train to Poland, Rabbi Koretz persisted in counseling patience and cooperation with the German authorities. Zvi Koretz died in Birkenau a week after the Allies liberated the camp, but his wife and son survived to bear his shame.

By 1945, 54,000 Salonika Jews had been transported to Auschwitz and Bergen-Belsen. It was by far the largest Sephardic community destroyed in World War II. Of the few hundred who survived the concentration camps, nearly all held Italian or Spanish passports.

WHEN MY MOTHER returned to live in Israel in the early sixties, she gave up all traces of modern Spanish and reverted wholeheartedly to the Ladino of her girlhood. She and her older sister Rebecca, who died five years ahead of her, were among the last practitioners of a vernacular that embodied, like the Celtic runes carved on stones in far-flung corners of the globe, the rueful folk wisdom of a wandering people.

Of all Mother's evocations of the remote past, the phrase I shall treasure to my dying day is one she blurted out in a taxi as we traveled from Tel Aviv to Haifa to recite the Kaddish over my father's freshly interred bones.

"*Adió*—" she exclaimed, alarmed by the rising fare on the meter, "*esto mos va' costar lo que costó el higo de Adam Harishon.*" ("This will cost us what the fig cost Adam the First Man.")

Astounded, I ventured to correct her: "You mean apple, don't you, Mother? The Bible says Adam ate an apple."

Narrowing her eyes in a familiar pose of studied indignation, she slammed her open palm on the car seat. "*El ditcho dize higo, e higo fue.*"

("The saying is fig, and fig it was.") Mother's exhumed epithet cor-
rected a popular misreading of the Bible story. The account in Genesis
simply refers to the "fruit of the tree of knowledge," and a fig—or perhaps a pomegranate—is far more likely to be the one intended, as apples
had no part in the Old Testament's Garden of Eden.

CHAPTER I

ISRAEL

What was, what is, the aim of the Alliance? . . . In the first place, to cast a ray of the Occident into communities degenerated by centuries of oppression and ignorance; next, to help them find work more secure and less disparaged than peddling by providing the children with the rudi-ments of an elementary and rational instruction; finally, by opening spirits to Western ideas, to destroy certain outdated prejudices and super-stitions which were paralyzing the life and development of the communities.

—Declaration, Alliance Israélite Universelle, 1860

"WHEN WE LIVED in Montefiore, in Jerusalem, we were poor, but we had no *espanto*, no fears like we do today. We bought our fruits and vegetables from the Arabs, and they bought from us the fruit jams my parents prepared. We moved in and out of the Old City walls like they were our backyard—and in fact that's what they were. Those were the days before the Arabs wanted to push us into the sea."

My Aunt Rachel, youngest of my father's four sisters, has invited me to her apartment in Holon, a suburb of Tel Aviv, to reminisce about the old days. In her mid-seventies, she is a grudging memoirist, and has waited until the eve of my departure to confide some of her sto-ries. Her reluctance is fed by an unbending conviction that her four brothers and an older sister committed a fatal misstep when they emi-grated to the New World. In the mid-1920s my father and two of his brothers opened a department store in Guatemala City, where I was born. Aunt Rachel regards their departure as the source of the calami-ties that befell the family during the next half century. Of the five émigrés, only one is still alive, her youngest brother, Moshe, who to this day runs a shoe store in Guatemala City.

The sad truth is that Aunt Rachel's own fortunes have not been that much better, for all her adherence to family tradition and the patri-arch's injunctions to remain in the Holy Land. Her husband died of a coronary while still in his forties, and her firstborn son met the same fate at about the same age. On top of that, her two daughters have been unable to hold on to a husband; their success as career women cannot re-move the compounded stigma of childlessness and divorce.

Today, in her tidy, pincushion-size apartment, Aunt Rachel seems almost voluble. She recalls that in 1935, when she was in her teens, her eldest brother, Alberto, brought from America the first gramophone ever seen in the Holy Land. (They called it a "pati-phone.") Uncle Alberto played Caruso and Toscanini on his scratchy 78s, to the rapt wonderment of his mother and younger sisters.

"The truth is," Aunt Rachel confesses, "we were poor and terri-bly provincial, and could hardly afford a decent meal, much less luxu-ries like a patiphone. When your grandfather Aharon Haim gave me a piastra for a sweet on my birthday, it was an event. But we lived in peace with our Arab neighbors, and we observed our Sephardic tradi-tions. After my father died in Alexandria, Alberto came to take my mother and the rest of us back to America. But when she overheard him bragging that they conducted business on the Sabbath and no longer kept kosher, my mother put her foot down and refused to leave. My older sister Reina, who was already married with children, Simha, my little brother Moshe and I all stayed behind as well."

I have learned enough family history to ask questions that unlock memories. In 1980 I was invited to a two-month residence at Mishkenot Sha'ananim in the Yemin Moshe quarter of Jerusalem, which my aunt still calls by the name of its founder, Montefiore. After Israel's victory in the 1967 war, Jerusalem's mayor Teddy Kollek renovated the decayed buildings of Mishkenot and converted them into a sumptuous residence for visiting artists and scholars. During my stay there I discovered that I was two short blocks from the house where my father and his seven brothers and sisters had been born. My paternal grandfather, Aharon Haim, and his wife, Esther, had moved there in the 1890s from the Old City, where Aharon Haim's father, Yitzhak Moshe, lived until his death.

With the meteoric rise in property values during the past decades, Yemin Moshe has become gentrified, and now only the most successful artists can afford to live side by side with wealthy Jewish law-yers and businessmen, among them my cousin Avshalom Levy.

"Aunt Rachel," I prod her, "how was it when you were a girl? Can you describe a typical day in your life?"

"I already told you," she says testily. "We were poor but con-tented. The Turks and the Arabs left us alone. The problems began with the British Mandate. I remember, whenever my mother baked bread I would take two loaves to my great-aunt Rivka, who lived alone inside the Old City. I was eight years old, but I walked in and out of the Old City gates without fear. The Arab vendors liked me, and sometimes gave me an orange or a sliver of *halwah*." She shuts her eyes and sighs. "Today that time seems like a dream from another life."

"You say you were poor. How did you survive?"

Aunt Rachel turns on me her sharp-eyed look of reprimand. Her aquiline features and stern brown eyes convey a haughtiness that is only skin-deep. "You think because we had no fancy cars, no mansions and servants like you had in America, that we lived in misery? You think we had no pride? Your grandfather was a *shohet*. Don't you forget it. He butchered livestock and poultry according to the laws of *kashrut*, and he was paid well for it. In the winter he and my mother prepared jams and conserves from figs and other fruits, which they sold in the *shuk*. Our neighbors kept after my mother for her recipe, because their jams were thin and not as sweet as ours. Mother's secret was two spoon-fuls of flour she mixed in with the fruit before she sealed the jar; she con-fided in no one, and the neighbors never suspected.

"My father was highly respected in the community, even by the Arabs. His grandfather, also named Aharon Haim, had been the Sephardic rabbi of Hebron. When we lived in Montefiore, my father held services in the Old City. And then he took it into his head to travel, ignoring his father's admonition not to leave Jerusalem. Before the First World War, Father had traveled to Bukhara, a Russian prov-ince in Central Asia, as a religious envoy, and stayed so long his con-gregation asked him to take a second wife. But he turned them down after his father sent him a stern telegram. In 1922, when I was a small girl, Father sailed to Alexandria, and from there he never returned. He developed a canker sore—they call it 'rose of Jericho'—and as he had no one to look after him there, the canker festered and got worse until it killed him."

"And you think his death was connected to his father's admonition?"

"Only God knows. Your father and uncles also flouted the pro-hibition by traveling abroad. My grandfather's testament was pinned to the wall, but no one heeded it." In 1973 Aunt Rachel and her two older sisters Reina and Simha showed me a framed document be-queathed by my great-grandfather Rabbi Yitzhak Moshe Perera of Jerusalem. In a flowing, prophetic Hebrew he exhorted his sons and grandchildren never to leave the Holy Land without his consent, "from now to eternity": "If ye have need to go abroad on a religious mission then ye shall go alone, and in no circumstances stay away from thine house for more than six months. . . . If ye heed my command not to live abroad from now to eternity, ye shall earn all the blessings of the Torah." Three blessings are enumerated: wealth, honor and a long life. The testament ends: "If ye comply with the above conditions then I, Yitzhak Moshe Perera, Servant of God, forgive thee. . . ."

In the center of the document is the three-letter Hebrew word *Nahash,* or "Snake." In 1992 I learned from an Israeli specialist in such documents that "Nahash" is an acronym for *Nidui, Herem* and *Shamta,* which represent three degrees of excommunication. Evidently my great-grandfather meant business.

"Your grandfather Aharon Haim Perera was the first to break the pledge when he traveled to Bukhara and Egypt," Aunt Rachel reminded me. "He stayed only a few months in Alexandria, and then he died. After that your father and his brothers went to live in America, which my grandfather called 'the land of idolatry.' And look how they ended up."

In 1980 I traveled to Alexandria to retrace my grandfather's footsteps. In the Eliyahu Hanavi Synagogue I found a ledger recording the death of Aharon Haim Perera on January 22, 1923. But none of the surviving elders of the Jewish community remembered him, and I was unable to find his gravestone in the Jewish cemetery. Three years later, Aunt Rachel and one of her daughters traveled to Alexandria, but they had no better luck locating the grave than I had. She concluded that a lonely death and burial in a pauper's grave had been Aharon Haim's punishment for disregarding his father's commandment.

"Aunt Rachel, what was my great-grandfather Yitzhak like?"

"I don't remember. I was too little when he died. But my sister Reina remembers he was tall, had eyes like an eagle and a thick white beard, and always dressed in white. He never smiled."

"Where was he from?"

"I don't remember. I think it was Salonika. Or perhaps that was his father. At that time Salonika belonged to Turkey." I made a quick calculation. Twenty-three years after my great-grandfather Yitzhak Moshe wrote down his testament, the first trainloads of Jews left Salonika for Auschwitz.

Aunt Rachel turns toward me. "I just remembered something about your grandfather Haim." For the first time in my several meet- ings with her, her eyes appear to soften a little. Aunt Rachel's child- hood years are the only ones in which she remembers having known happiness.

"The best time was the New Year, Rosh Hashanah. That's when he had the most work. On the eve of Yom Kippur neighbors brought him their poultry, and he performed a *kapara* [sacrificial cere- mony]. He raised the chicken or goose by both feet and swung it over its owner's head, reciting a *berachah* [blessing]. Afterward they gave him part of the slaughtered chicken—the liver or breast, or a whole drum- stick. The next day we broke the fast with our richest meal of the year.

"Of the older generation, the one I remember best was my mater- nal grandmother, Rachel, who married David Pizanty. She had named me herself, and so I was her favorite." The color rises to Aunt Rachel's cheeks. The hard lines dissolve. She is a small girl once again. "When I was little, she used to sit me beside her and smile naughtily. Although nearly ninety, she was a large, handsome woman with long silver hair that she combed every evening before she went to bed.

" 'We were *maderos*—"sticks"—when we were young,' she would say in Ladino. 'We knew nothing of the world, nothing. I was promised to your grandfather when I was twelve, and I knew nothing, nothing at all. But he was a handsome boy of fifteen, a little pale from too much study. His father was as strict as your grandfather Yitzhak, and he went to prayers every day. I learned his hours, and knew exactly when he would pass in front of our garden on his way to the synagogue. I would climb on the swing in time for the wind to lift my skirts just as he walked by, so he would look in and catch a glimpse of my white britches. That way, he would arrive at prayers with his cheeks aflame, and I knew he was mine.' "

Aunt Rachel dissolves into laughter, her cheeks flushed by the memory as her grandfather's had been by the sight of her grandmother's britches more than a century and a half ago.

II

In December 1989 I arrive in Israel to look after my eighty-six-year-old mother, who is dying of old age. This is my fifth visit with her since she

and my father moved back to the Holy Land in 1960. Two years earlier, my father had sold his share of the department store in Guatemala
City to his younger brother, Isidoro, known to his sisters as Nissim. Father died of a heart attack at age sixty-three, four months after returning
to his place of birth. My aunts and cousins tell me that he died at peace,
reconciled with the patriarch Yitzhak Moshe and his harsh posthu-
mous judgment on his male descendants.

The discovery of my great-grandfather's testament had struck me
with the force of revelation, just as my aunts had intended. Among
other things, that parchment helped me begin to understand the tangled
motives behind the sacrificial rites that Father had performed on himself
and on me, starting with the day of my birth. Upon his arrival in the
New World, Father turned his back on the religious observances of his
forefathers. He resolved to slough off his inheritance and become a man
of the world—a conversion, I was to discover, that has ample precedent
in my family. Nearly all the Pereras (or Pereiras) in my ancestry have
been either rabbis and Talmudic scholars or successful men of business,
with a high percentage of crossovers. But that is for later.

When I was born in Guatemala City, Father ignored the standard practice in the Jewish community of sending for a *mohel* from
Mexico; instead he had me circumcised by a gentile doctor who cut my
foreskin with a book open at his side. When an Istanbuli rabbi was
hired by the community five years later, he learned of my unclean circumcision and persuaded my father that I should undergo a proper *brit,*
which the rabbi would perform himself. I have described that second
circumcision—and my father's role in it—in a memoir that I began
long before I had any inkling of my great-grandfather's testament.

Father, a lifelong Zionist, had studied and taught the Talmud in
Jerusalem. In hindsight, I can only surmise that he somehow hoped to
atone for his dereliction by putting an end to the Perera male line, embodied in myself. But the symbolic castration, although it scarred me
psychologically, failed to achieve its purpose. When I reached maturity,
I came to the conclusion that I had been the victim of double jeopardy.
As the firstborn son of a descendant of Yitzhak Moshe Perera, I was
condemned to excommunication by virtue of having been sired by my
father in the land of idolatry. By being born in Guatemala, I was rede-
fining original sin.

On the other hand, civil law in a democratic society states that you cannot be punished twice for the same offense and so, rather than confirm me as a Jew, that second circumcision gave me license to renegotiate my forefathers' covenant with Yahweh. As I delved into my roots, I conceived an affinity with Pere(i)ras who had converted to Christianity to escape the Inquisition, only to reconfront their Jewish-ness after they fled from Spain and Portugal.

In later years I took an ironic revenge on Father by saving his life on two separate occasions: The first time was when he suffered a stroke; the second followed his first coronary. My pious aunt Simha, who wor-shipped Father, firmly believed I became an instrument of God's design to fetch him back in one piece to the Holy Land and assure him proper burial in the sacred ground of his ancestors.

Whenever I questioned Mother about my second circumcision, she invariably placed all the blame on Father. "I pleaded with him to send for a *mohel* when you were born, but he was intent on adopting modern ways. The second time, I entreated him day and night not to scar you again; but he was immovable, like stone. Rabbi Musan lec-tured him on Talmudic law, which he had sworn to uphold. He said you were a heathen, and only a proper *brit* could make you a Jew. My tears and supplications were in vain."

From my earliest awareness I had a sense of my mother as an un-stable, egotistical woman who used me as a foil for her romantic fanta-sies. I did not believe in her tears and supplications to prevent my second branding. But following Father's death another side of Mother's personality surfaced unexpectedly. I would discover that she possessed a more sturdy, expansive self—a second bloom—that had lain dormant during her unhappy bondage in Guatemala.

Like Father, to whom she was a blood relation, Mother had been nurtured in a patriarchal religious tradition. Her father, Shmuel Nissim, had been a Jerusalem rabbi and a *shohet,* and a rival to Aharon Haim Perera. In 1973 my cousin Malka, eldest daughter of my mother's elder brother Jacob, took me inside the four underground Sephardic synagogues of Ben Zakkai, in the Old City. She pointed to the restored *bimah,* or raised altar, of the Istanbuli synagogue, the largest of the four, where our grandfather Shmuel Nissim had held prayer ser-vices. My paternal grandfather, Aharon Haim, and *his* father, Yitzhak Moshe, had led Shabbat services in the adjacent and far smaller Middle Synagogue. Like his cousin Aharon Haim, Shmuel Nissim was restless and ambitious, and traveled to Russia as a religious emissary. He arrived in Samarkand, where he was warmly received by the city's thriving Sephardic congregation, which invited him to become its head rabbi. Rabbi Nissim summoned his family to Samarkand, where Mother, her two sisters and older brother spent their early years. Around 1913, when Mother was seven, he sent them all back to Jerusalem, with the promise that he would soon follow. But World War I and Lenin intervened, and my grandfather could not get out. His congregation persuaded him to take a second wife, with the approval of the Beit Din, or rabbinical court of Samarkand; the Beit Din ruled that the marriage would be annulled the moment he was free to return to his first family in Jerusalem.

Grandfather was as good as his word. At war's end he left his second wife and two children behind and set out for the Holy Land. He traveled in a train crammed with Russian soldiers in the middle of a cholera epidemic. Grandfather caught the plague and died in a remote village in the Ukraine. He was buried in a common grave with hundreds of Russian soldiers who never came home from the front. Mother's brother Jacob traveled to the Ukraine to say Kaddish over Grandfather Shmuel's remains and to collect his prayer books and prayer shawl from the custodian of the cemetery. Like Aunt Rachel and her younger brother Moshe, Mother would grow up without the guidance and solace of a father.

Grandfather Shmuel's death when Mother was a young girl left her with a profound grievance against the world, an ineradicable sense of bright expectations forever dashed. "If my father had lived, I would have had a proper dowry, and another rooster would crow for me," she used to tell me, unmindful that if she had married another suitor, I would never have been born.

Following Father's death, Mother at last appeared to come to terms with her life. Her thirty years in the Americas gradually receded from her memory. She all but forgot her Guatemalan vernacular and went back to conversing in the Ladino she had known as a girl. She moved into a small apartment in Ramat Gan, two blocks from the flat of her widowed older sister Rebecca, who had been the rival beauty in the family. At fiftythree Mother was still a vivacious, attractive woman. But although she was not too old to remarry, she remained single, indulging in occasional flirtations with widowers and older married men.

． ． ．

WHEN I STAYED with Mother in the aftermath of the October 1973 war, she spent much of her time watching television and baking the Sephardic Middle Eastern dishes she loved: cheese and spinach *bur-recas,* carp in gelatin, ground-meat *kubes* and her favorite almond marzi-pan and other sweets. After the late news on TV she sat in the dark for a long time, sighing heavily.

"This war has had a bad effect on me," she would say, staring at her gnarled hands. "Morally."

Her grandnephew Oded, the firstborn son of her firstborn brother Jacob's firstborn son Moshe, had been killed in action in the Suez. Oded, of whom great things had been expected, was the first member of our family to be killed in one of Israel's wars. He would not be the last.

In the afternoons Mother visited her sister. Aunt Rebecca had spent her youth and middle years in Egypt, and returned to Israel with her husband and two sons after the establishment of the state. She had been a widow for nearly twenty years.

"How did you like Golda last night?" Mother would ask at the door, and they proceeded to discuss the prime minister's latest speech in the Knesset, the color of her dress, the type of handbag she carried.

"It was green, the size of a shopping bag," Aunt Rebecca re-membered, although she could not be certain because the image on her TV screen kept jumping.

"She's going shopping in the Knesset," Mother said, laughing aloud. "What a brave old lady," she added, shaking her head in admi-ration. "She flies around the world, telling everybody off, and she's al-ready seventy-five. I'm only sixty-seven, and look what it costs me to cross the street." She showed Aunt Rebecca her swollen ankles.

Golda Meir was the only Ashkenazic Jew my mother and Aunt Rebecca wholly approved of.

Afterward they talked of their children and grandchildren, the latest movies on TV, the dishes they had planned for the week. When they got around to the war and Oded, they began to sway and moan softly.

"*Qué negradea, qué negradea,*" my aunt said. "What a blackness. I knew him as a baby. He lived in my house a whole year when he was two." She wiped her eyes and pressed her chest to calm her heart.

"And poor Moshe," Mother said. "Alone in the family without his firstborn. It is all on his shoulders now." They did not speak of Nehama, Oded's mother, whom they regarded as proud and head⁄strong, a regrettable mistake. "With all the attractive Sephardic girls in Israel," Mother remarked when I first arrived, "Moshe had to go and marry a stuck⁄up German intellectual. She gives him no peace."

Aunt Rebecca brought us tea and sweets.

"No, no tea for me today," Mother said. "When I am in a state like this, tea swells my intestines."

Aunt Rebecca nodded sympathetically and drew her shawl tight. "I can't have tea either. My heart pounds all night. It has been black, black like my star—*como la estrella mía*—since the news of Oded." In hard times Aunt Rebecca's thoughts invariably returned to Alexandria.

"We were so happy there," she says, as her eyes roll toward the ceiling and her face lights up. "We had live⁄in servants, a wonderful old villa, the best French schools for my two sons, and the oranges—ah, the oranges were large and golden, like the sun. . . ."

I stayed on with Aunt Rebecca when my mother went shop⁄ping. She poured more tea and watched me eat her clover⁄shaped mar⁄zipan. When I finished she smiled girlishly and rubbed her hands. "Better than your mother's, no?"

The following day I escorted my mother and Aunt Rebecca to the home of their grandnephew Oded. Moshe, his wife, Nehama, and their fourteen⁄year⁄old son, Ofer, live in a spacious home in Ramat Hasharon, a fashionable Tel Aviv suburb. Moshe is a communi⁄cations expert in the Israeli Army and makes several times the salary of his postal⁄worker father, Jacob. I had last seen them in New York City, where Moshe was on a tour of duty. In Flushing I had attended the bar mitzvah of Oded, who was a rail⁄thin, intense youngster with extraordinary black eyes. After his high⁄school graduation, Oded had returned to Israel to enlist in the army. He was one of the first⁄born sons in our extended family who kept faith with the patriarch's commandment.

Nehama, a sabra of German and Lithuanian parents, has light skin and blue eyes. She looks more beautiful—and prouder—than I re⁄member. She greets me with a smile and a firm handshake. "Forgive me," she says. "I do not yet know how to show grief. I will learn." She holds her head high as she sits Mother and Aunt Rebecca in the far sofa, and immediately begins to speak of Oded.

Oded, she says, died in a commando operation south of the Bar-Lev line on the fifth day of battle. He was a captain in the reserves, hav-ing served his regular army duty two years earlier. Still, he had volunteered for four missions and insisted on going on the fifth, a diver-sionary maneuver that would be the most dangerous.

She brings out photographs and a newspaper account of the bat-tle, which is officially named "Battle of the Shades." Oded's intense black eyes look out from every photo.

Aunt Rebecca begins to sway and moan softly, but she is stopped by a sharp look from Nehama.

"Oded had to be first, always," Nehama says, addressing me. "He had always a very strong drive to excel. The day after he died, a scorecard arrived from the university, where he had studied engin-eering." She pauses, fighting back tears. "He had scored a perfect ten. . . .

"His strong competitiveness is partly my fault, I suppose," she says in a softer voice. "I have always been very strongly competitive, and I'm afraid I transferred much of it to my sons. I wanted Oded to be per-fect. Not just good or very good, but perfect."

I look once more at the photos of Oded and feel drawn irresisti-bly into the myth-making process. I sense that the soul of all Israel is in this house.

I am still looking at photos when Moshe returns from the syna-gogue, where he has been saying Kaddish for Oded. The moment he walks in, Aunt Rebecca and Mother give vent to their grief.

"Qué negradea, qué negradea," they wail antiphonally, swaying from side to side. "It is not worth the pain to raise children and grandchil-dren," Aunt Rebecca says, "only to have them killed in the wars."

As we embrace, I feel on Moshe's shoulders the accumulated weight of our rabbinical ancestors. Haggard and stooped, he slumps into a chair and begins to speak of the war, slowly, in a thin voice. "In this war we have lost the flower of Israel's youth; a whole generation has been maimed and killed. We have paid a terrible price for our unpre-paredness. It was not American pressure that kept us from protecting our borders; it was our arrogant assumption that the Arabs would not dare attack us again after '67."

He raises his voice. "It is written that the guardians of Israel can-not sleep, day or night. The Maccabees knew this, and the Zealots on Masada knew it also when they fought the Romans and destroyed themselves rather than be taken as slaves. Israel has always known war. The longest peace in this land lasted seventeen years, between the death of David and the later years of Solomon's reign."

"They are all our enemies now," interjects Nehama. "Everyone is against Israel. Look at Africa, where we invested so much money and technical assistance. We helped to bring them into the twentieth century, and they repay us by breaking relations with us. Well, let them go, let them all go. I say good riddance to them and all other fair-weather friends. Israel will survive without them."

"The Jews are always alone," Moshe says. "When they forget their traditions, tragedy results. This war is a punishment on Israel for its unpreparedness, for its excessive confidence and for the greed and materialism that were growing among our people. When Jews leave the path and forget their prophetic destiny, they find ways to bring about their own destruction."

Nehama agrees about the greed and materialism, but recasts it in her own terms. She is a disillusioned supporter of Golda Meir's Labor party. "This war has come in the middle of a wave of tremendous cor-ruption," she says. "Everyone has gotten rich almost overnight, but they want more, always more. There is no more real parliament in this coun-try. The Knesset has been taken over by power-mad, corruptible old men. Right now the young still do not have a voice in Israel's govern-ment. After peace is made this will be the main thrust of reform. The young soldiers who fought for this country will demand to be repre-sented. When this happens, then Oded's death will begin to have some meaning for me."

Moshe looks at Nehama in silence as she gives in to tears at last. I feel the close bond of love between them, and also the rivalry—a com-petition between two ways of grieving, two ways of seeing the world, Sephardic and Ashkenazic. I look down once more at the extraordi-nary black eyes, the fine light-brown skin and firm set of the jaw in all the photos of Oded, and I see in them the two forces that shaped mod-ern Israel.

Moshe gets up to pace the floor. "What is it about this piece of earth?" he asks, absorbed in Old Testament language and imagery. "What is it that made these young men burn and fight, burn and fight again? Where did they get the courage? I love my Oded, but I know he is no different from ninety-nine percent of the young men of Israel's army. They all want peace. They don't like to fight, but if their country is endangered they will not hesitate to die in its defense. Oded—" he says, sitting down. "My son Oded went to his death as if it were an important appointment." He buries his head in his hands.

III

When I next visit Mother in 1980 I find her calmer than she was on my previous visit, although her morale has still not recovered from the October war and its aftershocks. She has become obsessed with the Ayatollah Khomeini.

The night of my arrival she sets before me a heaping plate of boiled lamb and rice. "See? I serve you meat," she announces proudly, as if we were back in the Palestine of her girlhood, when meat was a luxury.

Mother spends most of her days and her flagging energies preparing for hard times, though she has inherited a nest egg of hard-earned dollars from my father. In the evenings she rehearses her old age, sitting for hours in her cozy chair, bemoaning her faded beauty, the price of milk and eggs, her aching bones and her unlucky star. *"Como la estrella mía,"* has become her yardstick for the world's calamities. She watches both Arabic and Hebrew newscasts, so she can sigh *"Dios mío"* twice over and click her tongue. Her favorite is the weekly Ladino radio newscast, whose soft-voiced announcer consoles her by treating *"Las locuras de Khomeini"* ("the antics of Khomeini") as the aberrations of a demented distant relative who will sooner or later be put to rights. The down-to-earth Ladino idiom creates an illusion of continuity ("this too will pass") by reducing global crises to the dimensions of Mother's living room.

In 1980 Mother rarely visited Aunt Rebecca, who was seventy-six and in failing health. Mother lived for her grandson, Daniel, my sister's only child, who was seventeen and had grown up in Kibbutz Beit Oren, outside Haifa. Daniel would soon be subject to the Israeli military draft, although he was born in the States and has retained his U.S. citizenship. Before long he would have to decide whether to join the army or return to California, where his mother lives. My sister has spent the past fifteen years in a halfway house in Santa Cruz, recovering in slow stages from a severe mental illness that struck her down in her youth. When Daniel was three Mother brought him to Israel because my sister was no longer able to care for him.

"Take Danny with you," Mother urged me every morning. "I don't want him killed in the next war, like Oded."

By evening she had changed her mind. "No, Danny belongs here with me. He is an Israeli now, and America would spoil his sweet temper. Why, he can hardly even speak English."

Which was true. Daniel, a tall, strapping young man who loves riding the kibbutz horses and is a long-distance runner, seems in many ways more a sabra than his sabra cousins. He is a nurturer who cut his eyeteeth on caring and cooperating rather than on competing. I could picture him one day as a first-rate veterinarian. On the other hand, when I tried to envision him in the Israeli Army, in another war, my mind drew a blank. The fate of Oded was too vivid.

Mother's return to her origins has honed her storytelling skills. For the first time, she speaks of the hard times in the Holy Land during World War I. "The happiest years were before the war, here and in Russia with my father. When I was small I had two grandmothers to pamper me; my grandfather Jacob's first wife, Rivka, was barren, and under Jewish law he was permitted to take a second wife to bear his children. Rivka was the kindest person in our family. Having no children of her own, she spoiled all of us with affection and frequent small gifts. Your great-uncle Yehuda Burla, who became a famous writer, wrote of my grandfather and his two wives in his story *Two Women*. At that time I thought our happiness would last forever. Although we were not rich by any means, we got by well enough. In Russia we were well treated by the Jews of Samarkand, who held my father in high esteem. Then the war came, my father stayed behind and died in Russia, and nothing has ever been the same again."

I ask her how they managed to survive during the war.

"The post office. My brother Jacob landed a job in the post office at Mount Tabor, and when I was sixteen they hired me as a mail sorter. The postmaster was a tall, kindly Britisher who complimented me on my excellent English. At sixteen, I already spoke seven languages, including Russian and Arabic. Jacob was married with two children and had mouths of his own to feed, so my small salary went for feeding my mother and sisters as well as myself. At an age when I

Tamar Nissim in Jerusalem Post Office, ca. 1924

should have been enjoying life, entertaining beaux and preparing my trousseau, I was the family's provider."

She showed me a photograph of the family taken after the war. The two beauties, Mother and Aunt Rebecca, stand erect and tall at opposite ends. Rebecca's right hand rests on the shoulder of her older brother. Uncle Jacob, who was to die in his sixties, looks care-worn and middle-aged, although he was not yet thirty. Mother's tresses nearly reach her waist. Their mother, Rachel, seated below, gazes sadly into the distance, her dignity intact. Between Mother and Aunt Rebecca stands Aunt Leah, not yet twenty, with steel-rimmed glasses and long black hair combed back behind her ears like a spinster's. My aunt Leah, who never married, would die of cancer in her early thirties. Mother seldom spoke of Leah, who lacked the cameo beauty of her older sisters and dressed in mourning black for most of her adult life.

"Leah became a victim of that terrible time," Mother acknowl-edges matter-of-factly. "We had so little to eat, a few crusts of bread and a fistful of potatoes or green beans. Mother boiled them with lots of salt to deceive our palates. But our stomachs were not deceived, and we went to bed hungry." Mother gazes at the ceiling, sorting out the images flickering before her eyes.

"Even after I started sorting mail at the post office we never had enough to eat. Mother and Leah were unaggressive, but Rebecca and I always got our share. If there were only two crusts of bread, Rebecca and I divided them between us." She reaches a thin, bony hand across the table and snatches at an invisible crust of bread. "Leah died of can-cer brought on by vitamin deficiency. She had no iron in her blood. My mother also died years before her time. She was undernourished, but it was the sorrow that killed her."

Mother sighs, hunched low over the table by the dowager's hump that would twist her body within a few years into the gnarled shape of a Gethsemane olive tree. "In the end we did not get enough iron either, Rebecca and I, and that is why our bones are so brittle." ("Iron, animal!" Mother would scream in Guatemala, shoving a fork-ful of spinach into my mouth. "It's full of iron!")

Tamar Nissim and family, ca. 1924

The early deaths of her mother and younger sister were not the only shadows cast over Mother's years in the Americas. She told me of another brother, Natan, who was born two years before her and died long before the family picture was taken.

"Of malnutrition?" I asked in consternation.

"No, of the *ayin hara.* He was a very pretty boy, and the neigh-bors cast the evil eye on him."

IV

In 1973 and again in 1980 I met with Dr. Eliyahu Eliachar, cofounder and vice president of the prestigious World Sephardic Federation and president for years of Jerusalem's Sephardic Council. Dr. Eliachar, a tall, aristocratic octogenarian whose family has lived in Jerusalem for eighteen generations, at first reacted skeptically to my proposal to write a chronicle of the Pere(i)ras. At the time I had only begun to probe the family tree, and the patriarchal legacy that had haunted the lives of my father and his brothers.

"You are evidently an educated, intelligent person," Dr. Elia-

Tamar with friend in Palestinian dress, ca. 1925

char remarked acerbically, "but in terms of understanding your ances-try, you are still in swaddling clothes. You come from a distinguished family with deep roots in Jerusalem, and you know next to nothing about them."

Having put me smartly in my place, Dr. Eliachar went on to ex-pound in his elegant English on the erosion of the Sephardic communi-ties in Israel and throughout the world. "The fate of the Sephardim may well be decided in Israel within your lifetime. The problem is most acute here, for we comprise well over fifty percent of Israel's population. The tragic reality is that we are losing not only our religion but our cul-tural cohesiveness, and to a large extent we have only ourselves to blame. We have permitted ourselves to be exploited by unprincipled Ashkenazic leaders who turn us against one another by playing on our feelings of inferiority."

Dr. Eliachar denounced the efforts of Israel's first prime minister, David Ben-Gurion, to prevent what he called the "levantinization" of Israel by segregating the North African and Oriental Jews from the Eastern Europeans and the established Sephardic families. "Most of the Iraqis and the Moroccans never lived in the Iberian Peninsula, and they do not speak Ladino," Dr. Eliachar conceded, "but they are our blood brothers all the same. The sad truth is that we too have our 'Uncle Toms'—Sephardim who give lip service to solidarity with the North African and Oriental Jews but have sold their souls to the state. Unfor-tunately, your great-uncles Yehuda Burla and Nissim Ohanna, who was chief Sephardic rabbi of Haifa, fall into this category. They became leading spokesmen for the state's discriminatory policies. The Ash-kenazim have come to me as well, offering me laurels, pensions and whatnot. I tell them, 'I don't need your honors. I distribute them.'

"Our present decadence," Dr. Eliachar continued, with his silken inflection, "began a hundred and twenty years ago when the Al-liance Israélite Universelle, an international Jewish body based in Paris, began to erect elementary schools—lycées—all over the world. They were established with the best of intentions, to help raise the standard of living in poor Sephardic communities. Under the guise of eliminating centuries of Oriental superstition and backwardness, however, the Alli-ance did irreparable damage to our Sephardic traditions and customs. Throughout the Middle East and North Africa, lycées began to super-sede and replace the yeshivas, which had provided not only excellent religious training but a sound secondary education. These yeshivas were the backbone of our Sephardic identity. Many of our brighter young men, who formerly would have gone on to rabbinical studies, contented themselves with elementary schooling in these lycées and then went on to white-collar occupations to earn money for their families. This, in essence, is what befell your father's and mother's generation in Jerusalem."

His introductory lecture over, Dr. Eliachar pulled from his bookshelf a biographical dictionary of illustrious Jerusalemites and thumbed through it, picking out Pereras and Pereiras who had made their mark in the Holy Land over the centuries. There were Kabbalistic rabbis, noted scholars, and Abraham Israel Pereira, a Dutch Marrano businessman and author who had founded yeshivas in Jerusalem and Hebron in the seventeenth century without ever setting foot in the Holy Land.

"These are only the tip of the iceberg," Dr. Eliachar assured me. "To get the full story you will have to dig into the Inquisition archives of Portugal, Spain, Holland and the New World. Your great-great-grandfather came here from Salonika, whose Sephardic community, as you know, was all but exterminated by Hitler. But your roots here go back much farther. To find them, you will have to go back to the beginning and work your way to the present. In the process, you may be able to find the link connecting the Dutch Pereiras, who were Marranos, or secret Jews, with the Portuguese Pereiras who are your direct ancestors. I suspect you will find ancestors who played a role in the Sephardic Golden Age in Spain. You will also have to discover your ancestral Jewish name before the Inquisition foisted on your family the name Pereira, and engraved the pear tree on your family escutcheon. Once you have dug up your original Jewish name, you can trace your origins prior to the Iberian Peninsula, possibly all the way back to the Twelve Tribes. It should be an interesting journey, and one full of surprises. I wish you the best, and do keep me posted on your progress." Dr. Eliachar rose stiffly to shake my hand, signaling an end to our interview.

As he showed me to the door, I presented him with a photocopy of Yitzhak Moshe Perera's testament. Dr. Eliachar's impeccable composure faltered, and his face paled. "I have written a similar document for my sons," he said.

Eliyahu Eliachar died two years later. His widow, Hava, a stately Russian Jew imbued with Dr. Eliachar's patrician dignity as well as his dry humor, is carrying on her husband's life work. At our first meeting she offered to make his extensive library available to me. And then she voiced regret that their two sons had emigrated to America, and showed little interest in family history. Dr. Eliachar's sons had, it seems, disdained their father's testament as resoundingly as my grandfather had evidently ignored his father's.

V

Aunt Rebecca, who lived with her elder son Morris, died of cervical cancer in 1987. Two years later my mother moved to a state nursing home in the heart of Ramat Gan. Her sister's death deepened Mother's despondency, which never left her after the death of Oded. Israel's invasion of Lebanon in 1982 had soured Mother on Menachem Begin, who had been favored by most Sephardim. She switched her loyalties to David Levy, Begin's Sephardic housing minister, who later became foreign minister under Yitzhak Shamir, although he speaks hardly a word of English.

In 1989 a second tragedy struck an enlisted young man in our family, this time on my father's side. Eighteen-year-old Boaz, a tall, gangly grandson of Aunt Simha, was killed in a car crash during a weekend leave from his army posting on the West Bank. The story made all the papers after his seventeen-year-old girlfriend, who announced that she had no desire to live without Boaz, was killed a week later in an automobile accident in Eilat. Boaz, a Peace Now supporter, had been a prison guard in the Gaza camp of Jebaliyah, a bitter experience that had poisoned his sympathy for the Palestinians.

"All the best of our young men are dying," Mother remarked when I informed her of the death of Boaz. Mother had been close to Aunt Simha and her children, the only family members on Father's side who continued to show an interest in her.

At the nursing home Mother declared, "I have grown old *en un dos por tres,*" a Ladino phrase that roughly translates as "in a trice." Arteriosclerosis was clouding Mother's memory, and her dowager's hump had caused her frame to shrink several inches. During her last year of life, she weighed less than she had as a twelve-year-old girl, and stood no taller. Still, her spirits rallied whenever Daniel or I came to visit, and although she was by no means the youngest, she was by all accounts the liveliest resident of the home.

When Daniel and I were both abroad, her most frequent visitor was her nephew Morris, a sixty-year-old bachelor who had transferred his nurturing vocation from Rebecca, his mother, to his last living aunt. "She is the last of her generation," Morris reminds me without reproach as he presents Mother with *burrecas* and her favorite sweets. Mother returns his favors by calling him a prince and "my salvation." She made a point of complimenting Morris whenever Daniel and I were in the room. And she invariably greeted me with the rebuke, "Why can't you be more like your cousin Morris?"

Childhood stories poured from my mother with the least encouragement. The color rose in her emaciated cheeks, and her hands moved with a life of their own. Although her eyes were clouded with rheum, she could still peer into space to snatch at a memory and render it marvelously whole. Her favorite childhood recollection was the voyage to Samarkand, when she stayed on deck for hours on end. *"Bailaba y bailaba sin pena ni verguenza,"* she would say. ("I danced and danced without guilt or shame.") The ship's captain, as Mother tells it, was so smitten by her that he wanted to buy her, and actually quoted her mother a price.

Toward the end of her second year in the nursing home, Mother's sclerosis worsened, and her spirits declined markedly. She complained constantly of bad food and of surly nurses who stole her dentures. When someone in the ward screamed, Mother invariably remarked, *"está pariendo"* ("she's giving birth") even if the scream came from a man. Mother prayed to God to deliver her from old age as she had once prayed to be delivered from Guatemala. "Why doesn't He take me? I have no teeth, my eyes are gone, and I have to be wiped clean like an infant. I am ready for the rabbi to give me the blessing."

One morning she accused an Arab orderly of having raped the nine-year-old granddaughter of her roommate, a senile Polish woman who spoke no Hebrew. And yet the Palestinian was the only male nurse she would allow near her after dark to change her underclothes and tuck her into bed. Mother's ambivalence toward Arabs is a family trait. She loved to watch Egyptian films on Jordanian TV, and she fondly recalled her childhood expeditions to Ein Kerem, outside Jerusalem, where the Arab residents invited her to pick oranges from their trees.

On the evening news Mother learned of Saddam Hussein, and he soon replaced Khomeini as her favorite monster. Mother assured the Iraqi nurse who served her dinner that Saddam was a new Hitler who would never rest until he had destroyed Israel. "He has no pity," she said aloud to anyone who would listen, "no pity at all." It would have amused her to know that President George Bush—among others—might have considered her a prophet.

Toward the end, Mother found kind words even for Father, whom she had often criticized for not having given her more child-ren. "He was the only one of the Perera brothers with any brains," she said in one of her typical snap judgments. "The others were *calabazas*" (pumpkins).

Crouched in her wheelchair, Mother glances up to reproach me for not having married and given her more grandchildren. When I re-mind her that I had been married for twelve years to an East Indian woman she never approved of, she attempts, after thirty years of ada-mant silence on the subject, to make amends.

"I had nothing personal against your Hindu bride, but you have to understand I was brought up in a religious family. My father was a *shohet.*"

My hopes rise that we might yet make peace of a kind before her death. But on my next visit she gives me a sidelong glance and says, "You're waiting for me to die, aren't you, so you can remarry your little Hindu?"

The closest Mother and I came to reconciliation was during one of my last visits to the home, before she lapsed into incoherence. She concluded one of her oft-repeated reminiscences with a Ladino phrase she had not used before: *"Agora ya kaparates mi storia."* ("Now you know my story.") And then, as if to emphasize that the gift of her life story did not come without strings, she added, *"Dices las vedrades, tienes que pagar."* ("You tell truths, you must pay.")

An old friend of Mother's who had known her in Guatemala advised me: "At bottom, your mother wished the best for you and your sister. And naturally she wished the best for herself. She could not al-ways tell the difference." I have come to regard this syllogism as Mother's epitaph.

·   ·   ·

MOTHER DIED in June 1990 and was buried in a new cemetery in a Tel Aviv suburb. The state, which takes responsibility for its citizens when they are born, when they apply for marriage and after they die, turned down her request for a grave site next to her sister Rebecca, on the mistaken ground that it was already taken. As the next of kin, I was invited into the morgue to identify Mother's body, and I noted that her face was contorted in a grimace, as though she had died in struggle. The coarse shroud that covered her body was labeled *isha* (woman); only the men are buried in their prayer shawls. She was laid in the ground, enclosed by four slabs of concrete.

A Sephardic prayer maker recited the Kaddish at her funeral. The prayer maker, who mispronounced her name "Ferrera," as though she were Italian, snipped the top of my worn T-shirt with his scissors as a token of bereavement and extended his hand for payment before I had finished my recitation. The summer sun was pitilessly hot and bleached the sky of all color. There were no trees in view—not even the obliga-tory cypresses—only sand dunes and rows upon rows of incised granite or marble tombstones from Hebron. Despite her seven languages, her brief career in the post office, her thirty years abroad and her irrepressibly alert, lively mind, Mother lived her eighty-six years unable to conceive of a life lived outside the traditions of her forefathers. What would she have made of the startling hypothesis that the original Five Books of Moses were composed by a woman?

Seven months after her death, one of Saddam Hussein's Scud missiles landed in Ramat Gan, a few short blocks from Mother's nurs-ing home. Two elderly people, the first casualties of Hussein's attacks on Israel, died of heart attacks. They could have been Mother and Aunt Rebecca, had their lives been prolonged by an iron-rich diet when they were young.

CHAPTER II

SEPHARAD
(SPAIN AND PORTUGAL)

[The Earth] has the shape of a pear, which is all very round, except at the stem, where it is very prominent ... like a woman's nipple....
—Christopher Columbus, 1498

And among these nations shalt thou find no ease, neither shall the sole of thy foot have rest: but the Lord shall give thee a trembling heart, and failing of eyes, and sorrow of mind; and thy life shall hang in doubt before thee; and thou shalt fear day and night, and shalt have no assurance of thy life. In the morning thou shalt say, would God it were evening! And at evening thou shalt say, would God it were morning! For the fear of thine heart wherewith thou shalt fear, and for the sight of thine eyes which thou shalt see.
—Deuteronomy XXVIII, 65–67

TOLEDO

ACCORDING TO Jewish tradition, a number of noble Sephardic families, including the Ibn Dauds and the Abravanels, conserved genealogical trees tracing their descent from King David. Their warrior ancestors, members of the tribe of Judah, were taken captive by Nebu-chadnezzar when he seized Jerusalem and razed the First Temple in the sixth century B.C. The Babylonian king subsequently banished many of these captive warriors—or, in another version, they escaped—to the Iberian Peninsula, where they settled and founded the noble Sephardic lineages. If these claims have any validity, it means Jews arrived in what is now Spain and Portugal three centuries after the first Phoenicians from Tyre and Sidon, and concurrently with waves of Greek mer-chants and Carthaginian navigators from North Africa. These three groups, with historical and blood ties to the ancient Hebrews, amal-gamated with the Iberians and Celts who had lived in the peninsula since prehistoric times to forge the Hispanic and Portuguese races.

A number of Sephardic historians, among them Edmond S. Malka, discovered that many old Spanish towns had Hebrew names.

According to Malka, Escalona derives from Ashkelon, Maqueda from Masada, Joppes from Jaffa. Barcelona was Bar-Shelanu ("our country-side" in Hebrew), and its origins are linked with the Sephardic family Barchilon. Sevilla was Shevil-Yah, "line of God," later modified by the Muslims to Ishbilia. Similarly, Calatayud derived from the Arabic *Kalaat el-Yahud*, or "quarter of the Jews." The belief that Mérida and Toledo, or Toledoth, Hebrew for "generations," were founded by noble Jews released from Babylonian captivity is supported by Flavius Josephus, whose *History of the Jews* includes the Iberian Peninsula among Nebuchadnezzar's conquests. (In Malka's opinion, "Toledo" derives not from "Toledoth" but from *Toltel*, an old Hebrew term for "exile.") In the Old Testament, "Sepharad" refers to the westernmost lands on the Mediterranean, present-day Spain and Portugal. The term "Sephardim" was already being used for Iberian Jews when Jesus of Nazareth walked the hills of Galilee.

The belief that biblical Hebrews were among the Iberian Peninsula's earliest settlers was propagated by Christian prelates during the Middle Ages. Rodrigo Jiménez de Roda, archbishop of Toledo in the twelfth century, claimed that Hispania was first settled by descendants of Tubal, a grandson of Noah.

I like to think that a Perera, by whatever name he was known at the time, was among the Hebrew sages of Toledo who are said to have been consulted by Jerusalem's rabbis regarding the trial of Jesus. After careful consideration, the Toledo elders concluded that he was an honest man and a prophet, and they urged the rabbis to overrule Jesus' death sentence lest his martyrdom result in a second destruction of the Temple. Although the letter of exculpation—if it ever existed—evidently had no bearing on Jesus' crucifixion, this ancient tradition attests to the prestige that adhered to the Iberian Israelites 1,100 years before the birth of Maimonides.

Although I have not been able to trace my family name farther back than the fourteenth century, my visits to Toledo beginning in 1958—and the ghostly sense of familiarity I always experience there—have nourished my conviction that my direct ancestors were among the city's early inhabitants. The town once known as the Iberian Jerusalem is harsh and austere as only a Castilian town can be. No storks from Africa roost on the rooftops of Toledo or hazard to nest in its battlements, as these migratory birds still do in towns farther to the south. From a distance, the granite-gray citadel of the Alcázar, perched high

above the gorge of the muddy Tagus River, presents as haunting a prospect today as on the day El Greco painted it.

As I enter the city through the old Gothic portal of Besagro, the
words *peñosa* (rocky bluffs) and *pesadumbre* (gloom) leap out of Cervantes' dedication, engraved on a pilaster. Spain's preeminent literary
genius, who lived not far from here, eulogized Toledo as "the light of
Spain"; but in truth, that light had been extinguished the century
before Cervantes was born. Like other would-be hidalgos of question-
able lineage, Cervantes lived in the shadow of the Inquisition, obsessed
with proving the *limpieza*, the "purity" of—that is, the lack of any Jewish taint in—his bloodline. Beginning in the sixteenth century, anyone
seeking office in the military or religious orders had to prove they were of
pure Old Christian descent for at least seven generations. The *limpieza
de sangre* statutes remained in the books for more than three centuries.

It was in Toledo that riots first broke out against Jews accused of
crucifying Christian children and desecrating the Host in the course of
performing diabolical rituals. And Toledo was also the setting, in
1449, of the first clashes between Old Christians and recent converts
suspected of practicing their Jewish religion covertly; these recidivists
were contemptuously called Marranos, or "swine," a label that carried
the added connotation of accursedness. Three decades later, the Holy
Office confined and tortured my New Christian ancestors in its castle
dungeons and burned them alive in spectacular autos-da-fé that were
timed, as often as not, to add luster to a royal wedding or coronation.
At their height, the autos-da-fé outshone the bullfights as a popular
spectacle. And they offered the spiritual dividend of participation in an
uplifting religious event.

The Inquisition tribunals persecuted and humiliated New
Christians for the unforgivable apostasy of secretly nurturing the ancient
Jew they bore in their veins. And regardless of whether the accused
were "relaxed" to the secular arm which then burned them at the stake,
or were reconciled to the church and purged of their sins, their worldly
goods were invariably confiscated and divided between the Inquisition
tribunals and the royal treasury.

After Portugal introduced its own Inquisition in 1547, thousands of Jewish converts, a score of Pereiras among them, sought asylum in Spain. Toledo's was the first Spanish tribunal to fill its jails and
stoke its fires with Portuguese Marranos, known as *judaizantes,* or "Jud-

aizers," a term no less odious for its jarring dissonance. And Toledo went on burning converts well into the eighteenth century, after the other tribunals in Spain had suspended activities.

The courage of Marranos who paid with their lives for refusing to abjure their heritage is enshrined in the silver Magen David's and other Jewish mementos sold in Toledo's tourist shops. General Francisco Franco, a Galician of *converso* descent and Hitler's ally in World War II, had a change of heart after Germany's fortunes in the war began to decline; starting in 1943, he granted free transit to some 30,000 Jews in flight from France and the Balkans. Later on, Franco restored Toledo's two ancient synagogues to their original splendor. In 1411, following outbreaks of anti-Semitic violence, the Torah scrolls had been removed from the Ark of the Chief Synagogue; the gold-leaf rosettes of Solomon that shone from Mudejar cornices were hidden behind the niches of Catholic saints, and this noble edifice became the chapel of Santa Maria La Blanca. (Fifty years later, it served for a time as a convent for fallen women.) During the Napoleonic Wars the former synagogue was used as an arms depot by the French Army. El Tránsito Synagogue, the other jewel of Mudejar architecture erected in the eleventh century by the legendary royal treasurer, Rabbi Samuel Levi, has also been restored, and a collection of rare books and manuscripts has been made available to investigators.

But these gestures were too little, too late. The Toledan nights are still weighted—*pesadumbradas*—with the dull sound of Toledo steel impaling itself on innocent flesh; and they also resonate with the exploding grenades and machine-gun fire of the siege of the Alcázar by Republican troops in 1938. The narrow, labyrinthine Moorish alleys and cobbled plazas are shadowed by the hatred of neighbor for neighbor, by suspicions of *mala raza,* tainted blood and imported ideologies. The blood not only of Jews and Marranos but of thousands of Muslims and Christians has reddened the brown waters of the Tagus in the recurring slaughters variously named Reconquest, Inquisition, and Civil War.

Early in the seventeenth century, after El Greco returned from Crete, Toledo's Marranos began to appear in his canvases, as evidenced by the melting Semitic eyes and the swaying, davening movements of Domenico Theotocopuli's subjects in his so-called visionary period. Although El Greco's commissioned work was handsomely rewarded, his life had as strained an ending as that of any Moor or Jew exiled from

Toledo. Recently uncovered records indicate that El Greco never lived in "Casa del Greco," nor are his bones to be found in the mausoleum that bears his name.

During its heyday in the Middle Ages, the fortified Jewish quarter, or *aljama,* contained ten synagogues and as many as 7,000 residents. The *aljama* was governed by rabbinical councils and courts that interpreted Halakhah, or scriptural law, and applied it to every facet of religious and secular existence. The sages of Toledo carried on a lively commerce with Talmudic scholars—*geonim*—in Baghdad and Cairo. In the Plaza de la Judería, the *alcana* (Jewish market) displayed Persian carpets, silks from Damascus, shawls from Kashmir and spices from Ceylon and India. And when a Castilian monarch had business to conduct with a Jewish financial backer, a minister or a physician, his envoys required a rabbi's safe-conduct before they could enter the quarter. In the thirteenth century, the love-stricken Alfonso VIII visited the quarter after nightfall to pay court to his Jewish mistress, the legendary Raquel. (The love affair, which according to one tradition lasted for seven years, climaxed with the murder of Raquel in the royal palace by the knights of Castile, followed by the chastened monarch's reconciliation with his English queen, Leonore.)

The *aljama's* autonomy was breached by the pogroms of 1328 and 1391, from which the Jewish community of Toledo never recovered.

When the Jews were expelled from Spain in 1492, many Toledans took with them the keys to their houses. On returning to Toledo centuries later to remove the remains of their ancestors from their old burial plots, the descendants found that their keys still opened the ironwork doors to their former homes.

Although my ancestors may have been among the peninsula's first Jewish settlers, the earliest Pereiras of whom I have documentary evidence lived in Portugal. In his 1934 genealogical study *Noble Families Among Sephardic Jews,* Isaäc da Costa quotes Pereiras who claimed direct descent from Ruy (Rodrigo) Pereira, "O Bravo," a fourteenth-century nobleman. His great-grandson's great-grandson was Count Dom Manuel Pereira, who possessed a document signed by João III of Portugal in 1535. The document proved that the king descended from converso Pereiras through the female line, which is now extinct.

A surgeon by the name of Isaac Pereira who lived in Leiria in the fifteenth century was named a servant to the royal court, possibly a case of favoritism shown by the monarch to a close relation.

The noble Pereira family's coat of arms was a cross in gules, or a crimson setting—fleur-de-lisée. (Pereira, or Perera, is a pear orchard, or one who cultivates pears.) In the Jewish branch of the family the peral (pear tree) took the place of the cross. In Los Angeles some years ago I met with architect William Pereira, a practicing Catholic, who showed me his family arms; it was a fleur-de-lis shield with a cross and a pear tree intertwined.

Isaäc da Costa traces the Portuguese Pereira line to the Jewish Abendanas, who originally wrote their name as "Aben"—i.e., "Ibn"—Dana (son of Dana). The Abendana arms displayed an eagle on a globe turned toward the sun, and the family crest was a left hand. The patriarch was Heitor Mendes de Brito, who lived in Lisbon in the sixteenth century. A descendant of his, Antonio Lopes Pereira, was a New Christian nobleman who upon arriving in Amsterdam declared himself a Jew; his relations adopted the ancient name Abendana. In his landmark History of the Marranos, Cecil Roth writes that five daughters of Manoel Pereira Coutinho were nuns in the Convent of La Es-perança in Lisbon, at the same time that his sons were living as Jews in Hamburg under the name Abendana. In Amsterdam, the reclaimed Pereiras lived in close proximity to the Abendanas, bound together by their presumptive descent from a common ancestor. The seventeenth-century Amsterdam Marrano poet and chronicler Daniel Levi de Barrios rendered Aben Dan as "precious stones of Dan," which sug-gests direct descent from the tribe of Dan. (In modern Arabic, how-ever, dana translates as "moneylender.")

The earliest reference to an Abendana in Toledo involved the chandler Abraham Abendanno, son of Mair Aben Dagnon, who on March 15, 1350, purchased a vineyard from María Díaz, daughter of Diego López the parchment maker. The vineyard bordered on one owned by David Abendanno, also a chandler. A century later, in 1462, Meyr Abendanno, great-grandson of Abraham, sold the title to his property in Santo Tomé, a quarter of Toledo, to Juan Díaz, shield-bearer to the king. The last Abendana in Toledo's records was Sule-man Abendanno, who was compelled to leave Spain by the 1492 Ex-pulsion decree before he could settle the debts he owed to a local official.

The Abendanas who settled in the Netherlands in the seventeenth century later moved to London, subdividing by marriage into Abendana de Brito, Abendana Mendes, Abendana Belmonte, and the like. Only a few of the Abendanas continued to practice their ancestral religion. Today Abendana and its variants, Avendaño and Bandeña, are common among Jesuits and other practicing Catholics in Spain and Latin America; nearly all of these distant kin whom I have met acknowledge their ancient Jewish lineage.

IN THE IBERIAN Peninsula, relations between Hebrews and the primitive Christians began on an even keel, solemnized by the practice of mutual benedictions. In one of the earliest references to the Hebrew settlers, the Proclamation by the First Spanish Council at Elvira in 320, farmers were interdicted from offering their harvests for a Jew's blessing, and intermarriage was expressly forbidden. By then Toledo had become known as a town dominated by its Israelite tradesmen, artisans and scholars. (The Spanish town of Lucena, and that of Santarem, in what is now Portugal, were almost entirely populated by Jews.)

The waves of Vandals and Visigoths who overran the peninsula had little immediate impact on the status of the Israelites. They continued to ply the Mediterranean with their merchant ships and to carve epitaphs on their gravestones in Hebrew and Greek as well as in the Visigoths' Latin.

The Jews' troubles began only after the Gothic kings, who practiced a non-Trinitarian Christianity, became Catholics. In the 589 Council of Toledo, at which King Reccared I announced his conversion, new decrees barred Jews from owning slaves, chanting psalms and holding public office. Although these restrictions were more honored in the breach than in the observance, they are signposts to a progressive deterioration in the Jews' standing in Christian realms that led, step by step, to the introduction of the Inquisition 800 years later.

When the first combined forces of Berber, Arab and Syrian invaders crossed the Straits of Gibraltar in 711, their assaults on Visigoth citadels may have profited from intelligence supplied to them by the Jews, who were only too glad to cast off the yoke of slavery imposed by the zealous Catholic king Egica. Jews joined Berber battalions in the conquest of Córdoba, and their rulers repaid them with a grant of religious freedom. (This and other privileges were also extended to Christians.) In parts of Castile these allies of the Muslims are still referred to as *Judíos traicioneros*—"treacherous Jews"—by Old Christians who conceived the dubious slander that Jews not only aided the Muslims but invited their invasion out of bitter hatred of the Catholics.

After a period of upheaval in the eleventh century, the Jewish communities prospered once again. A learned Hebrew, Hasdai ben Ishak, became physician and minister to Caliph Abd al Rahman II, a royal appointment that would be matched by many other Jews in the coming decades. (The caliph's heir, Abd al Rahman III, who ruled Granada for fifty years, gained a reputation as the most enlightened and just of Spain's Muslim rulers. In old age he made a tally of the days of perfect happiness he had known, and counted fourteen. Disillusioned, the caliph counseled his subjects to disdain all worldly splendors and temporal attachments.)

Jewish civilization in Spain reached its apogee under the Omayyad caliphs between the tenth and twelfth centuries. The Jewish population grew to more than 50,000, as thousands of emigrants were drawn from North Africa and the Orient by the fabulous wealth and the religious tolerance of the caliphs. Until the arrival of bloody-minded Almohade Berbers in 1146, bent on implanting Islam in all of Europe, Spain's Jews generally lived at peace with Muslim rulers and their Christian subjects; and they thrived culturally and commercially as never before or since.

The bones of contention between the Koran and the Torah have remained constant over the centuries. The Koran accords freedom of worship to Christians and Jews—"People of the Book"—provided they render tribute to Islam and abase themselves before its rulers. All other "infidels" must choose between conversion and the sword. The extraordinary trajectory of Maimonides, who composed his scientific and theological treatises with equal mastery in Hebrew and Arabic, and who at one time considered converting to Islam, suggests the extent to which Hebraic and Arabic learning cohabited in the minds of the great sages of Al-Andaluz. Moshe ibn Ezra, the first of Spain's great Israelite poets, translated the Hebrew classics into Arabic and used Hebrew grammars written in Arabic script. In the thirteenth century, the Castilian king Alfonso the Wise recruited Christian, Jewish and Muslim sages to compile an encyclopedia of astronomy, entitled *El Libro de Saber (The Book of Learning)*.

To be a learned Jew or Muslim in Al-Andaluz presupposed more than the mastery of Arabic and Hebrew, and the ability to dis-

course in flowing ornamental phrases on astronomy, theology, medicine, literature and the ancient Greek classics. To be learned, one had to
take an active part in shaping the historical currents that nourished the
two languages and cultures. The honing of language into a civilizing
instrument that is at once *dolce et utile* epitomized the Jewish Golden
Age in Spain.

The degree to which Arabic and Hebrew cross-pollinated
would be difficult to exaggerate and, given the present antagonism between these two Semitic peoples, impossible to reconstruct. And yet a
Sephardi is still marked by the inner dialogue between the ancestral Jew
and the Christian and Arab "others" who inhabit his psyche. This
triadic bond defines the Sephardi's role in the modern world—as
Eliyahu Eliachar understood so well—and despite our century's un-
precedented, transforming traumas, this bond continues to define the
Sephardi's place in Eretz Israel as well.

THE MASS KILLINGS of Granada's Jews in 1066 by fanatical
Almoravide Berbers were a prefiguration of worse slaughters to come.
By the end of the twelfth century, thousands of Jews had fled north to
the Christian kingdoms of Aragon and Castile, which offered them
sanctuary in exchange for vassalage and the payment of feudal taxes. In
Castile, where the royal court honored Jewish scientists and philosophers, Jews were enlisted to fight Moors as vassals to Alfonso X and his
successors. When Jewish soldiers took part in the recapture of Seville in
1248, the monarchy rewarded them with a "village of the Jews."

In 1261, Alfonso the Wise's Code of the Seven Partidas guaran-
teed Jews the right of free worship and other legal safeguards; but a Jew
who cohabited with a Christian woman was condemned to the sword.
In their habituated fealty to both Christian and Muslim rulers, Spain's
Jews were to fight on both sides of the protracted and tortuous Reconquest that finally ended with the liberation of Granada from the Nasrid
caliph Boabdil in the *annus mirabilis* 1492.

II

THE GOLDEN AGE

Neither Pereras, Pereiras nor Abendanas appear among the names of illustrious Jews of the so-called Golden Age of Spanish Jewry, from the tenth to the end of the twelfth century. But my ancestors were in Toledo all the same, holding court with Rabbi Samuel Levi when he enter-tained Pedro the Cruel in his palace, whose grandeur is said to have ri-valed Granada's Alhambra. Ostentation on such a scale is always hazardous for a Jew, and Levi—according to a popular Christian tra-dition—paid for his fabulous wealth with his life. King Pedro's churchmen, covetous of the rabbi's great fortune, convinced their mon-arch that he was carrying out God's judgment when he ordered the exe-cution of Levi and all his relations.

As so often happens in Spain, there exists a Jewish countertradi-tion alleging that Samuel Levi retained the favor of Pedro the Cruel— also known as Pedro the Just—to the end of his days. At his death, according to this view, Levi's body was escorted from the palace by a sumptuous funeral cortege.

My forebears were also in attendance—I know this in my bones—among the circle of Castilian and Córdoban scholars and mys-tics who surrounded Moses ben Shem-Tov de Leon, the thirteenth-century compiler of the *Zohar*. This collection of mystical formulas, rabbinical dialogues and biblical exegesis constitutes the masterwork of the Kabbala, and was traditionally, though falsely, attributed to Rabbi Shimeon Bar-Yohai, who lived in Jerusalem around the dawn of the Christian era. As my Kabbalist great-great-grandfather later would in Salonika and Jerusalem, these Córdoban forebears pored over every vowel, period and cantillation mark of Holy Writ to free of its fetters the living God's radiance, or *shekhinah*. With the great Sephardic mystic Nahmanides, they believed each portion of the Torah, and all actions and events pertaining thereto, to be infused by the miraculous.

In the same century, Spain's Jews quivered to the yearning for Jerusalem immortalized in Judah Halevi's canticles; and they marveled at the metaphysical word play of Solomon ibn Gabirol. These were the two seminal poets of the Golden Age, whose lyrics enrich both Sephar-dic and Ashkenazic liturgies. But whereas ibn Gabirol's subtle philo-

sophical writings—many composed in Arabic—struck deeper reso/
nances with Muslims and Christians, Judah Halevi has been enshrined
as Judaism's greatest poet, and its first Zionist. Halevi's pilgrimage to
the Holy Land was replicated centuries later by my great/great/grandfa/
ther, not from Granada but from Salonika. Like Halevi, Aharon Ra/
phael Haim Perera was driven by the conviction that only in the land of
Canaan could a Jew live truly the Torah's commandments and fulfill
the prophecy of redemption; everywhere else he was an exile, from him/
self and from God. Unlike Halevi, who according to tradition was
pierced through the heart by an Arab horseman at the portals to Jerusa/
lem, Aharon Perera arrived in the City of Light to fulfill his biblical
destiny.

In Amsterdam in 1663, Jacob Abendana translated from He/
brew into Spanish Judah Halevi's *Kuzari,* an imaginary dialogue be/
tween three scholars—a Jew, a Christian and a Muslim—and the king
of the Khazars. The core of the text, which includes a brief history of
the Khazars, is the rabbi's arguments establishing the supremacy of
King David's Elohim over all other gods and religions. When Halevi
wrote the dialogue, the Khazar kings of Central Asia and Eastern
Europe who converted to Judaism in the eighth century had already
passed into legend. Abendana's *Kuzari* is a crisp and persuasive rendi/
tion of a text exalting illumination over reason, as befits a man recently
reborn to his Jewish faith. But it suffers from a serious and revealing de/
fect. Yosef Yerushalmi, among other modern scholars, has criticized
Abendana for drastically abridging the Christian position, which is
presented at far greater length in Halevi's original text.

Halevi, who was trained as a physician, was the first to posit a
doctrine of the elect based on the natural order. Man's ability to speak
and reason give him dominion over all the other natural beings. Israel is
the crown of creation by virtue of the gift of prophecy, which God
granted to the Jews alone. Only in the Holy Land, which God prophe/
sied for the people of Israel, can they complete the redemption promised
on Mount Sinai. Thus, although the king of the Khazars, owing to his
gentile birth, can never be one of the truly elect, he can actualize his
"good intention" by converting and sharing in the fulfillment of Israel's
destiny.

Today Halevi is embraced as a prophet not only by Sephardim
but by ultranationalist Ashkenazim. Leaders of the Orthodox Israeli
Gush Emunim movement welcome Halevi's implicit rejection of Ish/

mael as Abraham's "bad seed" and adopt his reasoning to justify expelling Palestinians from the West Bank. Elhanan Naeh, a Talmudic professor at Hebrew University, considers much of the *Kuzari* to be "dangerously racist." As evidence, he cites passages like the following.

> . . . any Gentile who joins us unconditionally shares our good fortune, without, however, being quite equal to us. If the Law were binding on us only because God created us, the white and the black man would be equal, since He created them all. But the Law was given to us because He led us out of Egypt, and remained attached to us because we are the pick of mankind.

My Golden Age kin favored the mystical, elitist Zionism of Halevi above the cosmopolitan rationalism of Maimonides, who argued that Israel was chosen through the free will of its fathers and sons after they received the true faith on Mount Sinai. In principle, anyone who embraces the Torah and its binding commandments can rise to the ranks of the elect. Maimonides, who lived much of his life as physician and minister to Muslim rulers, believed that Islam and Christianity ("Ishmael and Edom") came into being to prepare Gentiles to receive the Torah. In his masterwork, *Guide to the Perplexed*, Maimonides dissects and interprets the Old Testament as allegory and parable, reconciling it with a rational belief in God.

Distrustful of rationalism, my ancestors heeded Halevi's admonition: "Let not Greek wisdom tempt you, for it bears flowers only and no fruit." Israel, they believed with Halevi, was the heart of humankind, the "Light unto the Nations." But they also concurred with Maimonides that the Messiah would appear not as Divinity—"a Voice from the Whirlwind"—but as a prophet of flesh and blood who would deliver them from bondage.

In the tenth century, Jews, Muslims and Christians converged to form a new civilization, the whole of which was immeasurably richer than the sum of its parts. With the dissolution of Muslim Spain and the expulsion of the Jews, the spores from this providential graft were disseminated to North Africa, Western Europe and the Levant. For observant Jews worldwide, Maimonides' codification of the Talmud remains the crowning achievement of Spanish Jewry. The Kabbala of Shem-Tov de Leon and Nahmanides found a home in the study rooms

of Jerusalem and in Isaac Luria's Safed, while the twelfth-century messianic movement resurfaced five centuries later in the Shabbatean cult.

The Muslims expelled from Al-Andaluz for the most part reset-
tled in North Africa, where the descendants of Abd-el-Rahman and
Boabdil can be found today. Like the Jewish Marranos, many of the
expelled Muslim converts who settled in Tetuán, Tunis and Algiers
conserved the Andalusian language and music, as well as the Christian
traditions of their Iberian past. Thousands of them lived as Arab Marranos, disdained by both Christians and Muslims. Spanish travelers
who find their way to these North African communities are astonished
to discover heads of families who, like their Jewish counterparts from
Toledo, still have the keys to their homes in Spanish towns and cities.

III

1391: THE AFTERMATH

Through most of the thirteenth and the first half of the fourteenth century, Jewish communities prospered in the Christian kingdoms of Castile and its rival Aragon, which included all of what is today Cataluña,
Valencia and parts of Andalusia. The great Talmudists, poets, astrono-
mers and philosophers were replaced by royal physicians, tax collectors
and ministers of the treasury. Those loyal to Pedro the Cruel would pay
dearly after he lost the thirty-year Civil War to his brother, Enrique II.
But Enrique, too, ended by seeking out the Jews' services and entrust-
ing to them the farming of royal revenues because, as he complained in
1367, "we found no others to bid for it." The chief business of Spain's
monarchy and nobility, during and after the end of feudalism, was
making war. Trade, commerce and agriculture were largely delegated
to slaves and captives, whether Jews or Muslims.

Even after such rabble-rousing evangelists as the Dominican Vicente Ferrer and Archdeacon Ferrán Martínez of Seville goaded Christians into rising up against Jewish unbelievers, the kings of Aragon and
Castile entrusted their well-being to Jewish physicians and employed
Jews to manage their finances. Royal treasuries were perennially on the
verge of bankruptcy. The huge financial drain of the three-century-long
campaigns against the Moors was largely stanched by Jewish merchants

and moneylenders who controlled Spain's foreign trade and absorbed most of its floating capital.

The extravagant wealth they amassed made these merchant fami-lies the focus of Christian resentment. Churchmen fanned hatred by railing against the Jews' ostentation and the moneylenders' interest rates, which rose as high as forty percent per annum. Andrés Bernáldez, chronicler of the Catholic monarchs, justified popular hostility toward Spain's Jews with the following depiction:

> . . . merchants, salesmen, tax-gatherers, retailers, stewards of the nobility, officials, tailors, shoemakers, tanners, weavers, grocers, pedlars, silk-mercers, smiths, jewellers, and other like trades; none broke the earth, or became a farmer, car-penter or builder, but all sought after comfortable posts and ways of making profits without much labor.

Self-effacing humility has never been the Sephardi's strong suit. Halevi pointed to the abyss between the humbleness owed to God and the self-abasement imposed by gentile rulers, proof of the exile's impo-tence. And he proclaimed defiantly, "If you could, you would slay your oppressor." Four centuries later, the nagid, or "prince," of Con-stantinople's Sephardic community was accused of counseling his counterpart, Nagid Chamorro of Spain.

> As the king takes your property, make your sons merchants that they may take the property of the Christians; as he takes your lives, make your sons physicians and apothecaries, that they may take Christian lives; as he destroys your syna-gogues, make your sons ecclesiastics, that they may destroy the churches; as he vexes you in other ways, make your sons officials, that they may reduce the Christians to subjection and take revenge.

The dissemination of this apocryphal letter, cited by the re-spected historian Henry Charles Lea, produced a revulsion in medieval Spain comparable to the surge of anti-Semitism caused by the publica-tion early in this century of the *Protocols of the Elders of Zion*. (The *Proto-cols* are a tendentious forgery in which fictitious Jewish rabbis and bankers are depicted hatching a conspiracy to take over the civilized world.)

The Spanish Jews' fortunes took an irreversible turn for the worst with the massacres and mass conversions that erupted in 1391 in Seville, Granada, Toledo and other towns and cities of Aragon and Castile. The old blood libels resurfaced as Dominican friars accused Jews of sodomy, prostitution and "perverse obstinacy" in denying the true Messiah. Even Jewish physicians were accused of killing one of every five patients as part of a diabolical plot against Christians. Once again, every calamity from crop failures to the outbreak of plagues and epidemics was blamed on the Jews.

The greatest damage was often inflicted by new converts who de-nounced their former coreligionists with the fervor of born-again Chris-tians. The anti-Semitic riots and synagogue burnings of 1391 were foreshadowed in the diatribes of Abner of Burgos, a Jewish scholar and Kabbalist who converted in 1321 when he was already advanced in years, and took the name Alfonso of Valladolid.

In Alfonso's shadow rose other New Christians whose animus toward the Jews helped to lay the foundation for both the Inquisition and the Expulsion. At the core of their metamorphosis lies a mystery no less baffling than that of Rabbi Koretz's collaboration with the Nazis in Salonika. Rabbi Don Solomon Halevi, who became convinced that Jesus was the true Messiah, converted and as Pablo de Santa Maria rose to the rank of Bishop of Burgos, in which capacity he composed homi-lies undermining the rationalist foundations of Maimonides' theology. One of his adversaries, Joshua Lorki, also converted and wrote *He-braeomastix*, a shrewd polemic that used Talmudic disquisition to ex-pose its sundry textual contradictions and impugn its authority.

As Gerónimo de Santa Fé, Lorki led the debate against learned rabbis in the Disputation at Tortosa of 1413. He alluded to a Talmudic tradition that predicted the Messiah's arrival at the time of Christ's birth in Bethlehem. How could the rabbis deny their own Talmud? The rab-bis argued that the Messiah might indeed have arrived but had not been ready to reveal himself. The two-year debate, closely attended by the monarchy and three rival pretenders to the papacy, ended with the rab-bis backing away from a defense of the Talmud—under threats and in-timidations—after it was accused of containing heresies.

Most damaging of all may have been the fulminations of another convert, Alonso de Espina, confessor to Enrique IV. This Franciscan friar was among the first churchmen to press for an Inquisition to punish New Christians who reverted to Jewish practices. Espina's extreme austerity, coupled with his call for the forcible baptism of Spain's Jews, and the expulsion of the obdurate ones, would serve as inspiration for Queen Isabella.

Within a few years of 1391 the unremitting slaughters resulted in the death of 50,000 Jews, or nearly as many as had inhabited the peninsula at the start of the eleventh century. In Aragon, approximately 100,000 Jews accepted baptism, according to Henry Charles Lea, and at least that many converted in Castile. In Toledo, the eloquent proselytizer Vicente Ferrer virtually clinched his canonization by converting 4,000 Jews and Moors in a single day.

New laws were passed restricting the Jews' movements and limiting their livelihood to moneylending and petty commerce. They were confined to *juderías* (ghettos) and made to wear distinguishing yellow badges. Intermarriage between Christians and Jews was declared a capital offense; Jews were forbidden to assemble with Christians or erect new synagogues. In the wake of the pogroms, the enforced conversions and tightening curbs, thousands of Jews fled to Portugal, North Africa and the Middle East. Thousands of conversos married into titled families to start the New Christian lineages that would infiltrate, within a generation, the Spanish and Portuguese noble orders, the church hierarchy and the monarchy itself.

The decades leading to the Inquisition were best summed up by Lea in a characteristic sentence: "Antagonisms which before had been purely religious, became racial, while religious antagonisms became heightened, and Spain, which through the earlier Middle Ages had been the most tolerant land in Christendom, became, as the fifteenth century advanced, the most fanatically intolerant."

IV

INQUISITION

Isabella of Castile, who was herself a candidate for sainthood on the fivehundredth anniversary of the expulsion of the Jews and of Columbus's voyage to the New World, entrusted her finances to a Jew. Abraham Seneor, one of Castile's fabulously wealthy tradesmen, had been, with Isaac Abravanel, the chief financial backer of the Crown's reconquest of Granada. Seneor also acted as intermediary in Ferdinand's courtship of Isabella, and supposedly raised the 40,000 ducats for his wedding gift of a silver necklace. This gesture apparently backfired by calling attention to Ferdinand's humiliating dependence on wealthy Jews, an indebtedness inherited from his father, King Juan III, the last royal patron of Spain's Jews. (Ferdinand had a Jewish converso greatgrandmother on his mother's side, the famous beauty Paloma of Toledo.) In the end, the taint of Jewish blood in Ferdinand's veins served only to magnify his Machiavellian ambitions and harden his heart against his former protégés.

The campaign to canonize Isabella, spearheaded by the ultraconservative Opus Dei movement, rests on the presumption that the Inquisition she helped set into motion was inspired by her exemplary religiosity. This view prevailed in much of Europe among Isabella's contemporaries. Even such secular humanists as the Italian Pico de la Mirandola praised the Spanish monarchs for an act of "necessary cruelty" that helped to preserve the *castedad* (Catholic purity) of the new Spain. Modern scholars point to racial bigotry as a driving force behind the Inquisition, along with economic and political imperatives.

Ferdinand, preoccupied with consolidating through marriage the union of the kingdoms of Aragon and Castile, convened with Pope Sixtus IV to authorize the establishment of the Inquisition in 1480. With Isabella's enthusiastic approval, Ferdinand named her confessor, the Dominican friar Tomás de Torquemada, the first inquisitor general. Torquemada and his fellow inquisitors wasted no time. During his eighteenyear tenure, as many as 2,000 lapsed Jewish converts were "relaxed" to secular authorities and burned at the stake; 3,000 were relaxed in effigy, the usual penalty for those who had died in prison or fled the country; and nearly 40,000 were "reconciled" to the church after being sentenced to a typical penance of lifelong confinement in jail. (This sentence was often commuted to a shorter term.) The penitents were marched through the streets holding long tapers, to the jubilant jeers of the crowds. They were garbed in tall, coneshaped hats and smocks, decorated with demons and souls in agony, which were called Sambenitos. Public floggings were commonplace, with an obdurate penitent receiving fifty to one hundred lashes. Afterward the Sambenito was hung in the church of the penitent's hometown or village to ensure that his obloquy lived on after him. None of the penitents were allowed to confront their accusers until the sentence was about to be carried out. In nearly all cases, the goods and assets of those accused by the tribunal were sequestered or confiscated to defray the Inquisition's expenses and replenish the royal treasury.

Although influential New Christians appealed to the Holy See in Rome to intervene on their behalf, Ferdinand held firm against the pope's pleas for ameliorating the Inquisition's worst abuses. In this he was staunchly backed by Isabella, who honored her predecessors Espina and Vicente Ferrer by calling for severe penalties for all relapsed converts. The thirty- to forty-day grace period introduced through the Holy See's intervention, which ostensibly allowed the accused to clear his name or repent and become reconciled without penance, was instead used to gather damning evidence from informers and cooperative neighbors. And the penitent was obliged to denounce all those who had conspired in his heresy. At the expiration of the grace period, all the evidence gathered would be used against the penitent, as well as to open proceedings against the acquaintances or relations named in his testimony.

Although both Ferdinand and Isabella were trained in ruthlessness, each having gained the throne after poisoning a sibling who preceded them in the royal line, Isabella proved to be the more unswerving in pursuit of her goals. As queen of Castile, she had been notorious for establishing summary tribunals in which wealthy defendants—whether Old or New Christians—were routinely found guilty and stripped of their possessions. The svelte and striking Isabella is pictured by popular tradition marching at the head of the monarchy's armies. It was she and not Ferdinand who first entered the Alhambra's Court of the Lions to accept the surrender of King Muhammed XII, known as Boabdil, the last of the caliphs of Granada. For all her legendary piety, Isabella fully endorsed Ferdinand's assertion of monarchic authority over the church, and she turned a deaf ear even to the pope when his designs ran contrary to hers. On balance, the Inquisition was Isabella's creation as much as or more than it was Ferdinand's. For the king, the tribunals were a means toward the paramount end of subjugating Spain's warring feudal societies under an absolute monarchy. His ambitions extended beyond Sicily and Sardinia—which already belonged to Spain—to the whole of Italy, and beyond that to France and Turkey, which he dreamed of incorporating into a greater Iberian empire.

To accomplish these objectives, a great deal of money was required. The Inquisition proved convenient to Ferdinand so long as it assured a steady income for the Crown through an incremental confis-cation of the wealth amassed by converted Jews. And the expulsion of practicing Jews in 1492 proved convenient for precisely the same rea-sons. But the monarchs did not count on the expense of the monstrous bureaucracies they had set into motion. At Ferdinand's death, the royal treasury was nearly as empty as it was on the day he and Isabella inher-ited it.

V

EXPULSION

The majority of those Jews who refused to convert regarded their Mar-rano brethren with a mixture of pity and contempt. They distinguished between coerced converts, or *anusim*, and voluntary converts, or *me-shumadim* (literally, "destroyed ones"); these old Hebrew terms convey the faithful Jews' prideful condescension toward their converted breth-ren, an attitude that remains very much alive today.

Ferdinand exploited this animosity by ordering unconverted rabbis to unmask crypto-Jews among the converts and to cast ana-themas on them. In their desire to maintain favor with the monarchs, the rabbis often complied. And yet there are numerous accounts of Jews who helped save lapsed converts through the famous "underground railroads," a modern term for the secret contacts and expeditions used to smuggle persecuted Marranos out of Spain.

Pamphlets have resurfaced in which rabbis counseled crypto-Jews in how best to endure the torture of the inquisitors. They were to fix the four-letter name of the Almighty between their eyes, and upon being asked to repent and accept Jesus Christ to be spared further tor-ments, they were to respond: "What are you asking of me? Indeed I am a Jew. A Jew I live and a Jew I die. Jew. Jew. Jew."

As remarkable as the conversions of learned rabbis to a zealous Christianity were the opposite, equally sincere conversions to Judaism by Old Christians at the height of the Inquisition. Among the note-worthy cases is that of Don Lope de Vera, a chevalier of Saint Clemente who studied fourteen years at the University of Salamanca. Vera's stud-ies in Hebrew and Arabic scripture persuaded him of the superiority of

Mosaic law to the Christian sacraments. His avowed conversion forced the tribunal of Valladolid to detain Vera as a Christian Judaizer. His skillful rebuttal of the inquisitor's arguments and pleas led to a protracted trial, during which learned men from all Spain were brought to Valladolid to attempt to wean Vera from his apostasy. All the arguments failed. In the Inquisition's jail Vera adopted the name Judah and circumcised himself with a bone. He was finally led to the stake, reiterating to the end: *"Viva la ley de Mosen!"* ("Long live the law of Moses!")

Friar Francisco de Torrejoncillo, who established the precedent that a person could be found guilty of Judaizing even if only the smallest fraction of his blood was contaminated, insisted that Vera had not acquired his heresy from books but had suckled it from the breasts of a Judaizing wet nurse.

Among those profoundly impressed by Lope de Vera's example was Juan Pereira, a young Marrano of Portuguese descent who was standing trial in the Valladolid tribunal. Pereira swore he had seen Vera after his death, riding on a mule and shining from the sweat on his skin as he was led to the pyre.

News of Lope de Vera's unshakable devotion to his adopted faith would reach Marrano communities in other European cities. Amsterdam philosopher Baruch Spinoza, who heard of Vera's martyrdom as a small boy, described it to a colleague years later as if he had lived it inside his own skin.

Tomás de Torquemada, whose influence grew proportionately as the revenues from confiscations mounted, appears to have exerted a Rasputin-like influence on Queen Isabella. Now a bishop, he convinced her and Ferdinand that the presence of Jews in Spain was polluting the New Christians with their contumacious heresies. Torquemada, whose own grandmother may have been a Jewish convert, authored the slogan "One People, One Kingdom, One Faith." Ferdinand had the queen's staunch support when he signed the Order of Expulsion from Spain of all unconverted Jews on May 1, 1492. The document, which faithfully reflected Torquemada's warning against the contamination of converts by Spain's Jews, concludes:

> . . . we have agreed to order the expulsion of all Jews and
> Jewesses in our kingdom. Never should any of them return
> and come back. . . . And if they are found living in our
> kingdoms and domains they should be put to death.

Abraham Seneor and Isaac Abravanel are believed to have mas-
terminded an attempt by the Jewish community to rescind the Expulsion order with an exorbitant bribe. The reported offer of 600,000
crowns, enough to provision Spain's battalions and fit out its Armada,
caused Ferdinand to waver. If the scene described by the inquisitor Luis
de Páramo can be believed, Torquemada then erupted into the royal
chamber with crucifix held high: "Behold the crucifix whom the
wicked Judas sold for thirty pieces of silver!" he exclaimed, at the same
time tendering his resignation, so that Ferdinand would be left to answer to God all alone were he to accept the Jews' bribe.

The Expulsion Decree was confirmed and set to be enforced in
July 1492, allowing the Jews a scarce four months to either convert or
dispose of their properties and quit the kingdom. Seneor, witnessing the
failure of all his negotiations, retained his standing with Isabella by ac-
cepting baptism and founding the New Christian lineage of Nuñez
Coronel. Abravanel, his close associate, chose to depart Spain with his
extensive family. (From Italy, Abravanel declared that Gentiles would
always suspect New Christians of remaining Jews in secret, no matter
how sincere their conversion.)

And Tomás de Torquemada became forever in the popular
imagination the archetype of the fiery-eyed, satanic Grand Inquisitor to
whom sinners freely surrender their souls. In life, Torquemada lived in
terror of assassination by one of his innumerable enemies, to the extreme of providing himself with an armed escort of 250 footmen and
valry. On his dinner table he kept a unicorn horn as a charm against
poisoning.

VI

PORTUGAL

It is not clear when the Pere(i)ras who converted after 1391 and those
who bowed to the Inquisition and accepted baptism a century later decided to leave for Portugal. Documentary evidence suggests that many
left early in the sixteenth century, not long after Spain's Jews were expelled by the infamous edict whose quincentennial was commemorated
in 1992. Whatever the date of their departure, their travails must have

been enormous. But they did not approach the scale of the tragedy that befell the Jews who refused to convert.

Historians vary wildly in their estimates of the total number of Jews expelled from Spain. No one questions that Spain's Jewry was the largest in medieval Europe. The meticulous Henry Charles Lea quotes a figure of 165,000 emigrants, and 50,000 who accepted baptism. Higher estimates place the total figure at more than 400,000. Tens of thousands of Marranos and persecuted Muslims, in concert with the Portuguese who were on a war footing with Spain, might have closed ranks with the Jews to escalate a popular rebellion into all-out civil war. But the rebellion never materialized.

Questions similar to those that plagued Jews in the aftermath of Hitler's Final Solution continue to be raised regarding the Spanish Jews' feeble and seemingly self-defeating reaction to the Inquisition and the Expulsion. Any attempt at an explanation has to take into account the centuries of Jewish fealty to Aragonese and Castilian kings, a fealty that emigrant Jews would extend as well to Portuguese monarchs. And it must also be acknowledged that with rare exceptions, the Jews' loyalty was reciprocated by Spain's monarchs, even during periods of militant anti-Semitism—until, that is, the accession of the Catholic monarchs Ferdinand and Isabella.

Once the Inquisition was established, attempts at organized resistance were mounted in a number of cities, among them Seville, Teruel and Saragossa, where in 1485 the inquisitor Pedro Arbúes was killed by assassins in the hire of local conversos. Arbúes was instantly declared a Christian saint. In return, inquisitors tortured and burned all the influential Aragonese New Christian families that might have conspired with them. Resistance in Teruel, Seville, Valencia, Barcelona and other cities of Castile and Aragon fared no better. An uprising like that of the Warsaw ghetto had about as much chance of success in the Spain of the 1490s as it did in the Poland of 1944.

The effective date for the Expulsion was fixed by Queen Isabella as August 2, 1492. Historians have made much of the striking coincidences that Columbus set sail on his voyage of discovery the very next day, and that a number of his crew were converts and Marranos. Did the queen have any inkling of the far reach of events she helped set into motion, whose outcome would set a compass not only for Spain but for the destiny of Western civilization itself?

In their panic to leave Spain before the deadline, the Jews had to sell their homes and nonportable belongings at any price. Palatial villas were in some instances exchanged for a donkey, and a vineyard for a bolt of linen. In a gesture of communal solidarity the emigrants arranged hasty marriages for their offspring above the age of twelve. On old parchments there are depictions of elderly rabbis who encouraged women and children to dance and play timbrels as they accompanied the adolescent bridal couples on the road to Cádiz Harbor and exile. But this brave pageantry provided no protection against the pirates and brigands who fell upon the emigrants when they set sail for North Africa and the Levant.

Those who sailed to Morocco were often stripped of their belongings by the ships' captains, and the women were raped. On arrival in Fez, destitute and starving, hundreds were turned back by the king, and their last belongings were seized by robbers, who sometimes cut the men open to find the gold thought to be concealed in their stomachs. The thousands who managed to stay in Fez erected a sprawling *judería* composed of straw dwellings. When the houses caught fire, scores perished along with all their worldly belongings. Plagues and epidemics carried off several thousand more of the recent arrivals. Still, about 20,000 Jews managed to stay and found a lasting settlement in Fez.

Morocco, Italy and the Netherlands would be counted among the handful of countries that were hospitable to Jewish emigrants. The Holy See attempted to make amends by inviting the Jews to Rome. The Ottoman sultan Bayezid, heartened by generous donations from his Jewish subjects, welcomed the Spanish exiles to Constantinople, Smyrna and Salonika. Bayezid is credited with twitting Ferdinand with the famous rebuke: "Do you term this a politic king, who impoverishes his nation and enriches ours?"

Lea estimates that 20,000 Jews died in the years immediately following the Expulsion. Thousands of impoverished emigrants who attempted to return to Spain and accept conversion were turned away by Ferdinand's agents when they could not prove their ability to support themselves. In 1499, the Crown announced an edict prohibiting the return of all expelled Jews, on pain of death; and legislation was passed forbidding entry into Spain of all foreigners save those with royal license. In two strokes the monarchs put their seal on an isolationist policy that would become the prototype of a closed, intolerant and morally retrograde Spain, giving birth to the notorious Black Legend. The enduring effects of this Black Legend, accentuated by the decline of Spain's universities, and propagated by the Renaissance and the Protestant Reformation, persist to the present day.

IN PORTUGAL THE 100,000 arriving immigrants were granted eight-month residence permits, although those with money to bribe corrupt officials stayed longer. But their fate was no better than that of the Jews who fled to North Africa. In 1496, in the week following King Manoel I's marriage to María, eldest daughter of Ferdinand and Isabella, the Portuguese monarch bowed to his parents-in-law's wishes and issued an edict of expulsion for all practicing Jews. But King Manoel, who was of a relatively kindly and politic disposition, understood the economic advantages of having skilled Jewish tradesmen in his kingdom, and offered them the alternative of mass conversion. Persuaded by the monarch's tempered words that their Christianization would be in name only, allowing them to maintain their Jewish communal bonds more or less intact, the majority of the immigrants accepted baptism in a mass ceremony in Lisbon's Rossio.

In Portugal, the Inquisition was not formally introduced until 1547. The delay was in part due to the tributes paid the monarchs by wealthy Jews. If Torquemada's religious fanaticism and Isabella's obsession with *castedad* may be said to have offset Ferdinand's greed and megalomania as the driving force behind Spain's Inquisition, no such constraint marred the introduction of the Holy Office's tribunals in Portugal. The years of wrangling between Manoel I's intemperate heir, João III, and the Holy See revolved almost exclusively around the issue of how the expected revenues from condemned Marranos should be divided. In the end, a compromise was struck, paving the way for tribunals in Lisbon, Evora and Coimbra.

In spite of a late start, by the seventeenth century the Portuguese Inquisition rivaled its Spanish counterpart in savagery as well as scale, and as with its model, its life-span would stretch across three centuries, into the early 1800s.

CHAPTER III
PORTUGAL

The oral, rectal and vaginal pear: torture instruments. These instru-
ments are forced into the mouth, rectum or vagina of the victim and there
expanded by force of the screw to the maximum aperture of the segments.
The pointed prongs at the end of the segments serve better to rip into the
throat, the intestines or the cervix.

   —*Inquisition: Torture instruments from the Middle Ages*
   to the Industrial Era

TORRE DE TOMBO

THE LISBON TELEPHONE book, which I looked up in Madrid,
lists twenty-eight pages of Pereiras. Samuel Toledano, an elder of
Spain's Sephardic community, assures me that most of these hundreds
of Pereiras are of Jewish descent. The Pereiras gained notoriety in the
sixteenth century, when the Portuguese Inquisition ferreted out 200
Judaizers of that name from the province of Evora alone.

   Setting out on the trail of my Portuguese ancestors, I spend the
night in Badajoz and rise early to obtain my visa and cross the border
into Portugal on an early spring day in late February. The contrasts are
immediate and palpable. Even the more remote Castilian towns have
been touched by the new *Europeización:* My hotel in Badajoz boasts a
swimming pool and one-armed bandits, and the latest yuppie fashions
are on display in downtown store windows. In a little over a decade,
Spain has sloughed off half a millennium of xenophobia and joined the
European community of nations. Madrid boasts more automobiles and
VCRs per capita than any other European city. Spain's youth, the
disaffected grandchildren of Republican and Nationalist combatants in
the Civil War, are routinely featured in trendy magazines as Europe's
most narcissistic and "yuppified."

   Although Portugal, like Spain, is now a member of the European Economic Community and aspires to its prosperity, life in the
campo is mired in an earlier century. The groves of budding quince and
almond trees and the olive-clad green wheat fields are dotted with the
tumbledown hovels of dirt-poor farmers.

   The town of Elvas is overshadowed by the soaring arches of its

fifteenth-century aqueduct, and pigeons circle over the tiled roofs of Estremoz with an old, old familiarity. A few miles to the south is the ancient city of Evora, former seat of the largest of Portugal's three
inquisitional tribunals, and one that reputedly burned three-quarters of
its accused Judaizers. Today Evora is known for its university, its
Roman temple to Diana and an ossuary chapel in the church of São
Francisco whose walls are adorned with the bones of several thousand
pious Christians and an undetermined number of heretics. Perhaps,
on closer acquaintance, these towns resonate, as does Toledo, to drum
rolls of a distant Jewish Golden Age; and their castle dungeons are as
likely to conserve imprints of the inquisitor's *penas y penitencias.* In any
event, from the top of a double-decker bus this countryside presents a
far gentler prospect than that of Castile. Driven to industrialize and
gain ground on its western neighbors, northern Spain has declared
open war on its natural resources. Castilians are laying siege to their
sparse forests and waterways, banishing them from the landscape as
they formerly banished their Jews and Moors. In this self-defeating en-
deavor, as in the earlier ones, Portugal lags two steps behind. Flocks of
birds still fill the skies of Portugal, and the trees have not turned grave
and uncommunicative.

In preparation for a stint in Lisbon's Inquisition archives, I have
boned up on Portuguese poets unread since my student days in Ann
Arbor. I am dazzled by the lambent stillnesses in the sonnets of Luiz
Vaz de Camões, Lusitania's national treasure, and turned off by the
fustian excesses of the playwright Gil Vicente, an ardent patriot and
anti-Semite. Unlike Spain's great poets Góngora and Quevedo, who
like Cervantes were subject to the scrutiny of the Holy Office's censors,
Portugal's two laureates flourished during a brief literary and humanist
interregnum and remained above suspicion.

Camões died in 1580, a few months before Portugal fell under
the Spanish yoke. By then, autos-da-fé were a commonplace in Lisbon,
Coimbra and Evora, providing lurid entertainment for the avid multitudes, and a spectacle with which the bombastic plays of Gil Vicente
could never compete.

LISBON SEEMS a simpler city than Madrid or Barcelona. My taxi
driver eagerly seconds this initial impression, even as we stall for half an
hour in bumper-to-bumper traffic. "This is exceptional," he assures

me, waving a right hand that is missing a thumb and two fingers. "It is the last Friday of the month. Everyone has just been paid and is doing his shopping." The voluble taxi driver, whose name is João, assures me that he lives on cheese, wine and bread for a mere 500 escudos a day. "In Spain I would have starved to death years ago."

When I tell him my purpose in coming to Portugal, João straightaway announces that he is from Coimbra and has cousins named Pereira whom I should meet. "We may be related!" he exclaims, flushed with spontaneous fellowship. When I ask about his hand, he mimics a fireworks display and goes "boom! boom!" over and over until I get the point: His fingers were blown off by an exploding rocket.

Lisbon has two main thoroughfares and a theater named after Pereiras; the telephone directory boasts eight full columns of Vitor Pereiras. I also find several Isaac and Moses Pereiras, none of whom, I will soon learn, is an avowed Jew. Small wonder that in the seventeenth and eighteenth centuries any Portuguese met in the streets of Toledo or Seville was assumed to be a Jew or a Marrano, and was a candidate for lynching.

Ancient animosities between Portugal and Spain still lie close to the surface. Although João especially despised Castilians, he had little good to say about any Spaniards, lumping them generically as overbearing and niggardly *senhoritos* who are loath to do an honest day's work. He let down his guard with me only after I assured him that I was *americano* by birth. When I sought out Lisbon University's expert on Portuguese Jews, Professor María José Pimenta Ferro, she refused to meet with me until I learned Portuguese well enough to converse, although she has a perfect command of Castilian.

João deposited me in a middling-expensive hotel in Dos Montes perched high above the alfama, the former Jewish quarter. My first night in Lisbon I dream of a two-piece plaque with screw holes at each of its eight corners. I am to screw the two halves of the plaque together, but the screws are all different sizes, and the holes strip and rip apart when I press down. There is no way to join together the two halves of the plaque.

The next morning I follow the trolley tracks down to the alfama. I stop by the glazed tiled murals of Old Lisbon in a small park overlooking the Tagus River. I pause to admire the magnificent fountains of the Rossio, the municipal square overlooking the Tagus river. It was here that 20,000 Jewish refugees from Spain had to stand long hours without food or water until they accepted baptism. And it was in this colorful plaza, under the equestrian statue of King Pedro IV, that many of the autos-da-fé and public burnings were performed for the entertainment of royalty and visiting dignitaries. The red-sailed schooners of my previous visit here a quarter century ago are gone, replaced by humongous freighters and oil tankers. But the sloping tiers of houses lining the narrow streets have the same air of shabby-genteel intimacy and clutter typical of Jewish ghettos around the globe.

My sense of déjà vu is more attenuated here; but I have no doubt that these blocks of down-at-heel residences brightened by potted roses and geraniums were once my neighborhood, as much as the *aljamas* of Toledo and Córdoba ever were. And I also know that the Pereiras who lived here, and in whose veins flowed the same blood that courses in mine, came to a bad end.

At Easter 1506, a New Christian who scoffed at a miraculous crucifix in a Dominican church not far from here was dragged out by the hair and beaten to death. The Dominicans then paraded the crucifix through the streets, goading mobs into attacking any Jew or Marrano they could find. After three days of riots the surviving Jews and conversos had fled the city or gone into hiding, leaving behind several thousand of their brethren dead and maimed. Recent studies on the Lisbon pogrom of 1506, the bloodiest in Portugal's history, underscore the plague and drought that afflicted the city, and the residents' simmering resentments against Marrano tax collectors, who may have been the mobs' chief targets.

In the afternoon I am accompanied to the Inquisition archive by a senator who has put his *querida* (mistress) up at my hotel. The taxi we share takes us across town to the Parliament building, where the Torre de Tombo is located. When I tell him of my purpose in going there, the gray-haired senator nods and says a curious thing: "Politics is politics, here and everywhere else." He tells me he is a friend of Joshua Levy, a leading Lisboan Jew who might be of help in my research. Offering to write a letter of introduction for me, the senator leads me to the entrance of the archive without troubling to share the cab fare, and leaves me there to ponder what he meant.

The clerk at the desk writes my name down and escorts me inside after I mention Professor Pimenta Ferro—another plus for Portugal in my book. When I visited the Historical Archive in Madrid, I was

denied access to the Inquisition files even after I presented letters of introduction from Spanish scholars. (They insisted on a letter from the U.S.
Consulate.) Growing heated, I called the clerk a fitting descendant of
Torquemada, to which she responded with a gelid smile that chilled
me to the bone.

The files are stored with other ledgers in a single room with
barred windows and a domed ceiling at least fifty feet high. This will be
my penitent's cell for the next several days, as I pore over thousands of
two-by-two-inch cards with entries inscribed in a flowing calligraphy
and tied into bundles with string. There will be no computerized data
banks here, not soon, not for years to come.

The clerk brings me the files from the Evora tribunal, which was
not only the first and the largest of the three but also the longest-lived.
The last case of *judaismo* at Evora was tried in 1817. I begin taking
down the entries on Pereiras and am soon overwhelmed. Before I am
done I will have tabulated over 200 Pereiras who were tried in Evora
alone, and 150 others in Lisbon and Coimbra. Traced on a map, the
tribunals of Lisbon, Coimbra and Evora outline a deadly triangle that
cut the heart out of the Marrano communities of northern and central
Portugal. And Pereiras add up to nearly ten percent of the total. Only
da Silvas appear in greater numbers. I now understood why the name
Pereira aroused suspicion even when borne by inquisitors with impeccable Old Christian bloodlines.

My despair at finding a direct link to my ancestors abated only
after I realized that many of these Pereiras were arrested on the strength
of a single accusation. One family member, under torture, often implicated dozens of his relatives. The 350 Pereiras may have belonged to as
few as thirty-five to forty family groupings.

I look for Isaac, Moses, Jacob, Solomon Pereiras, common
names in my family for several generations; but I find none. The obvious explanation is that those with Jewish first names would have
changed them to João or Gonçalo when they converted, and then
passed on similar Christian names to their children. A separate file of
"Observaçoe" lists the specific charges against an accused person, their
place of residence, the sentence passed and the penances served, and
itemizes the goods confiscated or sequestered. (Confiscation indicated
goods permanently seized; sequestration referred to goods and moneys
held—and spent—while a penitent served his sentence.)

As I go over each card a second and third time, patterns emerge. Of the 200 Pereiras tried in Evora, nearly 150 were accused of *judaismo*. The earliest case tried on that charge was that of Antonio Pereira, in 1554. The latest was Henriqueta Xavier Pereira, in 1817—a span of 263 years! For the Pereiras the Inquisition was a holocaust stretched out over centuries.

Apart from Antonio, João and Francisco, the most common names on the list are Ana and Isabel. Among the hyphenated family names, the ones most often linked with Pereira were Lopes, Rodrigues, Nunes and Cardoso, all common New Christian patronymics. Surprisingly, the list of victims is almost evenly divided between males and females. Compared with Germany and France, where tens of thousands of women were burned as witches, the Spanish and Portuguese inquisitions were relatively lenient on the matter of witchcraft. But they did single out Marrano women, whom they labeled "Jewish prophetesses" bent on spreading their faith by necromancy and pacts with the devil.

During the first one hundred years of the Inquisition, the charges against Pereiras were almost invariably the same: *"judaismo, heresia, apostasia."* In the last century the charges more often included superstition, prostitution, homosexuality, blasphemy, bigamy, occult practices. None of these heresies was a capital offense, or carried the devastating penalties incurred by the accusation of Judaizing. And it was not necessary to have had two Jewish parents to be considered an apostate. *Judaismo* could be charged against someone with no more than one-twentieth of Jewish blood in his or her veins. (In another chilling anticipation of Nazi Germany, whose Nuremberg Laws forbade Jews to refer to themselves as "Herr," Pope Paul IV in 1555 banned the use of the honorifics "Don," "Seigneur," "Signor" or "Sire" in front of Jewish names.)

Another startling statistic was the age differential, which ranged from fourteen to over eighty. In Spain, several cases are on file of men and women tortured and/or burned at the stake when they were past ninety. And the Toledo tribunal regularly sentenced to penitence children under the age of ten. Among the women in particular, I found a disproportionate percentage between fifteen and twenty years old. Young women were evidently singled out, intimidated and tortured for the purpose of obtaining testimony that incriminated as large a circle of relatives as possible. And who would be more pliant in the inquisitor's hands than a fifteen-year-old New Christian virgin who had only recently begun to make confession and receive communion?

IN SCANNING THE evidence presented to back a charge of *judaismo* I found an impressive catalogue, beginning with "keeps the Sabbath"; "proclaims the Law of Moses"; "announces the Messiah"; "practices circumcision"; "uses home as a synagogue"; "observes Purim, Passover and Feast of Tabernacles"; "washes blood from meat"; "turns his face to the wall before dying"; "washes corpse with warm water"; "recites prayer to the dead and buries same in Jewish cemetery"; and descending to thin circumstantial proofs, physiognomic stereotypes and outright conjecture. Many of the Pereiras were arrested and charged on the testimony of neighbors who claimed to have seen them "changing linen on Friday evenings"; "refusing pork alleging medical reasons"; "preparing dishes with onions and garlic instead of lard"; "never buying meat on Saturdays"; "offering friends a repast before undertaking a voyage"; "absent from communion"; "deleting Ave Maria from the benediction"; "reciting psalms of David without saying Gloria Patri"; and "looking away from the crucifix."

Given the flexible criteria acceptable to the tribunals, a neighbor with a score to settle could give full rein to his imagination in seeking to put his enemy away. And, of course, the victim was not given the chance to confront his accusers or respond to the charges until he was condemned.

The tribunals had no need of paid informers to collect evidence. Apart from a suspect's neighbors, they could call on a fifth column of voluntary spies and investigators who were known as "familiars," and who often shared in the booty collected from confiscations. The familiars were an outgrowth of Queen Isabella's Santa Hermandad, the peacekeeping civilian militia. Over time, it evolved from a vocation for unemployed riffraff to a prestigious calling that attracted persons of high station. The Toledo tribunal alone was attended by nearly 900 familiars. Most of the complaints lodged against the Inquisition focused on the abuses by corrupt familiars; but the practice endured into the second half of the eighteenth century, when the revenues began to dry up due to the scarcity of monied victims.

The Inquisition's lists of confiscated goods were so meticulous as

to provide an inventory of the Portuguese Marrano community's predi-
lections in clothes, dry goods, furnishing, jewelry and other properties.
Isabel Pereira, daughter of Manuel Suarez, was found guilty of Judaizing and deprived of all her worldly goods, which included a home, several fruit and olive orchards, three fur blankets, a handcrafted oakwood
bed from Portalegre, three tambourines, three breadbaskets, wooden
cabinets and armoires, and a large number of metal objects, jewelry and
precious stones.

On occasion the inquisitors came up against steadfast detainees
who refused to confess or admit to a heresy. One such was Francisca
Pereira, widow of Francisco Lopes Castanho, a laborer. She was detained in 1715 and presented at an auto-da-fé three years later. Francisca
Pereira was finally absolved when she held firm in declaring herself a
"legitimate, entire and spotless Old Christian" ("*legitima, enteira e limpia
Crista-velha*"). The accusations brought against her by relations, who
may have been plotting to weasel her out of a portion of her estate, were
thrown out of court. She was released impenitent, and her two sequestered houses were returned. This was the single instance I found of a
Pereira who was released without having to forfeit at least a portion of
her possessions.

One of many peculiarities in the inquisitional procedure concerned the accused who died in prison or fled the country, and who
were sentenced and punished in *estatua* (effigy). Flight was seen as an
admission of guilt, and the culprits would be severely punished after
they were apprehended. Joanna Pereira, a fifty-year-old New Christian
married to a lawyer, attempted flight after her detention in September
1703. When recaptured two years later she was tied to a rack known as
a *potro* (pony), the commonest form of torture. She was given four turns
of the cord before she confessed her sins and begged for the sacraments.
Despite her confession and repentance, she was sentenced to "*penas e
penitencias espirituais*" for perpetuity in the Evora penitentiary, along with
the confiscation of her house and olive orchards.

An Ana Pereira who died in the tribunal's prison after twelve
days of detention was found guilty of Judaizing. Her remains were exhumed and delivered with her wooden effigy to the secular authorities,
which burned them together with those who had been sentenced to die
in person. The message in both these cases is unequivocal: Whether in
this life or the next, Judaizers can never hope to escape the long arm of
the Inquisition.

Along with the occasional pardons of New Christians by the pope, the officers of the Holy Office's Suprema could also in rare in-stances demonstrate leniency: for example, in a case where a swift and sincere repentance was elicited from a person of pedigree or outside influence. Andrés Pereira, a twenty-seven-year-old cavalry lieutenant and shield-bearer to a Castilian knight, fled from Estremoz to Badajoz after he was charged with Judaizing. Following his arrest at the Spanish border he was sentenced to mild penances and absolved of all further punishment. Nonetheless, the tribunal confiscated his horse, Damascene steel sword, two pistols, gold-braided uniform and regimental cape.

The case of Manuel Pereira, a twenty-year-old student at the University of Evora, would make a fine picaresque novel were the full particulars of his story to come to light. In the succinct account recorded on three two-by-two cards by the tribunal's secretary, Pereira is de-scribed as having traveled to Rome and then to Venice, where he ran out of money. He visited the city's famous Jewish ghetto and spent fif-teen days with a family that initiated him into Israelite ritual. Pereira was then escorted by other Jews to the island of Guelph, where he spent two weeks in the home of Rabbi Dom Samuel Seneor, a lawyer from Bayonne who instructed him further in the Hebrew religion. Dom Samuel advanced moneys to Manuel Pereira for his return to Venice, and from there he sailed directly to Portugal, where he turned himself in to the tribunal at Evora and confessed to Judaizing. Pereira cast off his indoctrination at once and declared himself a devout Catholic. After a course in Christian instruction he was reconciled to the church and re-leased. A note at the end suggests that Manuel Pereira's abjuration con-tained detailed information on Jewish rites that proved useful to the tribunal, and for that reason he was absolved without further penitence.

Among the last to be tried in Portugal was the adventurer Da Costa Pereira Furtado de Mondonça, who spent three years in prison, from 1802 to 1805, after he was sentenced by the Lisbon tribunal. In London several years later, Pereira Furtado wrote a chronicle of his per-secutions that itemized the tortures and afflictions resorted to by the Por-tuguese Inquisition as late as the nineteenth century. Publication of the account appears to have brought down more notoriety upon Pereira Furtado than censure upon the Inquisition.

.   .   .

NO CASE IS MORE affecting than that of fifteen-year-old Ana Pereira, who was the daughter of Belchior Lopes Pereira, a merchant, and Maria de Victoria, from the small town of Barcelos. Ana's case was presented to the tribunal in 1683, and she was detained on March 10, 1684, accused of practicing Jewish rites in the privacy of her home. At the auto-da-fé of March 10, 1684, she was convicted of Judaizing, heresy and apostasy. She was sentenced to wear penitential raiment and undergo spiritual penances in the Evora penitentiary.

Under "Observations," the tribunal lists fifteen family members, among them her sisters, cousins and brothers-in-law, whom Ana Pereira incriminated after she was subjected to *tormentos.*

I picture this adolescent girl dressed in white from head to foot, her brown or black eyes wide with terror as she is led to the *casa santa,* as the torture cell was called, and is placed on the rack by the secular tor-turer, who usually doubled as executioner. A representative of the bishop, a notary and a recording secretary would have been present as the inquisitor—perhaps a Dominican friar—admonishes the girl in a stern voice. Addressing her as "sister in Christ," he counsels her to con-fess all her sins in order to be spared the twists of the cords tied around her waist, wrists and breasts. To make certain that she understands what lies in store, he demonstrates how the cords will bite into her flesh until she screams in agony.

The majority of the accused, according to Inquisition records, confessed their sins and repented at the mere sight of the torture instru-ments, without having to be put through the ordeal. A few decades ear-lier Ana Pereira might also have been exposed to the water torture or the *garrucha,* a pulley from which a victim was hung and stretched until her arms and legs came loose from their sockets.

The interrogation would have included questions like the fol-lowing: Did she light candles on Friday night? Did her mother change the bed linens on Saturdays? Was pork customarily eaten in her home? When had she last received the Holy Sacraments? Why had she not at-tended Communion? After each question the inquisitor admonishes her to tell the truth and repent of her sins.

This may have been all it took for this young woman to confess her own transgressions—she had, after all, been brought up Catholic. Only recently had her mother told her the truth of her Israelite ancestry. New Christians who secretly practiced their Jewish religion rarely cir-cumcised their boys, and did not indoctrinate their children—if at all—until they were old enough to guard the knowledge of their origins with discretion.

The next stage, inducing Ana Pereira to turn in her kin, required more persuasive measures. A young woman of spirit might balk at taking that fateful next step in betrayal, and Ana evidently was such a young person, or there would have been no need for torments. Her white raiments are removed and she is tied to the pony. How many turns of the cord before she names her father's brother as one who kept the Sabbath? How many more before she confesses that her own sister refused to eat pork? The inquisitor must have repeatedly reminded her that if she fails to complete confession by naming all the Judaizers in her family she will be subject to relaxation as *renuente* (obstinate) or *negativa*. A Benjamin Gil of Toledo was declared *renuente* in 1670 and burned at the stake, although he implicated 213 relatives and acquaintances as fellow Judaizers.

We are told the inquisitors who participated in these events were moved by Christian piety and love for the penitents, and a sincere desire for their reconciliation with Mother Church. (In the autos-da-fé, only the unrepentant were burned alive; those who confessed and abjured their sins at the last moment were allowed the mercy of being garroted before the torch was lit under their bodies.) The fantastic depictions of sadistic inquisitors indulging their bloodlust on helpless innocents—a Black Legend tradition perpetuated in nineteenth-century European literature—had no basis in reality, according to the respected historians Henry Charles Lea and Henry Kamen. Kamen emphasizes the lengths to which torturers went not to spill blood or break bones, and to apply only the force necessary to elicit confession and sincere repentance. These factors add a paradoxical dimension to the inevitable questions:

Would there have been glee in the heart of the inquisitor after Ana named her fifteen relations, and rejoicing at the harvest of new souls to be set on the path to redemption? Where in this scene do we find the Christ of infinite mercy, the Christ of compassion toward the justly *and* the unjustly afflicted?

And what of Ana? How would she face her family, her friends, after she was paraded through the streets of Evora in the Sambenito and exposed to the ridicule of her neighbors? How did she fare in the penitentiary cell, where she was held for weeks on end without visitors or contact with other penitents, and where she slept—we are told—on a straw mattress in a damp cell not much larger than a broom closet? (Ana was relatively fortunate. In Valladolid a few years earlier, a four-teen-year-old girl and a nine-year-old boy had sat in jail for two years before charges were drawn up against them by the tribunal's arbiter.) What sentiments of remorse and forgiveness toward her adopted reli-gion could Ana be expected to embrace on being returned to Barcelos? Was she thankful at having been spared even worse cruelties at the hands of a jailer or a minor official—as had not been the case, for exam-ple, of the fifteen-year-old girl in Jaen, who was locked in a cell by the tribunal's notary, stripped naked and whipped until she agreed to testify against her mother?

The "Observations" conclude with the provision that Ana was not to leave the penitentiary until she had received the Holy Sacraments, and that she would require permission to attend mass.

The Inquisition's torturers may seem crude and unsophisticated compared with modern specialists in Latin America and the Middle East, but they achieved their intended purpose: to debase, scourge and afflict the victim's spirit until it was broken and he or she became an instrument of the inquisitor's will. There is no avoiding the conclusion that the soul was snuffed out of the living body of Ana Pereira as delib-erately and irrevocably as was the life of another young woman sub-jected to a twentieth-century version of state-sponsored evil, and whose name also happens to have been Anna.

COMPARED WITH THE 100,000 New Christians tried by the Spanish tribunals, Portugal's figures may seem relatively unimpressive. But that appearance is deceptive. The records of autos-da-fé in Portugal are spotty, as many of the files have been lost. The extant records ac-count for a total of about 40,000 Judaizers accused by the Holy Office's Suprema, or nearly half the Spanish total, out of a population less than one-third the size of Spain's. These figures include a nineteen-year pe-riod, 1581–1600, that saw a total of fifty autos-da-fé: In Evora 98 vic-tims were burned at the stake, 16 in effigy, and 1,384 received penance. The totals for the three tribunals between 1547 and 1765 were 1,800 penitents garroted and/or burned at the stake, 30,000 "reconciled" after receiving sentences of varying severity. Of the 200 Pereiras listed in the Evora files, only nine, or five percent, were burned alive in the *quemadeiro* for obstinately refusing to abjure their Judaism. Another six or seven were relaxed in person by the Lisbon and Coimbra tribunals. But this tells only part of the story.

Beginning in the 1600s, Portuguese converts fled to Spain by the thousands, only to revive the Inquisition's smoldering fires there. In 1602 wealthy Portuguese offered Philip III a gift of 1,860,000 ducats in exchange for a royal pardon to Judaizers for all past offenses. Tempted by such an exorbitant ransom, the Spanish monarch applied to Rome, and a papal pardon was issued in 1605. On January 16, the three Portuguese tribunals released a total of 410 prisoners. As Kamen points out, "By this astonishing agreement the Spanish crown revealed its own financial bankruptcy and its willingness to jettison religious ideals when the profits from a bribe exceeded those from confiscations."

This respite proved to be temporary, as the Inquisition resumed full-fledged activities in Spain and Portugal as soon as the terms of the pardon were met. By the middle of the eighteenth century, so thorough had been the extirpation of Judaizers in the New Christian communities that the Portuguese and Spanish tribunals had to turn their attention to other heresies, including witchcraft, homosexuality, bigamy and sacrilege, to justify their continued existence.

II

THE SYNAGOGUE

As I had feared, Professor Pimenta Ferro was not encouraging about my chances of isolating the thread of my direct ancestors from the thick skein of the Pereiras of Portugal. The few Abendanas listed in the Inquisition files proved of no help in establishing a lineage.

After a week of research in the Torre de Tombo I scanned the telephone book for "esnoga Israelita" and found two, a Sephardic one listed on Alexandre Herculano Street and an Ashkenazic one on Elías García Avenue. The Ashkenazic turned out to be a dead letter, but a voice at 59 Herculano said I could meet with members of the congregation at their Friday evening services.

Two strapping young men stopped me outside the tall steel gate and asked to see my passport and Jewish credentials. I was not flustered, as I had undergone similar security checks in synagogues all over Europe, but a sadness lingered. Had I been a Marrano seeking his Jew/ ish roots after centuries of anonymity, would I have been able to get past the gate?

The synagogue was instantly familiar. In fact, it bore a remark/ able resemblance to my father's Magen David Temple in Guatemala City, where he initiated me into the Jewish religion. An oblong *bimah* rises from the center of the prayer hall, flanked by two rows of pa/ triarchs' chairs; the benches in the rear are for transients and the women. The ark housing the Torah is made of fine polished wood, and displays the Ten Commandments inscribed on copper plates. The Hebrew leg/ end above the ark reads: "Behold, the Lord is the one in whose presence you stand."

The rabbi is a Moroccan immigrant of about sixty/five. After delivering the opening benedictions he turned the service over to his son, an apprentice *gabbai* (synagogue official) to recite the Sabbath lit/ urgy. Five middle/aged men in prayer shawls davened with a natural/ ness tutored by long custom, as their wives looked on from the rear. The five other worshippers who rounded out the minyan appeared to be novices or transients. A dark/skinned man sitting in the back with the women turned out to be an Angolan refugee who hoped to obtain fi/ nancial aid from the congregation so he could study abroad. It was not clear whether he was a Jew, although he wore a skullcap and cracked open the prayer book at least once.

As I tried to keep up with the prayers, I was overcome by a fa/ miliar sense of inadequacy and intimidation. My father had not had the patience to teach me my *aleph/bet*, and gave up on me altogether after having paid for the honor of my bearing the Torah during Rosh Ha/ shanah. I was barely ten at the time, and was so stricken by the fear of dropping the scroll and profaning Holy Writ, that my ankles turned to rubber and I barely made it to the *bimah*. From then on, Father delegated my Jewish education to an Auschwitz survivor, a Polish math profes/ sor who spent many of our sessions sighing and moaning aloud.

Now, after all these years, I have come to understand the paralyz/ ing guilt that underlay my father's impatience and outward insen/ sitivity. Burdened with the onus of violating his grandfather's commandment, Father turned his back on the religious orthodoxy of his forebears; and he all but turned me into a Marrano. It was a fate shared by many Sephardim of my generation, whose parents, upon arrival in the New World, lapsed into a desultory observance of Jewish ritual.

At the end of the service I approached one of the patriarchs, a corpulent man of about sixty-five who turned out to be none other than Joshua Levy, the prominent Lisboan mentioned by the senator. Levy, an accountant, is a third-generation Portuguese Jew whose great-grand-father arrived in Lisbon from Gibraltar in 1820.

He answered my questions with a formal distance verging on ir-ritability. As the secretary of the congregation he fields all questions from outsiders, which tend to be the same questions, repeated ad nau-seam—or so his bored manner seemed to suggest.

Exaggerated rumors to the contrary, Levy said, there are only about 350 practicing Jews in Portugal, most of whom live in Lisbon. Of these, only about fifty attend services, usually during the holidays, so it is often impossible to gather the ten men needed for a prayer quorum. "Since the war, 30,000 Moroccan Jews have been admitted to Spain, but only a trickle came to Portugal, our rabbi among them. We Gi-braltarians take a certain pride in having been here first, although we are in the minority.

"Pereira? There are no Jewish Pereiras in Portugal, and have not been for many generations. In fact, if you ring up the Cohens and Levis in the phone book, you'll find they are all Christians, every last one. They converted in the fifteenth and sixteenth centuries, and never both-ered to change their names."

"What about crypto-Jews?" I asked Levy. "I understand there is a functioning synagogue in the town of Oporto, run by Marranos."

"That one was founded by a Portuguese army officer named Barros Basto, a convert who reclaimed his Jewish identity earlier in this century. With the help of British Jews he passed out Old Testaments among Marranos in Oporto, reopened the synagogue and attempted to revive Jewish worship. Barros Basto was brought up on trumped-up charges by a fellow Jew, and the army court-martialed him. After he died in 1961 the synagogue closed down, and nothing more ever came of it. The Marranos there still fear repercussions if they practice their Ju-daism openly, and so they have returned to their secretive ways."

"And what about smaller towns? Isn't there an underground Jewish culture in parts of central and northern Portugal?"

"Of course, of course, there are pockets of Marranos all over Portugal. A couple from Belmonte writes us every year to inquire when the holy days of Yom Kippur and Queen Esther will fall so they can ob- serve them. These Marranos made contacts with rabbis in Israel, but they still cling to their curious tradition of fasting not only on the Day of Atonement but on Purim as well, which is a festive occasion. We keep them informed of the dates but do not otherwise encourage them. All of these people have received baptism; their sons are uncircumcised, and they know only the rudiments of their ancestral religion. To us they re- main *anusim*. We do not consider them formal Jews. In fact, if they came to Lisbon and asked to attend services, we would probably have to turn them away."

CHAPTER IV

MADRID

Stay in the middle of the road, Pereira.
—"Johnny with the Bandy Leg," Marais and Miranda

ARIAS MONTANO

BACK IN SPAIN I continued my research at the Arias Montano Institute, a center of investigation named after a seventeenth-century converso and biblical scholar who ran afoul of the Inquisition's censorship
commission. The Arias Montano opened in 1939, shortly after the vic-
torious Generalissimo Francisco Franco confirmed himself as premier
of Spain in perpetuity.

Ya'cov Hassan, curator of the Judaica division, extended a far
warmer welcome than I had received at the Historical Archive. I lost
no time in getting back on the track of my ancestors in the centuries following the Expulsion. The excellent library of 20,000 new and old
books and documents, the wealth of material published by the institute
itself and the superb guidance of the staff opened window after window
into the fascinating and inexhaustible saga of the Iberian Jews. Eliyahu
Eliachar had not exaggerated when he predicted that I would find
enough surprises to stitch together an original and singular chronicle.
And if the story of Iberian Jewry could be summed up in the experience of a single family, the Pereiras would serve better than most.

DESPITE THE CONCERTED efforts by the Inquisition to root
out all secret Jews from the body politic, and to curtail the power of assimilated New Christians in high office, by the middle of the sixteenth
century conversos had married into virtually all the noble families of
Aragon and Castile. Far from resolving the problem of "tainted
blood," the Inquisition drove thousands of Marranos to seek safeguards
against discovery and persecution in the highest redoubts of secular and
religious office. Descendants of conversos rose to be bishops, governors,
royal ministers and founders of financial empires.

In Portugal three Pereiras held the office of inquisitor at one time
or another. In Venezuela, Don Juan Pereira de Castro was the chief

inquisitor of Cartagena. Pereira de Castro was brought to trial on sixty-seven counts of corruption and abuse of office, chief among them a scandal involving a black Judaizer. The most intriguing case of all is that of Diego Lopes Pereira, a bishop and an inquisitor in Portugal during the eighteenth century, and a Marrano whose story unfolds below.

Pereiras also continued to appear prominently on the lists of victims of the Inquisition, not only in Spain and Portugal but in the New World colonies. Nunes Pereira, a Guatemalan of Portuguese birth, was burned at the stake in Mexico City in 1595 for "judaizing, heresy and apostasy." At least two other Pereiras from Portugal, Nuño and Baltasar, were tried by Mexico's Inquisition in the seventeenth century. Baltasar abjured his Judaizing and was reconciled after paying a 200-peso fine. Nuño, accused of writing obscene verses to Saint Felipe de Jesús, was fined and given 200 lashes before he was sent to prison for perpetuity in Spain. Juan Antonio Pereira was one of the last victims sentenced for Judaizing in Peru. He was burned alive in an individual auto-da-fé in Lima in 1737.

The fifty or so Pereiras who appear in Spain's Inquisition files after 1547 include a score of conversos who fled Portugal's Inquisition only to be found out and tried in Spanish tribunals. By the middle of the seventeenth century, Portuguese Judaizers made up the majority of penitents sentenced to autos-da-fé in Seville, Toledo and other cities with active tribunals, a trend that would continue for several generations.

In 1658 Francisco Lopez Pereira, a tax administrator in Granada, was called before the Inquisition tribunal on charges of Judaizing. Pereira had been tried eight years earlier on the same charges in Coimbra, Portugal, where he was born. After lengthy scrutiny, his trial was suspended, a rare reprieve for one bearing that family name. Not so fortunate was Juan Pereira, a doctor of Portuguese birth accused of *mala raza* in Jérez de la Frontera in 1745. Pereira launched a countersuit against the tribunal, alleging mistaken identity and defamation of character. He claimed that the Francisco Pereira tried for Judaizing a half century earlier was no relation of his. Unimpressed, the tribunal prohibited him from practicing his medical profession. Having tried so many of Pereira's blood kin, the inquisitors declared that the accused's surname was sufficient proof of guilt since "it is much noted among the cases of relaxation and reconciliation infected by Portuguese ancestry."

II

A MARRANO RENAISSANCE

In the sixteenth century, conversos and their descendants were to play a key role in the brief Spanish renaissance. The writings of Erasmus found enthusiastic disciples in Spanish humanists of Jewish origin like Juan Luís Vives and the brothers Juan and Francisco Vergara, as well as in biblical scholar Arias Montano, progenitor of the Royal Polyglot Bible composed in Hebrew, Chaldean and Greek. Charles V counted himself among the admirers of Erasmus's *Enchiridion,* which was trans, lated and distributed by Spain's proliferating printing presses. Another admirer of Erasmus was the reformist archbishop of Toledo, Cardinal Francisco Ximénez de Cisneros, who founded the liberal university of Alcalá de Henares. As inquisitor general from 1507, the humanist Cardinal Ximénez was the first—and last—inquisitor to attempt struc, tural reforms in Spain's Holy Office.

In the first quarter of the sixteenth century, books and ideas cir, culated freely in Spain, and its two universities, Alcalá and Salamanca, became the foci of humanities studies to which scholars flocked from all over Europe. Their divinity faculties led the world in Hebrew and Ara, bic studies, to the extent that Erasmus himself was moved to assert that his greatest following was to be found in Spanish academic circles. This brief interlude, however, was brought to an end by two develop, ments: the rise of Martin Luther and the Reformation, and the emer, gence of a mystical cult of Illuminists, or *Alumbrados,* who gained notoriety for sexual profligacy and other profanations in their obsessive quest for ecstatic union and divine revelation.

The Jesuit order under Saint Ignatius de Loyola was among the first to counsel religious tolerance toward Marranos and *moriscos* (con, verted Muslims). Loyola, who was called a Jew,lover and worse by his enemies in the church, denounced the cult of *limpieza* as "the Spanish bile." But even the Jesuit order capitulated after Loyola's death and adopted a statute of *limpieza* in 1593. (A 1608 amendment rendered the statute inoperative.) For nearly 200 years, the Holy Office persecuted Loyola's followers, many of them descendants of conversos, as tena, ciously as it went after Judaizers and Lutherans.

The Lutheran Reformation, which threatened the Catholic

heart of monarchic Spain, became increasingly identified with Erasmic humanism and "Jewish" thought. And the Illuminists, whose progenitors were Franciscan friars of converso descent, were denounced as an outgrowth of the Marrano heresy. After stamping out the Illuminists, the Inquisition targeted the Lutherans by attacking the universities where Erasmic Protestants had taken refuge, and by introducing the practice of book burning that endured into the nineteenth century.

The Inquisition's obsession with religious and racial purity was replaced by a preoccupation with impure ideas. Many of the writers singled out by the Inquisition's censors were of converso origin, or were accused of "Jewish Lutheranism." Francisco de Vergara, one of Spain's leading Greek and Latin scholars, was convicted in an auto-da-fé in 1535, and spent two years imprisoned in a monastery after being forced to abjure his errors. Juan Luís Vives, the greatest of Spain's humanist pedagogues, who secretly practiced Judaism in his youth, wrote: "We live in such difficult times that it is dangerous either to speak or to be silent."

Friar Luís de León, the great converso poet and scholar, was accused of taking "heretical liberties with the study of Scripture and theology" at Salamanca University, and spent four years in the Inquisition's jails. In prison he wrote several of the religious canticles that rank him one of Spain's three great mystical poets. (The other two, Saint Teresa of Avila and Saint John of the Cross, also had converso ancestors.) With the arrest of Luís de León and three of his colleagues from Salamanca—all of converso origin—liberal studies were all but expurgated from Spain's two universities, which entered a centuries-long decline.

The Holy Office's role as censor of heretical writings had only begun, however; its Index of Prohibited Books, first published in 1551, was progressively updated and expanded until it included most of Spain's literary classics, from *La Celestina* and *Lazarillo de Tormes* to Cervantes' *Don Quixote*. The Inquisition and the Expulsion, which would isolate Spain and contribute to its decline as a major economic and military power, paradoxically engendered Spain's greatest literary resurgence. The repressive policies that would make Spain an international pariah also sparked a veritable revolution in literature, architecture, music and the visual arts. This cultural explosion came to be known as Spain's Golden Age.

III

THE JEWISH TRADERS

What about Pereira?
He's no gentleman, Pereira: You can't trust him!
Well, that's true.
No it wouldn't do to be too nice to Pereira.
                    —*T. S. Eliot, "Sweeney Agonistes"*

In the early part of the seventeenth century, most of the Marrano Pereiras who would make their mark in the Diaspora arranged their departure from the peninsula. In 1628 a group of monied Portuguese Jews paid Philip IV more than 80,000 ducats for the authorization to enter Spain. After leaving Portugal, many of them traveled instead to the Nether﹨ lands, France and England. However, at least three Pereiras—Manuel, Jacob and Abraham Isaac—would reenter Spain separately as trades﹨ men.

Jacob Pereira, an Amsterdam merchant who slipped into Spain without permission from the Inquisition, was discovered and appre﹨ hended in Cádiz. After the count of Floridablanca vouched for Pereira, depicting him as "a man as honest as any to be found," the in﹨ quisitors acknowledged that he was a practicing Jew with no connec﹨ tion to Judaizers, "and one of the best of his kind." But before releasing him they interrogated him on the subject of Freemasonry, a heresy con﹨ cerning which Jacob professed total ignorance.

Manuel Lopes Pereira, brother of the legendary beauty Maria Nunes (of whom more later) traveled to Holland from Portugal in the late sixteenth century. In Amsterdam, Manuel had helped found the Dutch Sephardic community with his married sisters and his brothers Francisco and Antonio. Shortly after his arrival in the Netherlands, Manuel married his first cousin Brites Nunes and moved to Antwerp in search of better business opportunities. With his cousin and brother﹨in﹨ law Manuel Lopes Homen, Manuel Lopes bought shares in two mer﹨ chant ships and began a lucrative trade in figs and Madeira sugar as well as in West Indian hides and pearls and tapestries from the Orient.

In 1617 Manuel Lopes traveled to Seville with his sister Maria and his brother-in-law. A year later, in Madrid, he became an adviser to the count duke of Olivares, prime minister to Philip IV. In Spain he came to be known as "Antonio López Pereira," and that is how his name appears in most chronicles. Olivares had embarked on an ambitious program to reverse Spain's commercial, industrial and financial decline. A keystone of his plan was his efforts to persuade well-to-do Iberian Jews to return to the peninsula from North Africa and the Levant. During the 1630s, a period that coincided with a lull in the Inquisition's activities, the count duke of Olivares commanded considerable influence in court and in mercantile circles.

Manuel Lopes, alias Antonio López Pereira, gained a reputation as a mercantile expert, or *arbitrista;* he compiled and submitted to Philip IV's ministers economic proposals for improving Spain's foreign-trade imbalance. After he became a protégé of the count duke of Olivares, Pereira's enemies spread rumors of his Marrano origins, and of his relatives in Amsterdam who openly practiced Judaism. But Pereira's skills assured him of Olivares's and the court's protection, and in 1624 a junta of government ministers judged him to be a "man of great intelligence and dedication." After he was recommended for a royal grant, Pereira became a naturalized Castilian subject and accepted the post of royal auditor.

In the early 1630s he was put in charge of administering the revenues from Olivares's new salt tax. He soon proved his abilities and was promoted to chief auditor, with a seat in the Royal Council of Finance. Within a short time, the Marrano Antonio Pereira became privy to important and highly sensitive affairs of state.

As Pereira's initiatives gained favor with Philip IV's ministers, he pressed for direct trade with Antwerp and the Spanish Netherlands, bypassing Amsterdam altogether. Although his proposals for establishing a South Netherlands East India Company to compete directly with its Dutch counterpart were ultimately rejected, Pereira attained the position of chief *arbitrista* in charge of trade negotiations with both Amsterdam and Antwerp.

Rumors of Pereira's Jewish past pursued him as he made headway in Philip IV's court. His enemies circulated a false report that he had formerly been tried as a Judaizer in Lisbon. In fact, his brother Antonio, who reclaimed the ancient family name of Abendana (as did his brother-in-law Manuel Homen), had become a mainstay of Amsterdam's Jewish community. But the count duke of Olivares's determined protection of López Pereira kept the Inquisition's hounds at bay.

In the 1640s Olivares's reputation suffered a sharp reversal in court, perhaps because of his patronage of Marrano traders like Pereira and his overtures toward Jewish financiers in North Africa. "Count," Philip IV wrote Olivares in 1640, in the wake of one of Spain's re-peated military setbacks, "these evil events have been caused by your sins and by mine in particular." Philip IV came to the conclusion that restoring racial and religious orthodoxy was a higher priority for Spain than economic reforms. Once you started down that road, the king rea-soned, in tune with his forebears Ferdinand and Isabella, you opened the gates wide to the polluting influences of Jews, Protestants and other foreign contagions. Philip's mood of self-excoriation, which was mir-rored in the society at large, ideally suited the inquisitors' designs.

A fresh wave of detentions and autos-da-fé concentrated on Por-tuguese financiers, whose enormous fortunes were confiscated to shore up an empire that was on the verge of bankruptcy. This third major cycle of persecution of Judaizers would peak in the 1650s, which saw the highest number of autos-da-fé ever recorded in the 340-year-long history of the Spanish Inquisition.

The record loses track of Manuel Lopes, alias Antonio López Pereira, after 1640, except that he appears as one of the executors of Oli-vares's estate. As he does not show up in the Inquisition's files, the likeliest assumption is that Pereira lived out his days as a reassimilated member in good standing of Madrid's New Christian society.

In Amsterdam's Sephardic community, the story of the Marrano who reclaimed his Jewish ancestry only to return to Spain and recon-vert, continued to stir controversy as late as the nineteenth century. It is a Jewish success story with a double twist.

IV

BARON D'AGUILAR

The story of Diego Lopes Pereira, pieced together from Jewish histori-cal chronicles and diverse sources, would strain credulity to the break-ing point were it not rivaled by so many other accounts of remarkable metamorphoses provoked by the Inquisition.

The record opens in the late seventeenth century with Moses

Lopes Pereira's abduction in Madrid at the age of six by Dominican friars, after his father was charged with Judaizing and relaxed in an auto-da-fé. While his mother and sister went on living to all appearances as practicing Catholics, the boy, renamed Diego d'Aguilar, was groomed for a career in the church. Thanks to his keen intellect and his abilities as an administrator, Diego rose steadily in the sacred orders until he became a bishop, engaged actively in the work of the Inquisition.

One afternoon his mother, who has till now kept her identity a secret, appears in Bishop d'Aguilar's dispatch to solicit a pardon for her daughter, who has been tried as a Judaizer and is to be executed the following day.

"Why should I pardon a sinful heretic?" he demands haughtily.

She falls to her knees and cries out in despair, "*Miserable!* Don't you see it is your own sister you are condemning to death, and that I who am speaking to you am your mother? I have kept this secret to shield you, but I can do so no longer. Your name is Moshe Lopes Pereira, you were born a Jew, and you must do everything in your power to rescue your sister, and to save yourself and me."

One can only imagine the alteration in the inquisitor's demeanor as the revelation of his Jewish origins sinks in. The name "Moshe Pereira," the chronicle suggests, released a torrent of childhood memories. The tension rises another notch as his mother describes the death of his father in an auto-da-fé, a victim of the institution now embodied in his son. How many of his own kin has Inquisitor General d'Aguilar, alias Moshe Pereira, condemned to the stake? How weigh their lives in the balance against the fate of his sister—and that of his mother and himself if he chooses to do nothing?

Of course, Diego chooses survival. But his last-ditch efforts to save his sister are futile, and the noose daily tightens around his mother's neck. In the wake of the War of the Spanish Succession, Diego flees Madrid with her. She dies on the journey to Austria, where he is welcomed by Emperor Charles VI. They had met in Spain when the emperor was still Archduke Charles, a pretender to the Austrian throne. Bishop d'Aguilar had farmed tobacco revenues in Portugal, a fact the emperor remembers in his favor. As soon as he is settled in Vienna, Diego reverts to the name Moses Lopes Pereira and proclaims himself a Jew.

News of Pereira's high-level connections and administrative

skills has traveled ahead of him. The emperor makes him a baron, under his old name Diego d'Aguilar, and then appoints him lessee-general of Austria's tobacco monopoly. Charles's successor, Empress Maria Theresa, who had earlier given the then-bishop a gold chain during a visit to Spain, is so taken with Baron d'Aguilar that she names him one of her privy councillors. Among his first assignments is the restoration of the imperial palace at Schönbrunn, an undertaking he finances partly out of his own pocket.

At the same time, the baron has made contact with other Jews and reclaimed Marranos and becomes a champion of Sephardic causes, working indefatigably to rescue Jews in flight from the Inquisition. He also starts a banking firm and opens branches in London and Amsterdam.

At this juncture a darker element enters the story. Having disposed of the former bishop's sister as a Judaizer, the Holy Office is determined to apprehend Moses Lopes Pereira, alias Diego d'Aguilar. A *proceso* is opened against Pereira, charging him with Judaizing, heresy and apostasy. The Inquisition's spies make discreet inquiries in Vienna, apprising the court of their intense interest in the baron. After reminding the Austrian monarch of the long history of royal intermarriages between Hapsburgs and Bourbons, the Spanish government requests the extradition of Baron d'Aguilar. Empress Maria Theresa warns Pereira that he runs the risk of being kidnapped or deported if he chooses to remain in Austria. Under pressure from Spain, the empress regretfully denies him entry to court.

Pereira applies for protection from the sultan of Turkey, who intervenes on his behalf with Empress Maria Theresa. According to one version, Pereira is granted asylum in Turkey, where the Ottoman rulers had steadfastly favored their thriving communities of Sephardic Jews. Pereira's acquaintance with the international tobacco trade is of immediate service to the sultan, who appoints him his special envoy. Several years of prosperity ensue as the baron, who remains an esteemed *Hofjude* in Vienna, travels all over Europe and the Levant. But the Holy Office, relentless in its pursuit of a traitor to the Church, places obstacles in his path wherever it can. It aims constantly to remind him that there is no escaping the long arm and even longer memory of the Inquisition.

Eventually Baron d'Aguilar and his now extensive family of twelve children, numerous slaves and servants, move to London, where his brother Eugene Lopes Aguilar has preceded him. Nearly a hundred years earlier, Oliver Cromwell had ended a four-century-long banishment and reopened England's gates to Jewish immigrants. A persuasive factor in his decision—made against stiff Protestant opposition—was the proven mercantile value of the few wealthy Marrano families in flight from the Inquisition who had already found safe haven in England. A small but influential Spanish Jewish community welcomes the baron as a nobleman, banker and Sephardic elder of high repute. Pereira is once again in his natural element. He participates in Jewish communal activities and moves in court circles, as his banking firms in Amsterdam and London continue to prosper.

Upon his death in Bishopsgate in 1759, D'Aguilar left his title

Ephraim Lopes Pereira, second baron d'Aguilar. (From Encyclopædia Judaica*)*

and the bulk of his estate to his eldest son, Ephraim Lopes Pereira. Ephraim was not favored with his father's social graces, or his genius for commerce. After the American Revolutionary War wiped out his father's 15,000-acre estate in the colonies, the second baron d'Aguilar sold his father's three town houses and shut himself up in his father's manor in Islington. The baron became a notorious miser, starving his cattle and running his estate so parsimoniously that it became known as "starvation farm" by his hard-pressed retainers. At his death in 1802, the outwardly pauperized Ephraim Pereira left behind a fortune es-timated at some 200,000 pounds sterling, which his daughters found se-creted about the manor.

There are divergent accounts of Moshe Lopes Pereira's British connection. In fact, contradictory sources attribute Pereira's place of ori-gin to Lisbon, not Madrid, as claimed by Edmond Malka in his history of Portuguese Jewry. The archives of Vienna's synagogue, which might have shed light on this controversy, were destroyed by the Nazis during the infamous Kristallnacht of November 1938. Rabbi M. Papo, the former rabbi of Salzburg and son of Vienna's Sephardic rabbi in the early part of this century, describes Moshe Lopes Pereira as a legend-ary figure who founded the Turkish Israelite community of Vienna. In his contribution to *The Jews of Austria,* Rabbi Papo described a silver crown and a pair of Torah ornaments with the Hebrew inscription: "Moshe Lopes Perera—5498," which corresponds to the years 1737–38. The rabbi saw these objects in Vienna's Turkish synagogue, before the Nazis set it afire in 1938. (Rabbi Papo also recounts Moshe Pereira's early religious services in Vienna with Abraham Kamondo, Aaron Nisan and other notable Spanish Jews in house No. 307, inside the city walls.)

British historian Elkan Adler, in a 1930 study of prominent British Jews, claims Moses Pereira inherited the barony from the British crown, which had awarded it to his ancestor a century earlier "for ser-vices performed in favor of the British." Adler makes no mention of Pereira's career as bishop in Portugal. Of the Scrooge-like eldest son Ephraim, the second baron d'Aguilar, Henry Wilson writes in his book *Wonderful Characters* that he was twice married and divorced and lived in "great style" in Broad St. Buildings, in a house built by his fa-ther-in-law Mendes da Costa, Esq. After squandering his father's estate in America, the baron "renounced the character of a gentleman and be-came rude, slovenly and careless in his person and conduct, totally withdrawing into himself from his family connections and the gay world." Upon his death in 1802, the second baron d'Aguilar was interred in the Jews' burying ground at Miles End. His cortege was attended by half a dozen coaches carrying twenty to thirty prominent Jews. His father's valuable library of Hebrew and English books was sold at Shaftesbury Place. We are told nothing of Moses Pereira's numerous other progeny, and must assume that the Aguilar barony was terminated with the inglorious passing of his firstborn son.

There is a further twist to this byzantine tale. Among the descendants of the first baron d'Aguilar, whose memory was venerated every Rosh Hashanah until 1938 with a Kaddish in Vienna's Turkish synagogue, are—if Edmond Malka's genealogical tables can be trusted—the practicing Catholics who today own the Pereira banking firm in New York City.

V

THE TWO SPAINS

Ferdinand and Isabella's Edict of Expulsion remained in force until 1869. Jews were not permitted to practice their religion openly until the twentieth century, when the Spanish Constitution's Article II declaring Catholicism the official state religion was finally rescinded. In 1910 the first Sephardic community in more than four centuries was established in Barcelona. Its founder, Ignacio Bauer, an Alsatian Ashkenazi, was the first Jew to become a member of the Spanish Parliament. In 1924, the philosemitic dictator Primo Rivera directed the Spanish Cortes to restore Spanish citizenship to Sephardic Jews throughout the world. The order was implemented by the socialist Spanish Republic after it overthrew the Bourbon regime in 1931. Encouraged by these developments, a small number of Sephardim took up the offer and settled in Spain. By 1935 there were about six thousand Jews in Spain, several hundred of whom found themselves fighting on opposite sides of the Spanish Civil War. Franco's Falangist Party executed or imprisoned Jewish Loyalists who fought for the Republic, while hundreds of others fled the country.

Not until 1968, in the final decade of Franco's thirty-five-year rule, did the government grant a license authorizing a Jewish commu nity in Madrid. A handsome new synagogue was erected to replace the semiclandestine house of worship I had furtively visited ten years earlier in a shabby-genteel quarter of the city. On December 16, 1968, Justice Minister Antonio Oriol presented Samuel Toledano, president of the Federation of Spanish Jewish Communities, with a government proc-lamation officially revoking Ferdinand and Isabella's Expulsion Decree of 1492. Ten years later Israel's Sephardic chief rabbi, Ovadia Yossef, was welcomed in Madrid with elaborate state honors by King Juan Carlos and Queen Sofía. In 1990, the Spanish government gave its highest award, the Príncipe de Asturias Prize, to the World Sephardic Federation.

THE CULTURAL historian Américo Castro defined Spain's Christians, Moslems and Jews as three "castes" that labored over a span of eight centuries to produce the Iberian hidalgo. Spain's hybrid nobil-ity, Castro insisted, was Levantine at its core rather than European, and mid-twentieth-century Spain remained closer kin to Israel or the Is-lamic nations than to an occidental democratic republic.

The Catholic kings' obsession with *casticismo* (caste purity) was an inevitable product of the hidalgos' craving for domination over the other castes. In the 1880s José Amador de Los Ríos mordantly sug-gested that the Spanish nobility, in proclaiming its superiority over the Muslims and Jews and banishing them from the peninsula, had usurped the mantle of "chosenness"—itself a form of caste prejudice—from the children of Israel and of Mohammed.

In the century following the Expulsion, a collective psychosis overtook the Spaniard, who became so intent on proving his pure Christian descent that he eschewed all professions and intellectual pur-suits that had the slightest taint of Moor or Jew. In the view of the histo-rian Américo Castro, the Spaniard gambled all he had on the preservation—or the appearance—of blood purity and the "grandeur" of his individuality. Out of the nobility's anti-Semitic phobia and the exaltation of idiosyncrasy evolved the nineteenth-century *ocio* (leisure class), the dandified heirs of the Golden Age hidalgos and their convo-luted code of honor.

Earlier in this century, Ramón Menéndez Pidal argued Spain's need to heal its divided soul through a concerted effort at reconciliation. In Menéndez Pidal's view, Spain's older, African soul remained rooted in the Inquisition and its code of *limpieza,* while an emergent, forward-looking Spain gravitated toward Europe and liberal reform. Four centuries after the Expulsion the wounds inflicted by the two Spains on each other were far from healed, and they were to be opened anew by the catastrophic Civil War of 1936–39.

The Jew himself, the open, avowed Jew, was reduced to an almost mythic abstraction, a bogeyman invoked to intimidate misbehaving children. In 1958 I would meet many Spaniards who had no idea of the connection between the state of Israel and Jews, whom they believed to have disappeared centuries earlier.

In Castile and Andalusia, the Civil War's bitter aftermath and Franco's prolonged dictatorship induced a posttraumatic, trancelike state in which Spain's Middle Ages were preserved like a fly in amber. The Madrid of the late 1950s still resembled Cairo or Damascus far more than it did a European capital. Spain's Europeanization would begin in earnest only with the belated and unlamented passing of the Generalissimo.

VI

CANON BANDEÑA

In the spring of 1958 I traveled to Spain for a year of study in Cervantes and the Golden Age. I had been spurred on to explore my Iberian origins by my professor at Brooklyn College, Mair José Benardete, the first modern scholar to collect old Ladino ballads from Salonika, Rhodes, Sarajevo and other Sephardic outposts. Benardete, who had gained notoriety for his Quixotesque appearance, cutting remarks and histrionic outbursts, became my tutor after I sat in on his world literature class. When I failed to appreciate the Marrano nuances of Fernando Rojas's sixteenth-century classic *La Celestina,* Benardete raised both arms and declaimed, "Despair, despair, you have been corrupted by Yiddishistic values." Following my graduation, my father enlisted Professor Benardete to dissuade me from pursuing a career in writing. "You have no Hebrew and your Spanish is bastardized—how do you expect to be a writer?" Benardete admonished me. His prescribed cure for me, endorsed by my father, was a year of ascetic study in Spain, to be followed by predoctoral studies in Spanish literature at a prestigious university.

Soon after my arrival in the south of Spain I met the minor canon of Málaga, whose name was Bandeña. Ten years later I related this encounter in a lightly fictionalized opening chapter of my novel *The Conversion*. (After I passed my predoctoral exams in comparative litera, ture in 1963, I disappointed Professor Benardete and my father's ghost by dropping out of the University of Michigan and taking a staff posi, tion at *The New Yorker*. Although Benardete grudgingly approved of my first novel, he took me to task some years later for describing my fa, ther's genitals in a childhood memoir, *Rites*. "You have desecrated your father's memory!" he exclaimed when I visited his home in Brooklyn. Later that evening he lurched behind me as I drove away, waving his arms and shouting, "Don't forget the old man!")

I was introduced to Canon Bandeña by a boarder at my pen, sion, a medical student of twenty/six whom I called Luís. The canon, a Sevillian by birth and vocation, seemed delighted that I planned to study the Golden Age. He claimed a bond of kinship with the great Spanish writers of the sixteenth and seventeenth centuries, and with Cervantes in particular. Canon Bandeña lamented that unlike Se, villians, who suckled culture at their mother's breast, his Malagueño parishioners lacked intellectual curiosity and were entirely absorbed in their petty material concerns. At our first meeting, the canon (who seemed engaged in a perpetual struggle with his oversize clerical collar) complimented me on what he called my spirituality and intellectual ardor. He invited me to join him in peripatetic conversations he prettily named *convivencias*.

The canon had piqued my curiosity, and I decided to play along, hoping to gather some interesting material for my graduate thesis. The canon, of course, presumed I was Catholic. Little did I suspect that I would become the willing dupe in an atavistic game of cat and mouse.

Our first conversations touched on topics close to the canon's heart, such as the sixteenth/century Illuminists, who Canon Bandeña believed were resurfacing under the guise of Charismatics. He touched on the rising power of Opus Dei, the conservative, anticommunist ec, clesiastical movement. I did not challenge his effusive praise for their rigorous discipline and intellectuality, although I held a dim view of Opus Dei, believing it to be rigidly doctrinaire and intolerant.

The canon assailed what he called the "new prosperity," and its deleterious effects on the Spanish character. He blamed the North

Americans for fostering a "modern" and godless materialism, symbol/
ized by the U.S. military base outside Madrid. Later that week I
learned from Luís that Canon Bandeña owned a rather comfortable
casa de campo in a Málaga suburb that he used for "spiritual retreats."

Three weeks after our first dialogue, the canon and I were stroll/
ing along the Moorish citadel of the Alcazaba, on the brow of Gibral/
faro overlooking Málaga, when he casually asked why I had not
attended Communion. I stammered an excuse, and the canon alluded
to my religious upbringing. "I presume you were raised a good Catho/
lic, friend Victor, were you not?" The canon's voice, pitched distract/
ingly high to begin with, grated on my ears.

Flustered, I professed to be half Catholic only, as my mother was
Protestant by birth. Neither parent, I added, was an observant Chris/
tian and my religious education had been lax.

Canon Bandeña pounced at the opportunity to become my reli/
gious counselor and father confessor. He invited me to attend mass the
following day, and recommended a list of books, among them Saint
Teresa's autobiography, that would help set me on the right path. He
also gave me a sheaf of sermons on the topic of "Evangelization of the
Infidel" which he had composed himself. They were uniformly cheer/
less and tendentious. In one sermon he referred to the Inquisition as
"one of the highest expressions of the Utopian Quest," and "the terres/
trial manifestation of Saint Augustine's City of God."

At the pension that evening, Luís was particularly friendly. He
asked to visit me in my rooms to discuss a confidential matter. Over a
glass of muscatel, Luís told me of his fiancée, a very Catholic young
woman to whom he had been engaged for more than two years, and
whom he had never kissed. He was concerned that her quiet demeanor
concealed a "Gypsy panther" who would prove disruptive to his medi/
cal studies. Luís had not yet made up his mind whether to pursue his
medical career, or enter the seminary and aspire to the priesthood, or ac/
cept a managerial position in his future father/in/law's button factory.

Put on the spot, I advised Luís that his fiancée's Gypsy inclina/
tions could perhaps be bent in a spiritual direction with the proper
guidance. (Without knowing it, I had begun to parrot the canon's
mannerisms and peculiarities of speech.) Luís's sexual retardation made
me feel positively worldly, although at age twenty/three I could hardly
boast of any more experience in affairs of the heart.

I attended mass in the cathedral the following day, and afterward the canon and I took a stroll in the countryside. I vigorously assailed his views on the Inquisition, pointing out that most modern historians em﹍phasized the political and economic motives for its introduction; and then I confessed to the canon that I was part Jewish. Although it was clearly past time to make a clean breast of things, I still could not bring myself to admit that both my parents were Spanish Jews of rabbinical descent who had lived in the Holy Land for many generations.

"I knew it!" Canon Bandeña exclaimed in his unsettling fluting voice. And he proceeded to explain how he had accumulated suspi﹍cions about my Israelite ancestry. First, there was my reluctance to at﹍tend Communion. Second, friend Luís had spied on my night desk a prayer book in Hebrew characters. Stunned, I groped for an explana﹍tion, and at last recalled a Berlitz Hebrew phrase book I had in my lug﹍gage. My mother had packed it with my belongings for my projected trip to Israel. My confidant and fellow pensioner Luís, the faithful fa﹍miliar to the persistent inquisitor, had not only rifled through my possessions like a petty burglar but had managed to find out that I was circumcised.

I still cannot recapture fully the shock of finding myself the vic﹍tim of an inquisition *proceso*, 450 years after Torquemada gave up the ghost. And yet I had to admit that the canon's clumsy mousetrap had been partly of my own devising.

I accused Canon Bandeña of conspiring with Luís to commit a misdemeanor by tampering with my personal effects. Momentarily, the canon appeared stung by my rebuke. Then he countered:

"But lying about one's religion is also a crime, is that not so, my kinsman? That is tampering with one's soul."

The canon seized this opening to do some unburdening of his own. I did not then suspect, of course, that "Bandeña" was a variant of my own ancient family name Abendana, so that he and I were quite conceivably blood relations. Addressing me as "my kinsman" as his flushed cheeks sank deeper into his collar, Canon Bandeña confessed to suspicions concerning his own possibly tainted blood. There was the matter of his mother lighting candles on Friday evening; further, her disinclination to eat pork. The family had lived for many generations in the Barrio de Santa Cruz, the ancient Jewish quarter of Seville. At her death, he recalled dolefully, his mother had unaccountably turned her face to the wall.

"Now we can proceed with open hearts, is it not so, my kins-man?" the canon intoned in his thin, wheedling voice. It was now clear that he intended me to be a partner in a labor of spiritual reclamation. Through some quirky evangelical algebra, I would be returned to the fold as a devout Christian, and he would expiate the Jewish blot in his inheritance.

The sun was setting as we stood outside the sentinel's turret in the ramparts of the Alcazaba. I recall as though it were yesterday the trenchant odor of Canon Bandeña's cassock as he read out the titles of books he intended to place in my hands. All were testimonials of recent converts to Catholicism: South Africans, Australians, a former Nazi, even a Buddhist monk.

In a quavering voice I told the canon I was a one-hundred-per-cent Jew and had no intention of changing my religious affiliation, not a jot or tittle of it. I explained that I came from a long line of Jerusalem rabbis.

Without missing a beat, the canon reminded me that my ances-tors, even if they had started out Jewish, had lived as New Christians in Spain and Portugal for a number of generations. He had looked up "Pereiras" in his genealogical tables, and although he had not uncov-ered the Abendana/Pereira connection, he had gathered considerable information about my Marrano past.

As the canon rattled off the names of the exotic converts he had lined up for me, preparatory to immersing me in their redeeming epi-phanies, I burst into laughter.

In English, I shouted a reproach at the canon, to the effect that we were indeed kinsmen, bonded by our common hypocrisy. But I was barely coherent, and the canon would not have understood me even if I had spoken clearly. The idea of Luís concluding that I was a Jew be-cause I was circumcised, when over ninety percent of North American men are circumcised as a routine measure, fueled my indignation and added to a giddy sense of unreality. It did not occur to me then, though it has many times since, that we might have been reliving—literally—an episode from our common ancestors' past lives.

I shouted and laughed louder and louder to break free of the spell, as the canon repeated, "What are you saying? Speak Christian, my kinsman, I cannot understand you." The pungent odor of his cas-sock mingled with the scent of bat excrement emanating from the turrets. In fact, bats were pouring out of the turrets and flying all around us, but the canon chose to interpret the repellent whirr of their wings as something else entirely.

When Canon Bandeña rose on tiptoe and cupped a hand to his ear to catch the wing flutters of the angel he invoked to watch over our labors, I turned away and lurched downhill. Galloping full tilt in the near-total darkness, laughing and shouting at the top of my lungs, I ran down to the bottom of Gibralfaro and on to the alameda and all the way back to the pension.

The next morning I packed hastily and took a bus to Torremolinos, a small fishing village down the coast. On Luís's door I left the Berlitz phrase book, with a note expressing the hope that it would prove of some help in his marital trials ahead.

I have not seen Luís or my distant cousin the minor canon of Málaga again.

CHAPTER V

AMSTERDAM

*Sometimes the gates of prayer are open, sometimes they are closed. But
the gates of penitence are always open.*

—*Diaspora Museum, Tel Aviv*

Caute quia spinosa.
—*Baruch Spinoza*

MARIA NUNES

THE CONVERSO PEREIRAS who left the Iberian Peninsula in
flight from the Inquisition divided into two migratory streams, one in
the 1590s and another in the second half of the seventeenth century.
Those who emigrated to other European cities in the sixteenth century,
and who later traveled to the Levant, include the Portuguese Pereiras of
the *peral,* or "pear tree." This branch of the family, whose Iberian origins have been traced to the Abendannos of Toledo, are in all probabil-
ity my direct ancestors. They include the Marrano Lopeses and Nunes
Pereira, who landed on the shores of Holland in the 1590s and affirmed
their Jewish heritage, reclaiming their ancient family name, Abendana.
These Pereiras are counted among the progenitors of Amsterdam's
Sephardic community.

Thomás Rodrigues Pereyra arrived in Holland from Madrid in
1646, more than a half century after Maria Nunes and her kin. He settled in Amsterdam, renaming himself Abraham Israel Pereira. His
male descendance—which is now extinct—was headed by his sons
Isaac, Jacob and Moses Raphael Pereira, who became noteworthy philanthropists and elders of the Amsterdam Jewish community. The
blood links connecting the Portuguese Pereiras to the patriarch Abraham Israel have not, to my knowledge, been established. The genealo-
gist Isaäc da Costa adduced several arguments in favor of their descent
from a common ancestor. Chiefly, he cites the similarity of traditions
that linked the emigrant Spanish and Portuguese Jews, and the prestige
enjoyed by the two Pereira branches in the Grand Portuguese Syna-

gogue of Amsterdam, where they were regarded as "one pre-eminently noble and illustrious family."

THE ROMANCE OF the proud Marrano beauty Maria Nunes and her storybook encounter with Queen Elizabeth of England is probably the most widely circulated folk tradition involving a Pereira. As I delved into the suspect origins of this pretty tale, several alternative sce-narios unfolded that proved more intriguing than the original.

In his *Juden in Portugal,* Meyer Kayserling's seminal 1867 study, the author writes at length of a Maria Nunes who in 1593 embarked from Lisbon en route to Amsterdam with her brother Manuel Lopes Pereira and her uncle Miguel. Fifteen years before that, Holland had joined the League of Utrecht and adopted provisions forbidding reli-gious persecution. These liberal statutes drew crypto-Jews seeking sanc-tuary from the Inquisition, among them Maria Nunes and her family.

In mid-voyage they were intercepted by a British privateer that took the ship's passengers and cargo captive and transported them to England. The corsair's captain, a British duke, became so enthralled by Maria Nunes's beauty and aristocratic bearing that he proposed mar-riage to her before they reached port. Maria firmly turned him down. In London, news of the duke's infatuation reached Queen Elizabeth, who asked to see the Portuguese gentlewoman who had rebuffed her nobleman.

The queen, who in common with Lady Jane Grey and Princess Arabella Stuart fancied herself something of a Hebraist, was immedi-ately drawn to Maria Nunes and extended to her every consideration. In the evenings she drove her guest about London in her carriage to show off her radiant beauty. But Maria cared nothing for the attentions be-stowed on her by Queen Elizabeth, or for the lovelorn duke's insistent pleas, and asked only to be set free with her companions. Struck by Maria Nunes's fidelity to her Jewish origins, the queen graciously freed her and her party, assuring them safe passage to Holland, where they arrived without further incident. They were joined in 1598 by Maria's parents, her sister Justa and two more brothers.

Maria Nunes's years in Holland are far better documented than her London escapade. Seventeenth-century chronicles record that in 1594 or thereabouts, she and nine other Marrano emigrants passed through the German town of Emden, where they encountered an Ashkenazic rabbi, Uri Halevy. Rabbi Halevy urged them to travel on to Amsterdam, where they could practice their ancient religion in comparative freedom. Upon arriving in Amsterdam they were joined by Rabbi Halevy and his son Aaron; they circumcised the males and instructed them in the Torah, restoring to them their Jewish birthright. Another historical figure steeped in legend, Don Samuel Pallache, the Moroccan emperor's Sephardic envoy in Amsterdam—and a notorious pirate—invited the new arrivals to private services in his residence.

The first synagogue of Amsterdam opened for prayers in 1598, the year of Maria Nunes's wedding. Samuel Pallache, the elder Jacob Tirado and Antonio Lopes Pereira are among the founders of Temple Beth Jacob. Maria Nunes married her first cousin Manuel Lopes Homen there in a splendid ceremony attended by twenty-four of her relations, thus "inaugurating"—in Kayserling's words—the Dutch Sephardic community. (Amsterdam's city registers show a marriage contract signed by Maria Nunes Pereira and Manuel Lopes Homen on November 28, 1598.)

The inspiration for Kayserling's retelling of Maria Nunes's cautionary tale appears to have been a novel, *Jacob Tirado*, published in 1867 by Dr. Ludwig Philippsohn. Philippsohn's own source was a curious chronicle published in Amsterdam in 1683 by the Marrano poet Daniel Levi de Barrios, *Triumpho del govierno popular y de la antiguedad holandesa*. This fascinating hodgepodge of poetic narrative, quasi-historical tract and unctuous tributes to Levi de Barrios's rich patrons contains the earliest known account of Maria Nunes and the early years of the Marrano-Sephardic community of Amsterdam. We learn in these pages that only a handful of the Marranos arriving in Amsterdam had read beyond the Five Books of Moses, and they knew next to nothing of the vast rabbinical literature and jurisprudence.

As the community grew in numbers and prosperity, they employed rabbis from Venice and the Levant to instruct them in Jewish law, Halakhah. (The convoluted disclaimers in Levi de Barrios's chronicles, and the apologetic tone of much of his poetry, are two indications of how difficult these lessons proved to be to the newly reclaimed Jews of Amsterdam.)

Most scholars have approached Maria Nunes's story with understandable caution. Cecil Roth's reference to her in his *Short History of the Jewish People* (1936) is prefaced this way: ". . . an ancient legend, which need not be discounted in all its details, gives a most romantic origin for the Amsterdam community. In the year 1593, we are told, a brother and sister, Manuel Lopes Pereira and Maria Nunez. . . ." In 1968 Doctor Wilhelmina Pieterse published an annotated study of Daniel Levi (alias Miguel) de Barrios's *"Triumpho . . ."* which found his data on Amsterdam's Portuguese Jewish community "difficult to eval/ uate on their historical value." She goes on to say: "Half of the facts could not be verified and, what is even worse, fifty percent of the other half was found to be incorrect."

For all the doubts concerning his trustworthiness as a histo/ rian—and in part because of these doubts—Levi de Barrios remains one of the most intriguing members of Amsterdam's Marrano commu/ nity. He fled his birthplace in Vilaflor, Portugal, in the mid/1650s and lived with his first wife in Livorno, Italy. After they were divorced—an unusual event in those days—Levi de Barrios remarried and settled per/ manently in Amsterdam, where he became unofficial poet laureate of the Marrano/Sephardic community. No other Marrano poet of the time probed more feelingly the dilemmas posed by their dual heritage, Cath/ olic convert and Jewish. A prolific writer, Levi de Barrios left behind several tomes of poetry and prose narrative, composed in the course of a long and mercurial career. Levi de Barrios made the acquaintance of every person of consequence in Amsterdam. Like Menasseh ben Israel, he socialized with eminent public figures and artists of his time, not ex/ cluding Rembrandt, whose tender and mystical "Jewish bride" may have been modeled by Levi de Barrios and his second wife, Abigail.

NEITHER KAYSERLING NOR Roth foresaw the wealth of in/ formation that diligent investigators would dig up in the decade prior to the five/hundredth anniversary of the Expulsion. And with the quin/ centennial observances behind us, the mining for fresh data continues in earnest.

A book by Professor Jonathan I. Israel, *Empires and Entrepôts,* cuts through the fog of conjecture surrounding Maria Nunes. Professor Israel, whose 1990 study devotes a full chapter to Maria's brother, Man/ uel Lopes Pereira, cites a letter discovered in the 1920s by a Dutch his/ torian, Sigmund Seeligmann. The letter, dated April 1597 and sent to The Hague by the Dutch states' general agent in London, Noel de Carron, reports the British capture four years earlier of a ship from Flushing. The ship's passengers include five Portuguese refugees in flight from the Inquisition who are transported to London by the British ship's captain. (His name and title, regrettably, are not recorded.) One of the five passengers was "a noble lady" dressed in the garb of a man. The correspondent de Carron mentions that the young lady and her companions were on their way to Amsterdam, where she planned to be married.

Professor Israel's investigation further disclosed that in 1612, fourteen years after Maria Nunes married her cousin, he and her brother Manuel Lopes traveled to Seville, evidently passing themselves off as New Christian traders. The evidence suggests that Maria accompanied her husband to Seville, where they established a lasting, if not permanent, residence. This nugget of information, which appears to debunk the legend of Maria Nunes's unshakable fidelity to her Jewish origins, leads to another intriguing possibility.

Professor Israel credits his colleague Professor Angel García with discovering the striking parallels between Maria Nunes's story and Miguel Cervantes' cautionary tale *La española inglesa* (*The English Spanishwoman*). Like Maria, Isabela is captured by a British nobleman and brought to London, where she is presented to Queen Elizabeth. Struck by her extraordinary beauty and gentility and the subtlety of her wit, the queen immediately admits Isabela under her tutelage. In Cervantes' novella the *son* of a British nobleman, Recaredo, a secret Catholic, falls madly in love with Isabela when she is still a young girl. Queen Elizabeth, who grooms Isabela to be one of her ladies-in-waiting, declines to permit her marriage to the nobleman's son until he has proven his worth.

Recaredo affirms his valor as a navy captain in Her Majesty's service; but fate intervenes once more, in the guise of an irascible earl who has taken a fancy to Isabela during Recaredo's absence and is determined to marry her. Frustrated by the queen's refusal to break her word to Recaredo and deliver Isabela to her son, the earl's mother poisons Isabela. Miraculously, she survives, but only after forfeiting her beauty to the effects of the potion.

Recaredo's capture of the Portuguese galleon has providentially led to the reunion of Isabela with her parents, whom she decides to accompany back to Spain, with the queen's consent. Isabela, no longer beautiful but still beloved by the devoted Recaredo, vows to remain faithful to him and await his return. The ensuing two years are fraught with further tests for Recaredo, marked by the byzantine circumlocutions typical of Golden Age literature. In Recaredo's absence the adolescent Isabela, who has ripened into a young woman, recovers her rare beauty and radiant spirit.

Through all their trials and misfortunes, both Isabela and Recaredo remain true to their Catholic religion and to each other as devoutly as the folkloric Maria Nunes clove to her Jewish origins, and to the cousin she was pledged to marry. But the parallels between the two stories do not end there.

When at the end of two years Recaredo at last arrives in Spain to seek out his beloved and consummate their vows, Isabela, believing the report of his assassination by the jealous earl, is about to enter a nunnery; shunning all her numerous courtiers, Isabela has elected an ascetic life of seclusion and mourning for her deceased lover. Recaredo arrives in Seville as she is about to enter the convent. Calling out her name, he reminds her of their marriage vows. Isabela recognizes him as her beloved, and after they embrace Recaredo recounts his miraculous escape from the earl's assassins and all his subsequent adventures. Four days later, Recaredo and Isabela are married in a solemn Catholic ceremony. They settle in the Santa Paula section of Seville, where, the author piquantly suggests, they were still to be found, living in prosperous and idyllic contentment.

Cervantes, as it happens, was a frequent visitor to Seville at around the time of Maria Nunes's arrival there, and Professor Israel is tantalized by the possibility that they may have met. (Cervantes' cautionary novels were published in 1613, a year after Maria Nunes and her husband settled in Seville and three years before Cervantes' death.) By that time, the story of Maria's constancy and of her meeting with the queen of England—real or fanciful—had no doubt reached Spain.

The English Spanishwoman falls short of Cervantes' finest achievements. The plot's twists and turns exceed the bounds of literary convention; and the author's homilies on Catholic virtuousness are grafted onto the story line, which critics accurately describe as a Neoplatonic idyll. And it seems perverse to the point of absurdity to suggest that Queen Elizabeth of England, a Protestant, would admit under her protection an ardent Catholic like Isabela as readily as she presumably adopted Maria Nunes, an enemy of her enemies the Spaniards, and on that account a far more plausible ally. (Since no Jews were permitted to settle in England until Cromwell lifted the ban in 1656, Maria could only have been admitted as a fugitive convert.)

This flawed but intriguing novella tellingly betrays Cervantes' anxiety to affirm his Old Christian bloodlines and lay to rest suspicions of a Jewish taint in his lineage. By one of those alchemical transmuta/ tions that abound in Christian literature, Spain's supreme literary ge/ nius apparently seized on Maria Nunes's story of Jewish fidelity and converted it into a morality tale of Catholic constancy. Without excus/ ing the faults in the execution, one cannot help but admire the audacity of the intent.

In his short study of Maria Nunes in *Jewish History,* the late Rob/ ert Cohen proposed a third alternative; he suggests that Daniel Levi de Barrios may have "invented" the romantic version of Maria Nunes after he read Cervantes' novella. However, recent investigation has tended to buttress Levi de Barrios's account, save for the key episode of the love/ lorn duke and Maria's meeting with the queen in London, which reads, in effect, like a scene from a Golden Age play or novel. And there perhaps this speculation should rest, leaving further judgment to the reader's discretion, as both Cervantes and Levi de Barrios intended.

II

The first services in Amsterdam's Beth Jacob Synagogue were an odd syncretic mix of Catholic and Jewish rituals; rumors of these strange rites, spread by the refugees' neighbors, raised suspicions among Protes/ tant officials, who feared a papist plot to overthrow the newly estab/ lished Dutch Republic. On the first celebration of the Day of Atonement, the entire congregation was arrested and hauled into court for interrogation. As no one in the party spoke Dutch, the patriarch, Jacob Tirado (alias Simon Lopes da Costa), who had asked to be cir/ cumcised despite his advanced age, addressed the authorities in Latin. He explained that these worshippers were not Catholics but instead members of a reborn Judaic religion that was cruelly persecuted by the Catholic church in Spain and Portugal. Tradition has it that Tirado's tempered and lucid explanation, salted with hints of the potential com/ mercial advantages to the Dutch Republic if it took in the moneyed outcasts, fully satisfied the officials, who released the congregants and as/ sured them of the Protestant Dutch government's support. In fact, how/ ever, for nearly two centuries the Jews lived in Holland under numerous restrictions. They were forbidden to cohabit with Dutch women and denied membership in the all-important labor guilds, save for the emergent diamond polishers' and printers' associations. Small wonder that Sephardic Jews soon infiltrated the diamond trade, and established one of the largest centers of book publishing and distribution in Europe. The visionary jurist Hugo Grotius, after closely examining the Jewish question, proposed one of the most singular restrictions ever imposed on a Jewish community. Mindful of the huge debt owed by Calvinist theology to Israelite prophets and sages, Grotius recommended that Holland's Jews be obliged to cleave to their ancestral religion. His misgivings about the potential subversion of the Dutch Protestant Republic by Marranos who relapsed to their former Catholicism would be shared—for the same and additional reasons—by my forebear Abraham Israel Pereira.

As the number of immigrant New Christians returning to their ancestral religion multiplied, two more synagogues sprang up in separate quarters of Amsterdam. Maria Nunes's brother Antonio Lopes, who had taken the name Joseph Israel Pereira, served on the governing board of the Neveh Shalom Synagogue. Some years later, as Isaac Israel Abendana, he helped to found a Portuguese Jewish organization, with secret branches in Antwerp, Rouen and even Brazil, that provided dowries to indigent Portuguese Marrano girls seeking Jewish husbands. (Abraham Israel Pereira would continue this charity a half century later.)

Levi de Barrios relates an interesting anecdote regarding Maria Nunes's "celebrated" older sister Justa, who married her cousin Francisco Nunes Pereyra Homen. After Justa's first two children died in infancy, she refused to cohabit with her husband any longer unless he submitted to circumcision. Rabbi Uri Halevy was asked to perform the *brit* on Pereyra, who thereupon took the name David Abendana, and Justa became Abigail. Burial records at the famous Ouderkerk cemetery, south of Amsterdam, show that Maria Nunes's mother, Mayor Rodriguez, and brother-in-law Francisco Nunes Pereyra were buried there in 1624 and 1625 under the names Sara and David Abendana, respectively. They also certify that the renamed Abigail and the circumcised David Abendana bore a future *hacham* (wise man) of the Amsterdam community, Manuel Abendana.

This may be a legitimate instance of "rejudaized" Pereiras reclaiming their ancestral family name. But the use of aliases by Marrano businessmen in flight from the Inquisition frequently persisted after they reached safe harbor. In Amsterdam the multiple pseudonyms resorted to by Pereiras, Pintos and Cardozos were more likely to have been linked to the vicissitudes of commerce—and the evasion of fines and taxes—than to old family nomenclature. This is one of the factors scholars point to when questioning the Marranos' probity and the sin- cerity of their reconversions.

The separate congregations officially merged into a unified Sephardic community, "Talmud Torah," with the inauguration of the Esnoga, or Grand Spanish and Portuguese Synagogue, on the Amstel in 1675. It was in this magnificent temple, which remains one of the finest in Europe, that Sephardic congregants cast anathemas on inquisi- tors in Spain and Portugal who continued to persecute their Marrano brethren: "May the great, mighty and terrible God exact vengeance for the sake of His holy servant . . . who was burned alive for the sanctified unity of His name. May he seek his blood from his enemies by his mighty arm and repay his foes according to their deserts. . . ."

III

ABRAHAM ISRAEL PEREIRA

In April 1992 I traveled to Amsterdam to visit the ancient Grand Syn- agogue and cemetery, and to consult documents in the Jewish Histori- cal Museum and the Bibliotheka Rosenthaliana, a superb library of Jewish documentation housed in Amsterdam University.

The Grand Spanish and Portuguese Synagogue, erected in 1675 with the aid of wealthy former Marranos, among them Abraham Pereira, no longer stands on the Amstel River, as landfill has diverted its banks by several hundred feet. On approaching the synagogue, whose outer walls were modeled on King Solomon's temple, the visitor feels humbled by its massive scale, which is more appropriate to a cathe- dral than to a Jewish house of worship. A shiver coursed up my spine as I stood next to the fifty-foot Doric columns lining the synagogue's cavernous nave, which was undergoing restoration. The benches of the *parnassim* (lay presidents), where Abraham Pereira once sat, were hid- den behind huge sheets of plastic. The enormous branching copper candelabra, the raised *bimah* and majestic ark carved from Brazilian jacaranda testify to the Marrano entrepreneurs' conspicuous squandering of wealth to honor their reborn Jewish faith.

Across the square stand the twin structures of the former Ashkenazic Great Synagogue, erected only five years after the Portuguese synagogue, and every bit its match in scale and grandeur. In 1987 it was converted into the Jewish Historical Museum. Although the Sephardic beginnings of Holland's Jewish community are reflected in hundreds of documents and artifacts, the exhibits in the Joden Historisch Museum focus on Holland's twentieth-century socialist and Zionist movements, and on the annihilation of eighty percent of Dutch Jewry by the Nazis. Of the more than 100,000 Dutch Jews who perished in the Holocaust, less than 5,000 were descended from the Marranos who fled Spain and Portugal. Nowhere else in the world, not in the Holy Land or on the Iberian Peninsula, can one find two such monuments standing face-to-face to commemorate the two holocausts that darkened Jewish history in the second half of our waning millennium.

The Sephardim of Amsterdam entered a precipitous decline toward the middle of the eighteenth century, when Dutch trade with the Iberian Peninsula and the Caribbean colonies contracted sharply. Their power and influence were replaced by a growing and more resilient population of Ashkenazic tradesmen. Since World War II, the shrunken Sephardic congregation of a few dozen active members has frequently met in a small courtyard prayer hall rather than brave the cold drafts of the unheated, candlelit Grand Synagogue. Behind the small prayer hall is the marvelous Etz Haim library, which contains— among hundreds of other first editions from Amsterdam's seventeenth- and eighteenth-century Jewish printing presses—Portuguese psalm books, Daniel Levi de Barrios's poetic chronicles, Menasseh ben Israel's messianic tracts and Abraham Pereira's two religious polemics. The librarian, Mrs. Baruch, an Ashkenazi married to a Sephardic congregant, shows me a book of *hazkaroth* (memorial prayers) printed in Portuguese and Hebrew. She assures me that the prayers are still recited in the original version on Yom Kippur and Tisha B'Av, although the worshippers no longer understand the Portuguese blessings or the curses cast on the inquisitors who condemned their ancestors to the stake.

IV

Professor Jonathan Israel records that Thomás Rodrigues Pereyra (alias Francisco de Agurre, alias Gerard Carlos Bangardel, alias Abraham Israel Pereira), a resident of Madrid with family roots in Vilaflor, Por- tugal, fled Spain in 1646 on the heels of a financial scandal. Philip IV's ministers were threatening litigation over a large sum of money that Pereira—a former arms contractor to the Crown—had allegedly embezzled from funds allocated to resupply Spain's infantry.

Although Pereira was by no means the only Marrano entrepre- neur to leave Spain under a cloud—Fernando Montezinos and the brothers Rodrigues Cardoso were also accused of misappropriating funds—scandal and controversy as well as high honors would pursue the illustrious financier throughout his long, eventful life.

As Professor Israel records in *Empires and Entrepôts, 1646* was the last active year for the financial network of moneyed conversos assem- bled by the count duke of Olivares. Spain was at war in Flanders, Cataluña and Portugal. The drain on the monarchy's coffers had driven it dangerously close to bankruptcy, so that Philip IV could no longer repay the Marrano bankers who underwrote Spain's imperial adventures.

Another factor behind the precipitous departure of Abraham Pereira, his eight sons and daughters and his brothers Isaac Pereyra and Salvador Váez Martínez was the recrudescence of inquisitorial activity beginning in the 1640s. The downfall of Olivares was immediately fol- lowed by the appointment of Don Diego de Arce Reynoso—an austere and rigorous hidalgo—as the new inquisitor general. One after another, Marrano bankers and businessmen were accused of Judaizing and swept up in a wave of prosecutions. During the 1650s, forty-three autos- da-fé were recorded, the most of any decade of Spain's Inquisition. (According to undocumented reports, Pereira himself may have served time in the Holy Office's prisons.)

The Cardosos, the Pintos, the Pereyras and other prominent crypto-Jews began forwarding large amounts of cash from Madrid and Antwerp—seat of the Spanish Netherlands—to Amsterdam, Ham- burg and other European capitals.

Philip IV's ministers, alarmed by the huge capital outflow, suspected malfeasance and scrutinized the Marrano bankers' emigration papers for irregularities.

"I am advised," wrote one official, "that a personage named Thomás Pereyra left Madrid three years ago and came to Amsterdam, and having bankrupted there and taken from His Majesty a large sum that had been entrusted to him for remitting to Flanders and that this man, who is a Jew and lives now in Rotterdam and is very rich, if I had the necessary papers . . . I could pursue him through legal process and recover, if not all, at least part of what he has stolen and owes to His Majesty. . . ."

The threatened lawsuit was evidently dropped, perhaps out of fear of exposing the Spanish crown's own shady financial dealings. Be- hind an array of aliases, Abraham Pereira and his brothers continued their commercial ventures inside Spain. In 1658 they purchased a sugar refinery in Amsterdam that further swelled their considerable fortune. Shortly after their arrival there, Abraham Pereira and his sons became members in good standing of the Dutch Sephardic community, whose membership would peak three decades later at around 3,000.

Holland's rabbis were consistently indulgent regarding moneys gained illicitly by Jews in flight from persecution in Spain or Portugal. And it did no harm at all to Abraham Pereira's standing as an hon- ored *parnas* of Amsterdam's Sephardic congregation when he dedi- cated a portion of his fortune to found a yeshiva, which he named Torah Or (Light of the Law). The yeshiva opened the same year that the *herem* (ban) of excommunication was pronounced on the philoso- pher Baruch Spinoza, a ruling in which Pereira is believed to have participated. Three years later, Pereira gained lasting credit with the Holy Land's Jews when he founded a yeshiva in Hebron, which was named Hessed le Abraham (Charity of Abraham) in his honor. The yeshiva immediately became a center of messianic ferment, attracting Kabbalists and Talmudists from all over the Middle East. Three decades later, while his father was still living, Pereira's eldest son, Jacob, founded a second religious center, in Jerusalem. The Beit Yacov Yeshiva would exert an enduring influence on the Eternal City's heterodox Jewish community.

Jacob Pereira explained his decision to found the yeshiva with the biblical story of Zebulun and Issachar: "Zebulun and Issachar are partners. Zebulun is the traders living along the coast, sailing in their ships and trading and becoming rich; they support Issachar, who sits and studies the Torah: thus Zebulun is mentioned before Issachar, since Issachar's Torah exists only thanks to Zebulun." This biblical metaphor has a contemporary application in the American and European philanthropists who underwrite Orthodox houses of worship in Israel.

Apart from Abraham Pereira's philanthropy and an entrepreneurial genius that might have served as inspiration for Baron d'Aguilar and the fabulous Pereire brothers of Bordeaux and Paris, he is best known for two soul-searching religious tracts he composed in Spanish. *La Certeza del Camino (The Certainty of the Road)* and *El Espejo de la Vanidad de este Mundo (The Mirror of the Vanity of This World)*, published two decades after Pereira's arrival in Amsterdam, are of particular interest today for the light they shed on the seventeenth-century Marrano exile in search of rehabilitation and ultimate redemption.

I first stumbled upon Abraham Israel Pereira's writings in Jerusalem, in the Judaica division of Hebrew University. I had barely started serious investigation into my family, and Pereira's books struck me with the force of revelation. In the rare-book room, I painstakingly noted in pencil—ballpoint pens are not permitted—whole paragraphs from the yellowed pages of *La Certeza del Camino,* a polemic composed in a seventeenth-century Spanish that would have been perfectly familiar to my Jerusalem aunts, although they might have deemed it a trifle "modern" and lacking in color.

As though to offset the fulsome praises heaped on the author in the dedicatory pages by Isaac Aboab and other religious authorities, the author's prologue opens on a penitential note: "How errant are those who come to their senses late and do not try to mortify their bodies and warm their hearts with a live zeal and fervent devotion, to obtain forgiveness for their sins and regain so much time lost in offense of the Lord." Abraham Pereira included himself among those who had formerly mocked piety and charitableness and glorified commercial pursuits as the highest good.

Certeza del Camino was written as a latter-day "Guide to the Perplexed" addressed to Holland's Sephardim as well as to Marranos still living in "the lands of idolatry." Acknowledging his presumption in pretending to instruct others despite his ignorance of the Holy Tongue, Pereira confesses, "I labored on my part to incline those who, like myself, arrived late." Behind the book's didactic tenor and Pereira's insistence on the supremacy of Divine Law over all worldly affairs, lies a

profound crisis of conscience couched in two distinct voices, one theological and the other abjectly confessional. The first voice arises from the
author's efforts to come to terms with his great wealth and atone for it by
exalting a life of pious simplicity: "Whoever seeks repose and tranquility in life need only pass his eyes over the burdens and distractions of
troubled commerce and he will recognize to what extent God favors
those he helps to undertake the solitary life. The man of business arises
at dawn, kept awake by the cares that afflict even his dreams. . . ."

Pereira saves his bitterest scorn for the backsliding Marranos
who superficially embrace Judaism, only to slough it off when it gets in
the way of amassing wealth. In a passage that might have been addressed to his distant cousin Manuel Lopes Pereira, who like himself
had resided in Madrid, Pereira declares: "We discover every day that
many who are born and raised in Judaism, for lack of confidence in
their faith turn their back on God, and leave to seek their remedy in the
lands of idolatry. . . ."

Repeatedly homiletic to the point of sermonizing, Pereira condemns himself for his past avarice and other vices, as he attempts
through a live repentance "to rise above the swamp of my errors."

The more affecting confessional voice arises from the author's
impassioned search for his Jewish identity. As Abraham Pereira did
not know Hebrew, the texts available to him were mostly those of
Christian theologians, among them Friar Luis de Granada and Diego
de Estella, whose works were widely distributed in Holland. The investigator Henry Méchoulan has done a thorough analysis of the influence
on Pereira's writing of the Dominican Friar Granada, Estella and other
Christian theologians, and shows how Pereira adapted their arguments
to his own redemptive purposes.

J. van Praag was the first scholar to point out the heavy Christian overlay in Pereira's writings.

> La Certeza breathes a Catholic spirit: the profound concept
> of sin; belief in the demon . . . the necessity of faith and good
> works to attain life eternal, the preoccupation with the doc
> trines of free will and predestination, his recommendation of
> mortification and penitence; the vivid representation of the
> sufferings and agonies of hell—it is particularly curious how
> in this respect he recalls the torments of the Inquisition's

dungeons—and especially his placing above all else "the salvation of the soul." . . .

Méchoulan sets against these compelling arguments the traditions of penitence associated with the Days of Atonement and with the concept of *teshuvah* (repentance), both fundamentally Jewish traditions. If Pereira's thirst for redemption remains Jewish at heart, there is no arguing that he has clothed his search in the only trappings he knew during his long exile in Christian Spain. Méchoulan writes: "Deprived of religious instruction since 1492, crypto-Jews reduced Judaism to a vague memory of prohibitions and feast-days, and in most cases, to readings in the Old Testament." Pereira's road to redemption is paved in about equal measure with cobbles from Jewish and Christian traditions, as in the following passage from *Certeza:* "A feeling of repentance that is truly alive, a penitence that makes strict demands upon us—that is the way to secure God's mercy, and with it reconciliation to the divine grace."

Again and again, Pereira insists that "calling oneself a Jew" is not enough. As a former converso, he is well versed in the ruses and disguises employed by crypto-Jews to deny Holy Scripture and the true faith. Taking on the mantle of a prophet, Pereira sternly exhorts crypto-Jews who remained behind in the Iberian Peninsula.

> Remove idolatry from your sight, from your imagination and from your powers and do not imagine that, merely by saying that you neither serve or esteem idolatry, you will surely attain salvation, when, on the contrary, you deserve all the more affliction since, steeped in the grandeur of the Lord, you offend Him all the more by walking in blindness. . . .

The single greatest Jewish influence on Pereira was Menasseh ben Israel, the ex-Marrano printer and Kabbalist rabbi of the Amsterdam community, who at one time worked for Abraham Pereira and dedicated one of his books to him and his sons. Pereira was one of the chief funders of the Grand Spanish and Portuguese Synagogue on the Amstel, for which he was honored by Amsterdam's Sephardic rabbinate, and by ben Israel in particular.

Following the emergence of Shabbatai Zevi in Smyrna in 1666, Pereira repeatedly alluded to Menasseh ben Israel's Kabbalist tracts in support of Shabbatai's claim to be the true Messiah. Long before Zevi proclaimed himself the Anointed One, the *Zohar* had prophesied the arrival of a Messiah who would lead the dispersed Jews back to the Holy Land. In Jerusalem they were to rebuild the Temple and fulfill the redemption promised on Mount Sinai.

Isaac Luria and other seventeenth-century mystics rationalized the enormous tribulations brought on by the Expulsion as the "birth pangs" of the messianic age. They believed that God, prior to revealing himself in the person of the Messiah, conceals and contracts himself so that his holy sparks are diffused throughout the universe, hidden by an outer shell of impurity and evil matter. Only the deeds of holy men— *tzaddikim*—can pierce the outer shell and free the radiant light of God's grace, the *Shekhinah*. Isaac Luria carried the *Zohar*'s concept of redemption a step further by positing a Messiah who in breaking the yoke of Israel's bondage would bring about a cosmic reordering of the material and spiritual spheres. The end result, in Luria's view, was the Messiah's repair of the primal catastrophe known as the "shattering of the vessels."

In Menasseh ben Israel's writings, which were steeped in Jewish mystical tradition, Pereira sought to reconcile the tensions among his yearning for redemption, his great wealth, and a converso legacy of Christian guilt and self-abnegation. Ben Israel evokes God's blessings on those who are charitable to the poor and excoriates, with Isaiah and Ecclesiastes, the hollow vanity of piling riches upon riches to no loftier end than one's self-aggrandizement. Menasseh ben Israel's influence on Pereira crested when he announced the imminent arrival of the Messiah, who was the be-all and the end-all to Kabbalists of the latter part of the seventeenth-century, as he is once again today. What distinguished the messianic movement of Abraham Pereira's time, not only in Holland but in Salonika and other refuges of Iberian Jews, was the catalyzing fervor of former Marranos seeking a shortcut to redemption.

In 1663 the predicted signs and portents began appearing in Amsterdam, the first in the form of an epidemic that carried off 10,000 people. The following year a terrifying ball of fire with a long tail blazed across the night skies above the Amstel. The panic provoked by these events caused the states of the United Dutch Provinces to decree a day of fasts and prayers to ward off further calamities. The stage was set for the Messiah's appearance.

If Abraham Pereira's *Certeza* was suffused with his anticipation of the Messiah, his second book, *Mirror of the Vanity of This World*, is the bitter aftermath, published after Shabbatai Zevi betrayed his followers by converting to Islam. Although Pereira had no formal training in the Kabbala, he had implicitly regarded his "rebirth" in Judaism as a linchpin of the dawning messianic age. In *Mirror*, Pereira describes his departure with Isaac Nahar for the Holy Land, where he planned to join Shabbatai Zevi in the restoration of the Temple. This portion reads like a picaresque adventure: When their carriage breaks down in a German forest, Pereira and Nahar are taken prisoner by soldiers alerted by reports that they carried gold bullion. A timely Jewish emis-sary intercedes to help free Pereira and his party. They reach Frankfurt, and from there Pereira travels alone to Venice. In a perhaps uncon-scious emulation of Judah Halevi, who may never have got beyond Egypt, Pereira's own prophetic destiny would carry him no closer to Je-rusalem than the Adriatic port. In Venice he wrote diatribes chastising the weak-willed unbelievers who sold out their faith for material gain.

For the better part of a decade, Zevi's "Illuminations," during which God Himself appeared in a vision to pronounce him the Mes-siah, held in thrall Jewish congregations throughout Europe and the Levant, and pitched thousands headlong into a delirium that emulated Zevi's own raptures—the origins of which may have been manic-depression or, more likely, epilepsy. A younger visionary steeped in the Lurianic Kabbala, Nathan of Gaza, became Zevi's chief apostle after the two men met in 1665. He interpreted his master's illuminations to square with Kabbalistic prefigurations of the day of redemption, which Zevi predicted for June 18, 1666.

By 1671, four years after Shabbatai Zevi was detained by the Sultan's Grand Vizier, Abraham Pereira had heard enough of Zevi's hollow prophecies and suffered enough of his betrayals to conclude that he had been grievously misled.

Although Pereira eventually returned to Amsterdam, pro-foundly disillusioned, the Shabbatean adepts in Hebron's Hessed Le Abraham Yeshiva remained devoted to Zevi even beyond his conver-sion to Islam, rationalizing his aspostasy as a further act of self-abnega-tion on the road to redemption. In 1666 the head of Hessed Le

Abraham, Rabbi Meir ben Hiyya Rofe, wrote to Abraham Pereira to thank him for his generosity and to inform him that henceforth they no longer required his gifts, but that he wished he would come and join them "to behold the beauty of the Lord." They were joined in this view by the "Neo-Shabbatean" Dönme in Salonika and Smyrna, whose descendants remained faithful to Zevi until the present century. Zevi's conversion to Islam, the Dönmes contended, had been a necessary affliction on the path to redemption. (*Dönme* derives from the Turkish for "turn" or "convert.") Tens of thousands of Zevi's followers shared his affliction by converting to Islam, in what was the largest voluntary mass conversion in Jewish history. But the Dönmes continued to observe Jewish rituals in secret, as Zevi himself had done toward the end of his life. Until 1924, about 16,000 Dönmes in Salonika continued to practice their unique syncretic blend of Judaic, Islamic and pagan rituals. The "ceremony of the lamb" in March climaxed with a prolonged Dionysian orgy, the bastard fruits of which were consecrated to the rebirth of spring and its promise of the Messiah's return. (The Dönmes amended the Ten Commandments with eighteen "Injunctions" that retained Elohim's strict monotheism while rendering ambiguous the prohibition against adultery.) The last Dönmes in Salonika and the Holy Land emigrated or died out earlier in this century; three to four thousand Karakash Dönmes live on in Istanbul, where they maintain a cemetery and library as well as their own synagogue, known locally as "the Jewish mosque." In the first light of dawn, the Dönme elders intone their 350-year-old supplication in Turkish and Ladino: "Shabbetai Sevi, *asperamos a ti.*" ("Shabbatai Zevi, we await you.")

ABRAHAM ISRAEL PEREIRA'S illustrious life was accosted by heartbreak, and the unmasking of the False Messiah must have been uppermost among his disappointments. He shares that disillusionment with my great-great-grandfather Aharon Raphael Haim Pereira, who surely expected the dawn of a new messianic age in Jerusalem toward the end of the nineteenth century. Both men suffered the inevitable disenchantment of Jews, who, across the centuries, have insisted on clothing their messianic yearnings in earthly raiment. (My great-great-grandfather wrote three books of commentaries, published in Jerusalem in the 1870s, rooted in his faith in the Kabbala's prophecies.)

In *Mirror of the Vanity of This World,* written shortly after Abraham Pereira returned from Venice, he urges his coreligionists to practice self-flagellation and other mortifications of the flesh. In an ecstasy of self-excoriation, he calls on all Jews to atone for the frivolousness of spirit that he blamed for the postponement of the messianic age. Pereira's vigilance in the name of religious orthodoxy finally approaches that of the Spanish inquisitor, a rueful paradox that has not escaped the notice of his critics. Professor Henry Méchoulan attempts to refute these charges.

> In truth, Pereira yearns for a closely guarded community in which all heterodox deviation becomes impossible, in which all attempts against proper custom are repressed, but it cannot be affirmed that his desire for orthodoxy made him aspire, even unconsciously, for the establishment of an inquisitorial institution in the bosom of the community.

The mere idea of an inquisition, Méchoulan protests, perhaps disingenuously, is inimical to the teachings of the Talmud.

THERE IS COMPELLING evidence that Abraham Israel Pereira played a leading role in the excommunication in the 1660s of Baruch Spinoza. He had earlier signed his name at the foot of the document pronouncing a *herem* on another free thinker, the Marrano physician Juan Daniel de Prado. Prado, a contemporary of Spinoza's who had lived in Spain as a secret Judaizer, embraced deism after he failed to reconcile his readings in the Torah with the resurrection of the dead and the immortality of the soul, two of the 13 Articles of the Faith upheld by the Jews of Amsterdam. Prado obstinately resisted the community's ban of excommunication; after gaining reinstatement, he was banned again for relapsing into heresy, and was exiled to Antwerp. As Professor Yosef Kaplan discovered, Pereira employed a devious polemical artifice in *Certeza* to calumniate both Spinoza and Prado—who were close friends—in the same sentence: "In this world that is nothing but arid earth, full of thistles and thorns [*espinos*], a green pasture [*prado*] crawling with poisonous snakes. . . ."

As *parnas*—president—of Amsterdam's synagogue until nearly the final days of his life, Pereira wielded enormous influence with the rabbis who cast the bans on Prado and Spinoza.

Spinoza's efforts to redefine God by recourse to reason rather than faith or Scripture would ultimately alienate him not only from Amsterdam's Sephardic community but from the Dutch Calvinist church in which he sought refuge. Apart from Juan de Prado, Spinoza's other precursor was the Portuguese Marrano and autodidact Uriel da Costa, who was moved to return to Judaism by the message of social justice and "right reason" he found in the Five Books of Moses. After emigrating to Amsterdam and gaining acceptance in the Sephardic congregation, da Costa found himself repelled by what he regarded as the antirationalist authoritarianism of rabbinic literature and dictates; he concluded that the Torah was a human document rather than Divine Writ, and that there was no essential difference between Judaism and any other religious creed. Da Costa was twice excommunicated by the Amsterdam Sephardic congregation for his heretical views, and twice reinstated after an agonized and humiliating recantation. Like Prado, da Costa was loath to sever his links with the Jewish community, and tried to "act the ape among apes" even as his reason instructed him otherwise. In his recently rediscovered work, the *Examen dos Tradiçoes Phariseas,* da Costa wrote of the "fences" that Talmudic sages had erected around the Torah, which he felt had become laws unto themselves, more exacting than Moses' own law and nearly impossible to observe. In the end, the contradictions da Costa lived under proved intolerable, for they were turning him into a Marrano twice over, first among Christians in Portugal and then among his fellow Jews in Amsterdam. Unable to accept for the second time a religious orthodoxy he considered to be a restrictive and man-made fiction rather than God's handiwork, da Costa committed suicide in 1640. Even his chosen method of self-immolation—a bullet in the brain—contributes to the emerging view of him as a proto-modernist, a forerunner—with Juan de Prado—of the existential, secular Jew.

MORE THAN EITHER Prado or da Costa, the obdurate Spinoza would have topped Abraham Pereira's list of dangerous apostates guilty of "abominable heresies" and "monstrous deeds." Spinoza was only twenty-three when the Amsterdam community cast a ban on him. Since no writings of his prior to his excommunication have survived, we cannot know whether he advocated in them the three heresies commonly attributed to him, to wit: his claims that the Law of Moses is a fiction; that the soul dies together with the body; and that God exists only in a philosophical sense. These three assertions constitute a denial of the foundations of the Torah, an offense that Maimonides himself regarded as sufficient grounds for excommunication.

To Pereira, as to the rabbis who banned him, Spinoza was an atheist plain and simple, as was Machiavelli, whom Pereira relentlessly attacks in his chapter on politics. The author of *The Prince* is scathingly denounced for his impiety and for his efforts to divorce theology from politics, a charge that would also adhere to Spinoza. To Pereira, theological and temporal principles were indivisibly subsumed under God's divine law.

THE QUARREL BETWEEN Spinoza and Pereira, two Marranos who inherited the Spanish obsession with "purity" of blood and divine election, may be seen as a seventeenth-century extension of the medieval disputations between the followers of Judah Halevi and those of Maimonides. Abraham Pereira sought redemption in divine revelation, as had his forebears in the twelfth-century study centers of Córdoba and Granada, who labored in pious concert to induce the birth of Elohim's anointed. And it must particularly have galled Abraham Pereira that the youthful Spinoza could outthink his elder detractors and excommunicators.

Baruch Spinoza was preeminently a man of his time. His father had been a respected member of Amsterdam's Sephardic community, and in his youth Spinoza studied Menasseh ben Israel's Kabbalist tracts, as well as Maimonides and Moses ibn Ezra. But he also absorbed the teachings not only of Machiavelli but of Descartes and Thomas Hobbes, among other "modernists." His rationalist inclinations, like those of Maimonides, led him to seek redemption in this world, through a proper understanding of God's working in the minds of men and in the whole of nature. To speak of "Divine Will" is to commit an act of ignorance, and human liberty itself is an illusion fed by our own desires. Happiness is not the result of virtue, but the quality of virtue itself. And the highest virtue is the recognition and experience of God. All that is exists in God, and nowhere else, and nothing can be conceived of or known outside of Him.

As Méchoulan indicates, this view of God's immanence in the universe is diametrically opposed to Abraham Pereira's eschatological preoccupation with the Final Judgment. The doctrine of the elect, the

curse of exile, the concept of free will—all these traditional Jewish concerns are dismissed as sophisms and illusion by Spinoza, who in his
Ethics applied the laws of mathematics and physics to theological issues.
Like Halevi and Maimonides, Abraham Pereira and Spinoza "are two
worlds, in the fullest sense of the term, confronting one another, that of
faith and that of reason." And clamoring in back of both men, Méchoulan concludes, is the same Spanish thirst for immortality. From the
standpoint of the history of philosophy, Pereira's two tracts seem mere
footnotes to the age of Spinoza, whose family coat of arms, appropri-
ately enough, featured a rose with the legend *"Caute quia spinosa."*
("Take care, I have thorns.") After his excommunication, Spinoza renounced his Jewish first name and took the Latin Benedictus, thereby
completing the transition, as Harry Wolfson suggested, from the last of
the medieval philosophers to the first of the moderns.

I FOUND BARUCH Spinoza's modest apartment in The Hague,
where he spent the last seven years of his life. In the small square below,
Spinoza's statue is covered with pigeon droppings, and bouquets of
dried flowers rest at his feet. The caretaker, an elderly Dutchwoman
who claimed to know very little about Spinoza, showed me the tiny
room where he ground and polished lenses for his livelihood and the
garden where he sat and meditated in the evenings. The painter and re-
altor Van Goyen owned the house and rented a room to Spinoza for a
modest eighty guilders a year. Today the cow pasture he gazed out on
from his window has been replaced by The Hague's red-light district.
In the afternoon sad, overaged whores sit in their fish-bowl compart-
ments as middle-aged men and sailors ogle them. Spinoza's grave in the
courtyard back of the New Church, the only gravestone there, is austere, singular, redolent with alienation and exile. Spinoza died at age
forty-four of tuberculosis, which may have been aggravated by the dust
he inhaled when he polished lenses. (Spinoza had a lifelong interest in
optics, a corollary of the transparency he strove for in his writings.)
Spinoza never accepted baptism, and his grave site reflects the life he led
from age twenty-three as a lone, introverted, philosophical genius who
was light-years ahead of his time.

At the end of World War II, when a movement arose in Holland to recommunicate Spinoza, Solomon Rodrigues Pereira, chief

rabbi of Amsterdam's sadly dwindled Sephardic community, refused to have any part in it. He argued that no rabbi had the right to overrule the decision of previous rabbinates unless his judgment was wiser than theirs, which he did not believe to be the case. Rabbi Rodrigues Pereira concluded, "It would be just as ridiculous as trying to review the trial of Jesus."

In 1953 the chief rabbi of Israel at the time, Halevi Herzog, lifted the ban on Spinoza's writings, reasoning that the prohibition was in-tended to apply only during Spinoza's lifetime. When the Jewish Mu-seum of Amsterdam opened in 1989, Spinoza was the first to be honored as a Dutch Jew. It was a mixed blessing. So few Sephardim remained in Amsterdam that the Portuguese Synagogue's heteroge-neous congregation was headed by an Ashkenazic rabbi.

Had Spinoza lived today, the Orthodox rabbinate might have taken umbrage at his heretical views; but with Jews for Jesus and other New Age Marranist movements cropping up everywhere, who on earth would have troubled to cast anathemas upon him?

AT OUDERKERK cemetery south of Amsterdam I am greeted by its two caretakers, Rav Abraham Rodrigues Pereira, grandson of Rabbi Solomon Rodrigues Pereira, and his wife, Chava. Rav Ro-drigues Pereira, who is sixty and has a graying beard, traces his ances-tors in Amsterdam to the seventeenth century. His forebear Abraham Rodrigues Pereira was a contemporary and fellow *parnas* of Abraham Israel Pereira. I had heard the provocative story of the present Abraham Rodrigues Pereira from other Sephardim, but he has become nearly as notorious outside the community since he walked out on his first wife, the Jewish mother of his nine children, and married Chava, a much younger convert from the Dutch Reformed Church. This escapade cost Pereira his post as rabbi of Amsterdam's Ashkenazic congregation. He now makes his living as director of a Jewish nursing home and co-custodian with Chava of the Sephardic gravestones at Ouderkerk.

Rav Rodrigues Pereira and I are the same height and only a cou-ple of years apart in age, and although our blood links are attenuated, we recognize a distinct physical resemblance. He appears alternately mystified and intrigued by my quest. Before he sets out for the nursing home and leaves me in his wife's care, we shake hands and exchange smiles. His dark eyes sparkling piquantly, he suggests that I look up his relatives on Long Island, "even if they say not so nice things about their black-sheep cousin."

Chava, a tall, sturdy and rather dour Amsterdamer in her early forties, escorted me around the cemetery on a wet, early spring afternoon when the surrounding fields were carpeted with wildflowers. She led me first to the grave of Menasseh ben Israel, Abraham Pereira's tutor in the Kabbala, whose fame today rests on his efforts to persuade Crom-well to readmit Jews to England after a 400-year banishment. (The ban was not lifted until after ben Israel died on the return voyage to Amster-dam, embittered by the Parliament's refusal to grant Jews full English citizenship.) The graves of Baruch's parents Michael and Sara Spinoza, like that of the anti-Shabbatean Rabbi Ya'acov Sasportas, are among the few simple gravestones devoid of sculpted cupids, death's-heads and biblical scenes. Samuel Senior Teixeira's grave is orna-mented with a forbidden image of Yahweh revealing himself to Samuel. There is no mistaking the Marrano origins of these Sephardic gentry, who died ignorant or defiant of the Second Commandment's injunction against graven images.

The only exposed gravestone of a Pereira is that of Abraham Pereira's eldest son, Jacob. Above the Portuguese epitaph is carved the family coat of arms, which was unfamiliar to me. It represents a pear tree chained to a prancing lion of Judah. The highly stylized lion, a Castilian heraldic symbol, was adopted as its emblem by the new confederation of Dutch republics. As an aspirant to membership in Holland's gentry, Pereira may have shrewdly placed the lion on his family escutcheon to lay claim to three distinct noble lineages, Israelite, Marrano Catholic and Protestant. Pereira's ambitions for royal patron-age extended far beyond the Dutch Republic. In 1688 he was honored by William III of England for his sizable contribution to the military compaign that broke French dominance in Europe.

IN ABRAHAM Israel Pereira I discovered a direct patriarchal link to my great-grandfather. The didactic tone of *The Certainty of the Road* is close kin to that of Yitzhak Moshe's testament and to his father's Kab-balist commentaries. The memory of exile, and of generations of ances-tors who practiced a furtive crypto-Judaism burned alike in the souls of both authors. Like the eighteenth-century Marrano slave trader portrayed by Robert De Niro in the film *The Mission,* who penitently dragged his armor by a rope tied around his neck, Abraham Israel Pereira dragged behind him to the end of his days the mixed baggage of a Spanish Marrano heritage.

For his part, my great-grandfather signed his testament *samech tet,* or "ST," which stands for "Sephardi Tahor," or True Sephardi, as though to distance himself not only from Oriental Jews with no link to Spain but also from Marranos whose Jewish identity remained suspect. And this same shared inquisitorial memory apparently led Yitzhak Moshe Perera to pronounce the Kabbalistic injunction—with its veiled threat of excommunication if it were disobeyed—that prohibited his sons and their descendants from ever again departing Jerusalem for the "lands of idolatry." These two imposing figures, I concluded, would have recognized each other on sight. If Maria Nunes and her descendants are my blood kin, then Abraham Israel is my spiritual forebear.

IN PERHAPS THE final irony of his life, Abraham Pereira, who often praised the benisons of a short and virtuous life, survived into his late nineties, spanning the whole of the seventeenth century. He died at last, weighed down with honors and regrets, in the halcyon year 1699. I picture him on his *parnas*'s seat facing the raised *bimah,* a large-haunched *magnifico* who fills to the brim his place of honor. His red turban and cloak of fine damask silk, his heavily scored brow, deep-sunken eyes and white-bearded visage are bathed in the shimmering chiaroscuro of a portrait by Rembrandt van Rijn.

CHAPTER VI

THE FRENCH PEREIRAS

JACOB RODRIGUES PEREIRA

La poire de l'espoir (the pear of hope)
—Old French saying

. . . wishing for pears from an elm tree.
—Old Spanish saying

IN OCTOBER 1703, more than one hundred years after Maria Nunes arrived in Amsterdam, another family of Nunes Pereiras, led by the fifty-five-year-old paterfamilias Diego, disembarked in Bayonne, France. The register of passengers on the *Ville de St.-Malo,* which had sailed from Lisbon on September 27, reported the extended family of twelve Nunes Pereiras as having departed from Portugal "due to the vexations they were subjected to."

The passengers planned to settle in France, in accordance with the welcome extended to exiled "Portuguese" by the edicts of Henry II in 1550.

> The Kings welcome the Portuguese, known as New Chris-
> tians, inviting them to reside in our kingdom with their
> wives and families, and to bring with them their monies and
> portable belongings. . . . We regard favorably their good
> zeal and affection to live as our subjects, intending to
> become employed in our service and that of the republic of
> our kingdom; whose prosperity they desire to aid with their
> goods, manual skills and their industry, in recognition of
> which we are moved to receive them kindly and graciously.

The Nunes Pereiras, together with the Rodrigues, Lopes and other Marrano families in flight from the Portuguese Inquisition, found safe haven in Bayonne, Bordeaux and other port cities of the southwest. Like the Amsterdam Marranos, these Iberian families would find ways to prosper despite the persistence of age-old prejudices and restrictions in their host culture; and they would go on to found the powerful Sephar-dic dynasties of nineteenth-century France.

No other reclaimed Spanish Jews matched the meteoric rise and fall of the Pereire brothers, Emile and Isaac—who in the 1850s rivaled the Rothschilds in wealth and influence—or the prestige attained by their grandfather, the inventor and pedagogue Jacob Rodrigues Pereira. In the mid-eighteenth century Pereira pioneered a system for training deaf-mutes by devising a special manual alphabet and teaching clear articulation—a precursor of the integrated system used in deaf-mute education today.

In his authorized 1984 biography, *Les Frères Pereire: la bonheur d'entreprendre,* Jean Autin includes a genealogical tree dating to Jacob Rodrigues Pereira's grandparents, Juan-Abraham Rodrigues and Leonor-Abigail Henriques, who fled to Portugal from Estremadura, Spain, in the early 1700s. As with other family histories of that period, the record of the Rodrigues Pereiras' activities in the Iberian Peninsula is a thin quilt of documents and anecdotal material patched together by their descendants six or seven generations removed.

A striking leitmotif in the Pereira chronicle is the strong-willed, resourceful matriarch, who, in one generation after another, holds the family together during periods of adversity. The earliest of this breed on record is Leonor-Abigail Henriques, wife of Juan-Abraham Rodrigues and mother of Francisco Antonio-Jacobo Rodrigues Pereira. A native of Estremadura, she had fled Spain to settle with her husband and nine children in Bragança, a town in Portugal's province of Trás-os-Montes. In Bragança the family lived—as they had in Spain—as baptized New Christians, and Juan Rodrigues Pereira prospered in the silk trade. But suspicious neighbors alerted Portuguese inquisitors, who called Leonor Henriques to account. She was tried as a secret Judaizer by the Bragança tribunal and sentenced to perform daily penitences for one year at the portals to the town's cathedral.

This humiliation proved to be the last straw. Leonor convinced her husband that the time had come to leave the Iberian Peninsula for good. The liberal Treaty of Lisbon signed in 1668 with the intercession of Cardinal Richelieu, inclined the Rodrigues Pereiras in favor of emigrating to France. In 1734 Leonor and Juan sent their sons to explore possibilities in Paris as well as Bordeaux, Bayonne and other southwest port cities. Seven years later the majority of the family relocated to Bordeaux, where they shed their Christian names and reclaimed their Jewish religion. However, Beatriz, a daughter married to a Portuguese nobleman, chose to remain behind with her Christian husband. Another son, Manuel, returned to Spain, and a third, Louis-David, emi-grated to America.

A year after they settled in France, Abraham Rodrigues Pereira passed away. Jacob, the seventh of his nine children, assumed the obli-gations of primogeniture and became the family's provider. (Of his six elder siblings, four were women; his older brother Paulino was scant of ambition and the other, Manuel, was a poet and dramatist uninterested in family affairs.) The stage was set for the rise of Jacob Rodrigues Pe-reire—the French spelling—cited in Jewish encyclopedias and French histories as one of the outstanding personages of the eighteenth century.

Allowing for the doctoring of disagreeable facts and the closet-ing of skeletons that is to be expected of a family-authorized biography, Jacob Pereira still emerges as a fascinating enigma: an ambitious, com-passionate, immensely gifted man who was modest to a fault. It may be just as well Autin makes no attempt to reconcile these contradictory traits, which would resurface—unencumbered by the elder Pereira's modesty—in his two grandsons and heirs apparent, Emile and Isaac Pereire.

When Jacob Pereira arrived in France several years ahead of his parents, he dropped his Christian forenames, Francisco Antonio—al-though years later he signed them on a book of poetry as well as in arti-cles he published in Spain. He enrolled in medical school at age nineteen, hoping eventually to provide for his family with a doctor's wages. He had an omnivorous curiosity, which he focused on mathe-matics, anatomy and linguistics. A gifted polyglot, Pereira was in-trigued by the structure of language. His youthful companionship with a congenitally deaf young woman—who may in fact have been one of his sisters—would exert a formative influence on his life. The challenge of enabling her to communicate, enhanced by his natural bent for lan-guages, induced Jacob to embark on a pedagogic career.

After an initial success in teaching his companion to articulate vowels, Pereira devoted the next ten years to contriving a scientific sys-tem for teaching the deaf and dumb. In Bordeaux, he founded France's first school for congenital deaf-mutes. His studies in the physiology of speech led him to concentrate on vocalization. His first tool was a man-ual alphabet modeled on that of Juan Pablo Bonet, a Spanish peda-gogue who published his work in 1620. Pereira's other immediate predecessor was a Swiss physician resident in Haarlem in the 1690s, Jean Conrad Amman, a teacher of deaf-mutes who combined lipread-

ing with "artificial articulation." Pereira would absorb the accomplishments of these and other educators of his era and improve them with in-
novations of his own, such as a syllabic manual of eighty-odd signs that
came to be known as dactylology because it relied on the sense of touch.

In 1745 Pereira presented at the Jesuit college of La Rochelle a
thirteen-year-old Jewish deaf-mute, Aaron Beaumarin, whom he had
taught to enunciate the letters of the alphabet as well as several short
phrases. Among those in attendance was an influential man of affairs,
M. d'Azy d'Etavigny, who had exhausted a small fortune on fruitless
efforts to penetrate the wall of silence that shut him off from his deaf-
mute son. Intrigued by Pereira's achievement, he made him a straight-
forward business proposal.

D'Etavigny offered Pereira a one-year, 3,000-pound contract to
instruct his fifteen-year-old son on the following terms: The first 1,000
pounds would be paid when his son had learned to articulate a given
number of words; another 1,000 would be disbursed after his son was
able to "read, pronounce and conceptualize the greater part of visible
and ordinary things." The last third would be paid at the end of the
year, as mutually agreed, once the aforementioned conditions had been
met.

Pereira accepted, and arranged to instruct the boy daily at the
college of Beaumont-en-Auge in Normandy. The results of his labors
were presented on November 22, 1746, to members of the Royal Academy of Caen, under the presidency of the bishop of Bayeux. The boy
astonished the assemblage with his clear pronunciation of test words
like *chapeau, chemise,* and *épée,* and his ability to answer written questions
with a vocal *"oui"* or *"non."* But Pereira himself was met with cool for-
mality by the academy members, who appear to have been piqued by
his refusal to divulge his teaching methods.

Although he received the academy's official certification, that
cold reception evidently affronted Pereira's sense of dignity. And it may
also have deepened a distrust inherited from his Marrano past. He
turned his back on his sponsors and relocated to Paris to continue his
research. There Pereira began tinkering with mechanical devices, a
hobby that would ripen into a second vocation as an inventor.

News of Pereira's success with d'Etavigny's son spread beyond
Paris to other European capitals. Requests for his services came from as
far away as Sardinia, whose king offered him a handsome stipend to
work with his handicapped niece. Pereira turned down this and most

other offers, and decided instead to continue working with the young d'Etavigny, for whom he conceived a strong attachment.

These early experiences underline two personality traits that would indelibly stamp Pereira's private life and ultimately undermine his professional standing. The first trait was decried by his biographers as an unfortunate "timidity of character"; the second was an idiosyncrasy his contemporaries praised as a passionate—and reciprocated—devotion to his pupils. The first tendency manifested itself in Pereira's reluctance to publicize his teaching methods, or to publish professional papers to promote his achievements. The second and related trait, a consuming affection for his deaf-mute pupils of both sexes, may have verged in some instances on pedophilia. A lawyer named Coste d'Arnobat inadvertently drew attention to this idiosyncrasy of Pereira's in a fulsome tribute.

> His face pitted by the effects of smallpox, he had large eyes filled with fire and expressiveness; probity, sweetness, candor and humanity were painted on his physiognomy. One could not approach him without loving him; this was a man who honored human nature. His pupils of both sexes were so passionately devoted to him that prior to taking his leave of them their parents had to prepare for the separation, arranging to send for him every two weeks for some duration to make certain he spent one week of it with his charges. The pupils arrived at their teacher's home with the most affecting transports of joy; when it came time for them to depart at last, one cannot convey an idea of the pain endured by these children, who embraced him a thousand times and would not wrench themselves away until their teacher had pledged to visit with them often. . . . It is particularly difficult to represent the transports and the hurt of these small children, who could not be pried away from his arms, even as the kindly Pereira attempted in vain to conceal his own tender testimonials. . . .

Pereira's handicapped pupils, sealed off from the hearing world by a wall of silence, received their kindly tutor as a savior. For his own part, this retiring genius was evidently most at ease in the company of handicapped children and exceptional adults whose sensibilities were

Jacob Rodrigues Pereira and disciple. (Académie des sourds-muets, Paris)

as rarefied as his own. But of course his teaching methods by their very nature fostered a close interdependence and physical contact with his pupils.

A biographical study of Pereira published in 1847 by Dr. Ed-ouard Séguin, a physiologist and teacher of mental retardates, attributes Pereira's success with deaf-mutes to his grasp of "the fundamentality of the sense of touch." When teaching his pupils to vocalize, Pereira had them place both hands on his throat so their fingers could associate each syllable or word with the corresponding vibration from his vocal chords. Deaf-mutes, Pereira discovered, were able to translate tactile stimuli into cognate visual or abstract symbols; to that extent they could in effect "see" or "hear" with their hands.

Séguin's 1847 study of Pereira's methods, and another under-taken by Ernest La Rochelle in 1882, reveal the extraordinary measures he undertook to enable deaf-mutes to lead normal lives. Before taking on any new pupils, he first put them through a battery of tests to deter-mine the origin and extent of their hearing impairment and to evaluate their basic intelligence. (Pereira declined to take on mental defectives.) The tests he devised to classify deaf-mutes were decades ahead of his time, in both thoroughness and sophistication.

Pereira's extensive studies in physiology and anatomy convinced him that he could teach deaf-mutes abstract concepts by developing their visual, olfactory and even gustatory senses, which he regarded as modifications of the sense of touch. The patience and single-minded dedication this "wholistic" instruction demanded was comparable to a priestly calling, and evidently there was an alloy of mystical self-abnega-tion in Pereira's personality. Pereira's religious strain was a syncretic mix of Jewish and Christian principles; his equivocation and mistrust, even his resort to aliases, were hallmarks of a Marrano inheritance he shared with other distinguished coreligionists, among them Baruch Spinoza and Jacob's distant relative—and mine—the Dutch magnate Abraham Israel Pereira.

Pereira's determination to forge his choice pupils into useful, in-tellectually active members of eighteenth-century society can perhaps be best appreciated by reference to two remarkable women who lived ear-lier in our century: the sightless deaf-mute Helen Keller and her lifelong teacher and companion, Anne Sullivan. With Keller as her subject and collaborator, Sullivan made the following discovery: "Not enough emphasis has been put on the sense of touch, which is the great sense.

The whole skin sees and listens, and not only the skin but the entire body, bones and muscles. Psychologically, and as a matter of biological history, hearing and sight are only specializations of the sense of touch."

Pereira was so persuaded of this fundamental truth that he pre-sented it as a given in the brief "Observations" he submitted to the French Academy of Sciences in 1749. He remarked, for example, that congenitally deaf infants learn the words "Papa" and "Mama" in their parents' arms but forget them as they grow older. He concluded that deaf infants' acute powers of observation enabled them to associate the movements of the adults' lips and speech organs with the vocal vibra-tions passing through their skin. (This same insight has recently been expressed—and made use of—by the famed deaf Scottish musician Evelyn Glennie.) Given the radical novelty of this discovery, it is not surprising that Pereira was reluctant to reveal his methodology for fear of being labeled a crank.

And yet for all his modesty and retiring personality, Pereira counted among his acquaintances some of the outstanding names in French letters and sciences. His neighbor in Paris, Jean-Jacques Rous-seau, who often visited his small school, cited Pereira in his writings as "the only man of his time who could make the mute speak." Rous-seau's physiological theories were influenced by his acquaintance with Pereira, as is evident in sections of *Emile* and in others of his scientific writings. Pereira's companions included Diderot, d'Alembert and that inveterate world traveler the count de Bougainville, who persuaded him to compose a vocabulary based on his examination of a Tahitian native whom Bougainville brought to Paris.

In spite of Pereira's eccentricities, his achievements continued to draw attention, and pushed him into the public arena. On July 8, 1749, he at last agreed to set down his teaching methods in a presenta-tion before the French Academy of Sciences. His pupil d'Azy d'Eta-vigny was examined by a jury of distinguished scientists led by Buffon, the celebrated author of *Histoire Naturelle,* and Antoine Ferrein, a noted anatomist and professor of surgery. Their detailed report on young d'Etavigny's performance and on Pereira's brief memoir fully vin-dicated Pereira's system while praising his skills as a teacher. His pupil gave detailed answers vocally and in writing to the examiners' ques-tions, and repeated several prayers by heart; he also revealed a clear un-derstanding of French grammar and showed an ability to grasp abstract and general ideas. Pereira's syllabic manual was singled out as an original and useful invention. The panel unanimously recommended Pereira for membership in the academy, a signal honor for a Jewish immigrant.

Pereira's achievement opened an audible crack—and aimed a powerful shaft of light—into the dark, isolated world of the congenital deaf-mute; centuries before Aristotle, and for two millennia after him, the deaf and dumb had been lumped together with idiots and imbeciles as hopeless deviants beyond the reach of education.

Pereira was now flooded with requests to instruct the handi-capped children of titled families in France and abroad. Although he turned down most of these offers, he accepted stipends to instruct indi-gent deaf-mutes. The duke of Chaumes confided his son, Saboureux de Fontenay, to his care, while the marquis d'Argenson authorized him to open a small school for the handicapped in Paris.

In 1749 King Louis XV asked to meet Pereira, and honored him with the title of *"Portugais de nation,"* an honor that carried a yearly pension of 800 pounds. The award was recorded on a calculating ma-chine of Pereira's design, an invention that gained him an additional royal stipend. Dating from that honor, Pereira became known by the French form of the name, "Pereire."

Pereira's rising prominence drew the attention of France's grow-ing Portuguese Jewish community, which accredited him as its official agent. In pursuance of his duties Pereira often visited Paris's outlying quarters and villages, where anti-Semitic restrictions enforced since the Middle Ages forbade Jews to move about after sunset. Until the end of his life, Pereira persisted in his advocacy of immigrant Sephardim. It was through his endeavors in court that Portuguese Jews earned the legal right to settle in France in 1777.

There is a dark side to Jacob Pereira's advocacy that is not re-marked on either in Autin's biography or in the encyclopedias. On the advice of his friend and kinsman Isaac Pinto, Pereira used his cachet to persuade Louis XV to ratify a statute barring from France all foreign Jews not of Iberian extraction. Isaac Pinto, who was intimate with the duc de Richelieu, enlisted him to enforce the statutes. All but two Ger-man and Avignon Jews were banished from Bordeaux, a sorry episode in the history of French Jewry for which Jacob Pereira must bear partial responsibility. In extenuation of this blot on his character, his defenders argued—not very persuasively—that he was only capitalizing on a preexisting prejudice, given the favoritism French kings had consistently shown Portuguese Jews over their Ashkenazic brethren since Henry II.

For nearly a decade, Pereira's work kept him away from his mother and elder sisters, who had never left Bordeaux. Following an extended visit with his redoubtable mother, who died shortly afterward, Pereira returned to Paris with his sister Ysabel Ribka. She became his assistant in treating handicapped young women.

Pereira treated indigent deaf-mutes at his private school in Paris at his own expense. But whereas working-class pupils were taught little more than the skills they required for gainful employment, Pereira extended himself to the limit with his well-born charges. His most outstanding success was Saboureux de Fontenay, the young deaf-mute nobleman who in later years staunchly defended his tutor against his critics. Saboureux presented a lucid, succinct defense of Pereira's dactylological technique and lauded his unflagging perseverance in teaching his pupils the mathematical and physical sciences, literature, history and geography. Saboureux went on to astonish the scientific world by becoming an accomplished linguist, although he was totally deaf. Years after leaving Pereira's care he learned Latin, Italian and Hebrew. At the age of thirty-two he embarked on a study of Arabic and other eastern languages to "become acquainted with the metaphysics of primitive languages."

In 1766, having attained worldwide renown in middle age, Pereira turned his sights inward; he married his cousin Miriam Lopes Dias, who would bear him four children and afford him some of the happiest years of his life.

Pereira's career was capped by a second honor conferred on him by Louis XV, who named him royal interpreter. (In addition to mastering French, Spanish and Portuguese, Pereira was also fluent in Latin and Hebrew.) King Christian VII of Denmark and Emperor Joseph II of Austria sought to make his acquaintance. The Royal Society of London made him a member at the initiative of the French Academy of Sciences, as a result of which Pereira's work became known throughout the British commonwealth.

But just at his moment of greatest renown, Pereira's proudest achievement was eclipsed by a French abbot. Charles Michel de l'Epée devised his own scientific method for teaching deaf-mutes based on gesture, mimicry and a simpler, if less effective, manual alphabet. L'Epée taught his system in his own school for the handicapped and publicized his work in learned journals. Ignoring the earnest advice of his friends and colleagues, Pereira refused to challenge the abbot by publishing his own findings. In 1778, two years before Pereira's death, the council of Paris passed a decree placing the abbot's school for deaf-mutes under the protection of Louis XVI. Today it is the abbot's system that remains in use in France for teaching deaf-mutes, and that was used by an immigrant French teacher in the 1820s to create American Sign Language.

Pereira's season in the limelight came to an end. His "timidity" would erode his influence in professional circles and dilute the significance of his achievements. Testimonials of the time suggest that Pereira accepted his decline with an almost perverse equanimity. His life, like that of many other Sephardic fugitives from the nightmare of the Inquisition, was shadowed by a subtle and corrosive fatalism.

And yet his misgivings turned out to be at least partly justified. Pereira's Judaism became the butt of attacks by nationalists, anti-Semites and associates of L'Epée, who insinuated that he was teaching "alien ideas" to the sons and daughters of France's leading families. A detractor even accused Pereira of teaching his pupils to speak in his own "foreign accent." The abbot's simpler, standardized system of instruction did not require the wholehearted dedication and minute attention to detail that Pereira's methods did, and it was adjudged effective for the dissemination of sound Christian precepts among France's handicapped population.

None of Jacob Pereira's inventions received more than passing notice as novel curiosities. His calculating machine sat for decades in the vault of the Geneva banker Necker, who had commissioned it. In 1779 the marine minister Sartine persuaded Pereira to undertake the design of a wind engine to help speed France's growing fleet of transatlantic cargo vessels. The "windmill" engine foundered, soon to be overtaken by the first compressed-steam locomotives and ship engines, whose invention Pereira seemingly foreshadowed.

The premature death of his firstborn son, Abraham, plunged Jacob Pereira into a profound despondency from which he never recovered. Concerned in his last days with an Orthodox burial, Pereira obtained an ordinance to establish the first legal Jewish cemetery in France. A second son, Samuel, fell gravely ill and his death preceded his father's by several months. Both died in 1780 and were buried side by side in the cemetery of La Villette. At the *shivah* held in his home, three men recited the prayers of mourning for Jacob Pereira: a rabbi, a Catholic priest and a Protestant pastor, all of whom had been his close friends. The Portuguese Jewish community of Bordeaux convened to recite a prayer in Pereira's memory every Shabbat and feast day, offering a dram of oil on each occasion toward the repose of his soul. Besides his wife, Miriam, Jacob Pereira was survived by a twelve-year-old daughter, Abigail, and a nine-year-old son.

The Pereira standard was passed on to the following generation through Jacob's only surviving son, Isaac Rodrigues Pereire.

II

EMILE AND ISAAC

The death of her husband following closely on that of her son Samuel plunged Miriam Lopes Dias Pereira into a numbing despair. To worsen matters, her two surviving children, Isaac and Abigail, contracted the dread smallpox that had afflicted three generations of Pereiras. In December 1780, after Isaac and Abigail had sufficiently recuperated, Madame Pereira shook off her paralysis; she gathered her children and all their possessions and undertook the move back to Bordeaux.

The hard times persisted. Isaac continued in frail health, and the family's travails compelled him to abandon his studies and embark on a career in commerce. His father's slender inheritance all but exhausted, Isaac struggled as best he could to keep Jacob Pereira's legacy alive. He maintained contact with several of his father's faithful disciples, who were eager to cooperate in publishing Jacob's work and propagating his ideas. Unfortunately, in the unfavorable economic climate then prevailing, Isaac's career in maritime insurance stagnated; he was unable to lift the family above genteel poverty, or to advance his father's work with any effectiveness. In 1780 Isaac married Henriette Lopes Fonseca, a Portuguese Jew from neighboring Bayonne. Her vivacious, industrious spirit would give the family a much-needed boost.

France lived through a period of instability, suspended between the Peace of Amiens and the Treaty of Presbourg. In a few short years, Napoleon's armies would be on the march throughout Europe. Isaac Pereire became one of the casualties of the economic uncertainties of his

Emile and Isaac Pereire. (Bibliothèque nationale, Paris)

time. On the verge of bankruptcy in 1803, two years later he was unable to meet his payments. This humiliation apparently broke his delicate spirit, and he died a year later at the age of thirty-five. Isaac was survived by his mother and a twenty-four-year-old widow with two children, Jacob-Emile and Mardochée-Télèphe, a frail daughter fated to die in early childhood. At the time of her husband's death, Henriette Fonseca was eight months pregnant with a third child, a son she would name Isaac in his father's memory.

Once more, a resourceful widow would hold together the Pereire family and permit the tender heirs—Emile and Isaac—not only to survive but to attain a vigorous maturity and fulfill their brilliant destinies.

Intent on providing her two surviving sons with the best opportunities available, Henriette opened a notions boutique in Bordeaux under the name Au Juste Prix. Most of the revenues would go toward assuring Emile and Isaac a private-school education. But the persisting economic recession forced Henriette to close her boutique several years later and remove her sons from private school. The Portuguese Jewish community of Bordeaux, indebted to the memory of their benefactor Jacob Pereira, rallied to the family's aid. A prosperous relative and close friend of the family, Isaac Rodrigues, arranged for a dry-goods merchant to employ Emile and Isaac on a commission basis. Emile was eleven years old when he embarked on a career in commerce and public affairs, a distinction he would fling in the face of a detractor years later ("I have been in the business world for forty-one years . . . and from the beginning I have found by my sole enterprise, without the support of any personal capital, the means to provide for my existence and for that of many others besides.")

At age twenty, Emile joined the firm of Nunes and Hardel. Isaac at fourteen was hired as a copier with the firm of David Gradin. But Bordeaux's commercial prosperity was in decline, having peaked in the prerevolutionary years, when eight of every eleven money chang-ers were Jews. The brothers turned their sights to Paris.

Once more, their cousin Isaac Rodrigues came to the Pereire brothers' aid. He had settled in Paris years before, having landed a lu-crative position as an agent with the banker Achille Fould. He sum-moned Emile to Paris and placed him under the care of his two sons, Olinde and Eugène, who would prove stout allies and associates of the Pereires in their future enterprises. Emile undertook a course in accoun-tancy from Isaac Rodrigues, who had been a professor in that subject. In 1823 he married Rodrigues's daughter Rachel-Herminie, who brought a modest dowry of 4,000 francs. His younger brother, Isaac, ar-rived in Paris the same year.

The biographer Jean Autin points repeatedly to the stubborn pride of the self-made Pereire brothers; that and an entrepreneurial ge-nius absent in their visionary grandfather were to keep them afloat in the postrevolutionary, post-Napoleonic second quarter of the nineteenth century, at the dawn of the industrial age.

Emile and Isaac's grandmother Miriam Dias, who outlived her husband, Jacob, by nearly fifty years, never let her grandchildren forget their debt to their grandfather. His work on behalf of the Portuguese Jewish community would open doors for his heirs in Paris, as it had in Bordeaux. They soon set about repaying their debt.

The brothers knew that their grandfather's work had never been published, and his ideas had been appropriated by L'Epée and other specialists in deaf-mute education. But their mother was convinced that he had left the key to decoding his method with his disciples. Emile contacted the last of these, Marie Magdalene Marois, who was over-joyed to hear from the family of her beloved tutor. In answer to their father's first inquiries, in 1811, she had written to assure him that Jacob Pereira had been the sole repository of his teaching methods and had not imparted them to anyone else.

Not satisfied with this earlier communication, the brothers ar-ranged for Mademoiselle Marois to visit Paris from her home in Or-leans, and to bring with her any documents that would help to reconstruct Jacob Pereira's system.

She arrived in Paris with her notebooks, containing the rudi-ments of the manual alphabet Pereira employed in training deaf-mutes to vocalize. Marois had been Pereira's outstanding female pupil fifty years earlier, and although she was now nearly eighty, she still enun-ciated words clearly, with a distinct trace of Jacob's Gascon accent. Marois was more than eager to collaborate with her teacher's kin, but in response to their entreaties she could only repeat that their grand-father's kindness, patience and affectionate nature had been the real key to his success, beyond all his erudition and the scientific methods he employed.

Isaac collected all the documents assembled by Marois and pub-lished them under a single cover. In 1825 they presented the manuscript to the director of the royal institute for deaf-mutes, Abbot Perier. It was a symbolic gesture, as the brothers knew that L'Epée's methods had the Crown's official sanction and would not be challenged by these frag-ments of Pereira's work. The enduring legacy of Jacob Pereira was im-printed in the chromosomes of his heirs apparent, and that was perhaps how it had been intended all along. "Remember always," Miriam Lopes Dias Pereira admonished the brothers from her deathbed, "that you are the grandsons of Jacob Rodrigues Pereira."

In the 1840s Isaac Pereire commissioned the physiologist Ed-ouard Séguin to write his grandfather's official biography. *Jacob Ro-drigues Pereire: Notice sur sa vie et ses travaux* appeared in 1847 and garnered respectful notices from the press. But it did not receive the hoped-for recognition from the scientific fraternity.

In 1879 Isaac Pereire and his son Eugène—both members of the National Institute for the Deaf and Dumb—attended the unveiling of a statue of L'Epée. That same year Isaac honored his grandfather's mem-ory with a memorial conference and concert in the Théâtre des Nations. The event, with Victor Hugo as master of ceremonies, was attended by Paris's beau monde as well as leading specialists in deaf-mute educa-tion. The invited guests and the "orthoponists" heatedly debated the

advantages of lipreading and sign language against the benefits of vocalization: Should the emphasis be on training deaf-mute lip-readers and
signers or on turning out deaf speakers? The debate continues today.

TWO YEARS AFTER Isaac's death, Ernest La Rochelle published a new biography based on Jacob Pereira's collected documents.
But it was Séguin's study that would ultimately rescue Pereira's work
from oblivion.

In Robert J. Fynne's 1924 book *Montessori and Her Inspirers,* the
opening chapter is devoted to Jacob Pereira. Professor Fynne claims
that Séguin's brilliant exposition of Pereira's system exerted an indirect
influence on Maria Montessori, whose ideas borrowed heavily from Séguin's work with severely retarded children. Since Montessori's death
in 1952, her well-known pedagogical concept has been adopted by
thousands of teaching institutions throughout the world. Of particular
relevance to the Montessori method was Pereira's wholistic approach,
which relied on physiological observation to train the handicapped
child's unimpaired senses. Another plausible contribution was
Pereira's individual attention to the psychic and intellectual development of each individual pupil, and his insistence that they fulfill their
innate capacity to lead full, productive lives.

However, Montessori's concept of "spontaneous development,"
which presupposes a child's inborn capacity to educate itself, would
have been unthinkable to the paternalistic pedagogues of the eighteenth
century. It is unlikely that even Jacob Pereira would have coun-
tenanced the capacity for self-governance that Maria Montessori presupposed in a child.

Jacob Pereira and Baruch Spinoza, two geniuses born years
ahead of their time, shared two important predispositions from their
Marrano legacy. Both men sought to anchor their quest for redemption
on scientific bedrock. For all their alienating elitism, both had a rare gift
for friendship, and yet they were profoundly solitary men who lived and
died misunderstood and underappreciated by their contemporaries. In
spite of their secretive natures, both men valued transparency in their
private as well as their professional lives; if Spinoza strove for exact vision, Pereira's inner quest was for a psychic equivalent of perfect pitch.

Emile and Isaac's moral and spiritual indebtedness to their
grandfather is not easily defined. The stresses of survival in the financial

world and the prerequisites for acceptance by Paris's beau monde would gradually distance the two brothers—to varying degrees—from their Jewish origins. In its place they would embrace a social philoso'phy that glorified the entrepreneurial spirit as the engine propelling both economic progress and social justice. The founder of this new secular religion was the count Saint'Simon.

III

THE TRIUMPHANT PEREIRES

The spectacular careers of the brothers Pereire are a matter of record. In competition with the Rothschild dynasty they introduced the railways in France, beginning with Paris–Saint'Germain, and led the way in expanding rail lines into Switzerland, Spain and Russia. They founded the joint'stock investment bank or Crédit Mobilier, whose re'serves they used to buy up railway concessions, underwrite gas lighting and omnibus ventures in Paris, and expand steamship commerce beyond Europe to the New World. At the height of their success the Pereires held title to vast properties in Paris and owned luxurious villas, chalets and health spas in the south of France; they accumulated a superb art collection, hobnobbed with the great writers, artists and public figures of their day, and rivaled the Rothschilds in wealth and influence.

Although the astute Rothschilds eventually co'opted and par'tially eclipsed the achievements of the Pereire brothers, the name Pereire has an enduring resonance in France. The brothers personified Saint'Simonian ideas for social and economic progress espoused by Philippe Napoleon, Napoleon III and other rulers of the postrevolutionary Holy Alliance and the Second Empire. They hosted and dined with kings, struck up business partnerships with the cream of France's nobility. The Pereires also became known as social reformers for the thousands of articles they contributed to influential political and economic journals. Even after the demise of their credit banking houses, the Pereire broth'ers' audacity left an imprint on Europe's financial markets that endured until the eve of World War II.

A few years after the Rothschilds vilified the Crédit Mobilier as "Europe's greatest gambling casino," they reconsidered and introduced a modified version of it in Vienna. The Credit Institute for Trade and Industry (Creditanstalt für Handel und Gewerbe) survived the war, and, under another name, it remains Austria's largest private bank.

The Pereires' investments and influence spread well beyond Europe's borders. The Colón–Panama City railway was built on their recommendation; Ferdinand de Lesseps admitted that without Isaac Pereire's financial backing, he could not have laid the foundations for the Panama Canal. (Europeans also praised Pereire for deterring Yankee imperialistic designs, under the guise of the Monroe Doctrine, in Central America.)

Emile, the elder brother, became conservative with age, but to the last day of Isaac Pereire's life he propounded the Saint-Simonian gospel that capital was the ineluctable partner, with labor, of unlimited progress and the well-being of humankind. In their voluminous writings Emile and Isaac denounced child labor and supported workers' right to free association. They foreshadowed the labor-union movement, and warned that unrelieved oppression of the proletariat would lead to a social explosion. In 1831 Emile wrote in *Le National:* "In time the truth will be recognized that all social wealth is the product of labor, and that all taxes, direct or indirect, fall primarily on the workers. Who should draw up the state's budget? Those who generate the revenue, or those who spend it?"

The Pereires repeatedly attacked corruption in government and the church. They lobbied unceasingly for a standard European currency and were among the early harbingers of a European common market. In common with their grandfather Jacob, although perhaps less wisely, the Pereires sought redemption in hard work, leavened by a judicious philanthropy. In later years they envisioned themselves as architects of a grand design to move mountains, tame the seas and make the world habitable for rich and poor alike. Their joint-stock commercial ventures in the Americas—which included the shipment of 60,000 Chinese coolies to Cuba; the purchase of mining concessions in Honduras and Salvador; the importation of guano fertilizer from Peru and choice beef from La Plata—anticipated the unfettered expansionism of today's multinationals. Impenitent optimists, to cite Autin's felicitous phrase, the Pereires promoted the railways and credit banks as instruments of civilization as well as generators of profit. By turns acclaimed and reviled by their contemporaries as brilliant publicists, innovators and reformers, the Pereires fell far short of becoming revolutionaries—

although they were witnesses to the birth of modern socialism in Paris. They shared the spotlight with Karl Marx as well as Baron James Rothschild and fell somewhere in between. For all the Pereires' clamoring for social justice, when Marx and Engels published *Das Kapital* and proclaimed the emancipation of the proletariat, Emile denounced them as dangerous agitators who sought the overthrow of enlightened free enterprise. For Emile, as for Saint-Simon, progress and justice for the masses could flow only from a stable, established order.

As though to compensate for their grandfather's reticence, the Pereire brothers—no shrinking violets—broadcast their Saint-Simonian ideas through every channel of communication available to them. Emile became editor and columnist of *Le Globe* and *Le National*. Isaac Pereire founded the journal *La Liberté* and wrote for it eloquently during the last four years of his life, when his altruistic, quixotic nature overshadowed his entrepreneurial drive. "Give! give! give!" he exhorted his fellow entrepreneurs, echoing the Amsterdam magnate Abraham Israel Pereira. "Make amends for your wealth with your munificence!" Isaac Pereire's last article, published shortly before his death, was titled, "The Social Mission of Power."

Of the two Pereire brothers, Emile was the better publicist, with a nearly unerring instinct for grabbing hold of a promising concept— such as the railways—and disseminating it to the far corners of the globe, even as he rationalized his mounting revenues as the fruits of social progress. As the more aggressive of the brothers, Emile could be coldly calculating and contemptuous; in this tendency he mirrored his former employer and archrival Baron James Rothschild, who lampooned his competitors as "lap-dogs" and "boot-lickers" and referred to Emile himself as *"le petit Pereire."* Michel Chevalier, a close friend of Emile's, warned him in writing of the price he would pay in lost friends and influence owing to his "wounding manner, acerbic, cutting and lacking in *savoir-faire."* Chevalier's elegant advice evidently went unheeded.

By the 1860s the Pereires had become giddy with success, buying up hotels, a ninety-foot-tall castle, and a quarter-million-hectare estate in Armainvilliers with a casino and a health spa to distract Emile from his chronic asthma. But in the course of a single year, in 1867, the Crédit Mobilier in Paris, Madrid, Brussels and other European cities exceeded their investments and fell heavily into debt. The Pereires were forced to resign their bank directorships, one after the other; they also had to sell off their vast holdings as the credit houses were seized by the Banque de France, the giant financial monolith that represented every- thing the Pereires abhorred. (They had twice tried and failed to found a chain of low-interest "popular banks" whose chief beneficiaries would have been small businessmen and laborers.)

As a major stockholder in the Banque de France, Baron James Rothschild was instrumental in toppling the Pereire empire; but his victory proved to be short-lived, as he passed away the year after the Pe- reires' fortunes collapsed. The twenty-year rivalry, which grew from mistrust to hostility to outright hatred, did not end altogether with the death of the elder Pereires and Rothschilds. For years, guerrilla skir- mishes flared among the heirs. Early in the present century, François Pereire, a great-grandson of Isaac's by way of his son Gustave, formed La Compagnie Financière with Edmond de Rothschild, a second cousin of François (through Isaac's great-granddaughter Noemi Hal- phen, who had married Edmond's father the baron de Rothschild). Marriages of convenience between the two clans finally dissipated the interfamily feud that had spanned five generations.

Although they hardly died poor, the Pereire brothers lived to glimpse the apogee of nineteenth-century expansionism and the onset of twentieth-century mercantilism, with the opportunistic Rothschilds at the helm. The Pereire Hotel, La Société Pereire, Place Pereire, Boule- vard Pereire and the steamships named after family members all passed from the scene, or changed names and title. Gone forever are the gar- gantuan banquets thrown by the Pereires when they inaugurated the Gare Saint Lazare or started a new railway. The extravagant debut of the Paris–Lille line was attended by Victor Hugo, Lamartine, Alex- andre Dumas, Merimée, the Goncourts and the pick of France's titled nobility. Hector Berlioz led a 300-piece orchestra in a cantata he had composed for the occasion. Gone, too, is the opulent collection of Grecos, Goyas, Murillos, Velázquezes, Rembrandts, Fra Angelicos, Rubenses and Vermeers the Pereires painstakingly assembled only to have them slip through their fingers and show up decades later in far- flung museums. Their sprawling estate at Armainvilliers was damaged by Allied bombardment during World War II, which also destroyed part of the Pereire archives. After the war the new owner razed the old mansion and the palatial casino.

Like their prosperous forebears in Spain and Portugal, Emile and Isaac chose to consort with kings, who reciprocated their attentions only while the good times lasted. When rival financiers under Roth-schild's influence belittled the Pereires as common gamblers and specu-lators, and later when anti-Semitic ideologues took turns at bashing the Pereires for their greed and cosmopolitanism, the monarchs at first de-fended them, possibly to prevent a panic in the French money markets; but after the Crédit Mobilier foundered, the monarchs withdrew their favor, not all at once, but by degrees, so as not to appear impolitic.

Following the early death of Isaac's first wife, Laurence Fonseca, he began courting Fanny, Emile's vivacious sixteen-year-old daughter, who reciprocated his advances. To avert a scandal, the marriage con-tract between Isaac and his niece had to be approved by Napoleon III. Their union caused a lasting strain between the two brothers, which, however, had no discernible effect on their business partnership. Isaac, the more practical and down-to-earth of the two, often played the con-ciliatory mediator to Emile's uncompromising tycoon, working behind the scenes to smooth over contractual disagreements. As he grew older, Isaac also became increasingly aloof and uncommunicative, except in his writings. Forty years after his death, Isaac Pereire's daughter-in-law remembered him as a reclusive autocrat of the dinner table, engrossed around the clock in his articles and business affairs. Many of the ideas Isaac Pereire propounded in "On the Question of Religion," "Indus-trial Politics" and others of his best-known pamphlets, would be adopted by social critics in the first half of the twentieth century; to a postmodernist ear, however, Pereire's expansive rhetoric sounds bom-bastic and quaintly out of date.

Fanny outlived her husband by more than a quarter century. Autin's biography provides a 1904 photograph of Fanny with three generations of Pereires, among them her three children with Isaac. She was the last in a long line of Pereira matriarchs who endured the chang-ing fortunes of their men with a clear-eyed stoicism and devotion that shamed their fair-weather friends and outlasted their enemies.

It fell to Isaac's eldest son, Eugène, to continue the work of his great-grandfather. He republished Jacob Pereira's manual alphabet and personally worked with deaf-mutes, founding schools in Geneva and Paris. After Emile's death, his branch of the family became Christian. Most of Isaac's heirs remained Jewish, intermarrying with Dreyfuses, Halphens and Duponts as well as Rothschilds. The heirs have per-petuated the famous Pereire generosity to Jewish causes around the world.

Still, Isaac's Judaism was hardly one Jacob Pereira's forebears would have recognized or sanctioned. (Isaac's mother, anticipating my own grandmother Esther, refused to accompany her sons to Paris when she learned that they worked on the Sabbath.) In their writings both brothers embraced the "New Christianity" of Saint-Simon, which ex-alted Jesus Christ as a social reformer and benefactor of the disinherited. But the brothers also curried favor with the Catholic Church, and dur-ing his single term in the Corps Legislatif, Isaac voted to maintain the temporal power of the pope. In "On the Question of Religion," he fiercely attacked the Jesuits and Jacobins, while extolling the Vicar of Christ as a bulwark against the evils of socialism.

In his "Letter to a Jew," Isaac responded to a critic of his apos-tasy by quoting Saint-Simon's dictum: "The Laws of Moses are a co-lossal achievement, but they do not contribute to the happiness of mankind." He renounced Jehovah as a cruel God who visited the sins of the fathers on their children, and replaced Him with a God of love, wisdom and compassion.

Emile and Isaac each left five children and scores of grandchil-dren. Of the approximately 450 living descendants, the majority of whom are engaged in commercial banking, real estate and insurance, only two male heirs of Jacob Rodrigues Pereira—Arnaud and Marc-Emile Pereire—appear likely to carry his name—though not his reli-gion—into the twenty-first century.

CHAPTER VII

JERUSALEM: "I REMEMBER"

I want to remember the woman who kept a pear by her bed to sweeten her mouth.

—*Deena Metzger*

The pear is the grandfather of the apple, its poor relation, a fallen aristo-crat . . . preserving the memory of its prestige by its haughty comport-ment.

—*François Pierre de la Varenne, seventeenth-century chef*

"THE SOURCES SHOW that my father's grandfather came from Turkey to settle in the Holy Land. His father and his grandfather came from Italy, from the city of Ferrara in the north of that country. They may have gone there with many Jews who left Spain during the Span-ish Expulsion. They lived for a time in the city of Ferrara, years later in Turkey, and finally, they came to Palestine. Here the Jews found peace and quiet, albeit they were a minority, and they stopped migrating and did not leave the country."

Thus opens the memoir of my aunt Simha, younger sister of my father, Shlomo Perera. She sent me the manuscript in 1973 with the ex-pectation that I might find a publisher for it. The memoir is composed in a richly textured nineteenth-century Hebrew sprinkled with Judeo-Spanish phrases and refrains. On first perusing the manuscript, wres-tling with its cramped cursive lettering, I found it intriguing but rather rambling and repetitive. It would need a great deal of editing before it could be shown to a publisher, and I did not have the requisite Hebrew for the job. In any event, I was immersed in my work on Guatemala and as yet felt no urgency to record my family's stories.

Aunt Simha's manuscript sat among my papers for nearly two decades. In 1992, several years after Simha passed away, I got her daughter Penina's permission to translate it and incorporate it here. Yael Kopelman, a sabra journalist and a former student of mine, agreed to do the translation. On my rereading the memoir in Yael's sensitive rendering into English, the Jerusalem of the second decade of our cen-tury sprang to life. For all its desultory style, endless repetitions and archaic usages, Aunt Simha's memoir sets forth in vivid detail the day-to-day lives of my uncles and aunts, and rescues from oblivion not only my grandfather Aharon Haim and his wife, Esther, but the remote and formidable patriarch—Aharon's father, Yitzhak Moshe Perera.

Unfortunately, Aunt Simha is no longer around to answer questions and fill in the gaps. She had a casual, almost picaresque disregard for dates, names and biographical accuracy that peppers her memoir with inconsistencies. The "sources" she refers to existed, for the most part, in her imagination. The following is a partial re-creation of that era with the aid of Aunt Simha's memoir, and the faltering recollections of her older sister Reina and the youngest, Rachel, who died in 1993. In August of that year, I tracked down my uncle Moshe at his shoe store in Guatemala City, where he appended his recollections of Montefiore to those of his surviving older sisters.

From her early teens, Simha Perera regarded herself as the family chronicler and saved all her journals and the letters she wrote my father—her literary mentor—over a span of forty years. She had an additional incentive: "The final push to write came from the radio show on Saturday nights a few years ago, called 'Beit Avi' ['My Father's House']. I decided to write about the Montefiore neighborhood in Jerusalem, in which I was born and raised. To this day [circa 1972] I always visit it when I go to Jerusalem, above all to see the house we grew up in." Simha's memoir continues: "The Perera family was one of the oldest in Israel, and I am already the third generation born here. Being a sabra and a native Jerusalemite is considered a big deal these days. . . ."

Aunt Simha's pride was well founded. *Efer Yitzhak* (Ash of Isaac), one of three compilations of Kabbalistic formulas and commentaries published by my great-great-grandfather, gives the date and place of his death as 1880, in Jerusalem. This appears to confirm that it was he, Aharon Raphael Haim Perera, and not his son Yitzhak Moshe—as Aunt Simha suggests elsewhere in her memoir—who first emigrated to Jerusalem from Salonika in the mid-nineteenth century. Aharon's father, also named Yitzhak, apparently died in Salonika. (To compound confusion, Ferrara and Perera are spelled identically in Aunt Simha's manuscript, an anomaly attributable to Hebrew orthography.) My research has uncovered no noteworthy Pereras or Pereiras in Ferrara, although a number of Pereras traveled to Salonika from Livorno during the eighteenth and nineteenth centuries. Of all the émigré Jewish communities in Italy, none prospered as well or for as long as the

Iberian Marranos and the refugees from Turkey, Morocco and the Bal-
kans who settled in Leghorn (Livorno). By the eighteenth century they
numbered six thousand, and had attracted or produced hugely successful entrepreneurs as well as renowned scholars and Kabbalists like
David Azulai and Moses ben Jacob Cordovero, the Jerusalem-born
precursor of Isaac Luria. Cordovero, who died in 1570 in Safed, is
named by Aharon Raphael Haim Perera as the chief inspiration for his
Efer Yitzhak. My forebears probably left for Salonika well before 1750,
when Jewish communities in Italy entered a temporary decline, and lost
more than half their numbers to emigration.

On the side of my family related to Yehuda Burla, our roots in
the Holy Land can be traced back much farther. In 1992 Yehuda's eldest son, my cousin Oded Burla, presented me with a family tree that
traced the Burlas' residence in Jerusalem to the 1680s. (I am related to
the Burlas by both marriage and consanguinity: My maternal greatgrandmother, Reina Burla, is also my paternal great-great-aunt.)

Aunt Simha's impassioned subjectivity serves her well in her
evocations of daily life in Jerusalem and her anecdotes of growing up
with her sisters and brothers shortly before and after the outbreak of
World War I. Rabbi Yitzhak Moshe Perera, in Simha's telling, was a
God-fearing tzaddik, or holy man, beloved and respected by everyone
in the community. (Yehuda Burla described him in one of his books as
"a great scholar of Torah and practical Kabbala.") He gained a reputation for preparing potent amulets *(kameot),* for his mastery of therapeutic herbs and his success in saving many souls. Aunt Simha quotes a
thank-you letter from a family in New York, full of admiration for
Rabbi Yitzhak Perera for having cured their only son. That letter, unfortunately, has been lost.

In the Salonika of Yitzhak Moshe's father, according to historian Michael Molho, the art of preparing amulets against the evil eye
was a highly prized gift from God, possessed only by tzaddikim. The
rabbi or *escriba*—scribe—prepared parchments by hand, transcribing
passages from the *Zohar* and invoking the names of protective angels:
Uriel, Rafael, Gabriel, Michael. He might also write down the mira-
cle-working or healing formulae of Abraham Abulafia and other Kabbalist rabbis—as my great-great-grandfather did in his book *Efer
Yitzhak*—and place them on the doorjambs of his neighbors' homes or
inside the sleeves of their pregnant wives. Around the neck of a sickly
child, or of one considered pretty enough to arouse the envy of neigh-

bors, Yitzhak Moshe Perera might have hung a thread from the tallith of his father, or a small bag of garlic, salt or cinnamon stick. When his firstborn son sneezed, he would have exclaimed, *"Dios que te guadre"* ("May God watch over you") or the more poetic, *"Bivas, crescas y enflorescas como el pexe en el agua fresca."* ("May you live, grow and flourish like a fish in fresh water.")

My great-grandfather's studies in the Kabbala and his gift of healing went hand in glove. The primary, overarching purpose behind the medicinal amulets, the prayer-making and Kabbalistic formulas was to invoke God's protection to keep at bay the malefic influence of the *ayin hara* and its author, Shatan, the devil. Fear of the evil eye was so ingrained in the Jews of Salonika and their descendants in Jerusalem that without the intercession of the healers and scribes, the enchanters and tzaddikim, all family life would have been conducted behind closed doors and most daily activities would have ground to a halt.

Rabbi Yitzhak Perera lived in the Jewish quarter of the Old City, inside the walls. His home was in the Chakura Chatzer, a block of tenements in an enclosed courtyard *(cortijo)* next to the Rothschilds' Misgav Ladach hospital. The Rothschild family had bought blocks of apartments in the Old City that they then leased for three years by lottery to religious families, both Sephardic and Ashkenazic. Yitzhak Moshe was one of the privileged few who were awarded a permanent dwelling. (Could Baron Edmond de Rothschild's generosity to my great-grandfather have been connected, I ask myself, with little prospect of ever knowing for certain, to his kinship by marriage to Isaac Pereire?) Aunt Simha writes that the night watchman would unlock the iron gates for her grandfather late at night and he would make his way by lamplight to the venerable Yochanan ben Zakkai Synagogue, where he conducted the midnight services. "They said that when Grandfather prayed, he would do so in a great, thundering voice, as if he wanted his words to crash through the gates of heaven."

Aunt Simha's older sister Reina, who was born in the Old City, still remembers her grandfather's apartment in the Chakura Chatzer. Reina, my father and his older and younger brothers Alberto (alias Avram) and Isidoro (alias Nissim), regularly visited Yitzhak and his wife, Simha, when they were schoolchildren, and she would not let them go until each had eaten a full plate of rice, white beans and meat. In the beans she sprinkled some cumin seed, in addition to the fried onions, which gave the stew a spicy tang that warms Reina's recollections to this day. Grandmother Simha became ill and died when Reina was a small girl, leaving behind a family of six boys and girls, among them her firstborn son, Aharon Haim Perera, my grandfather. In his seven-ties Yitzhak remarried so there would be someone to look after him in his old age. His second wife is referred to simply as "Grandmother," and I never learned her name.

Yitzhak Moshe was a tall, handsome man in Reina's recollec-tion—even in old age—with a long white beard and a round face. When he came to visit his children and grandchildren outside the city walls, dressed all in white, "He looked like an angel." Reina awaited his arrival from afar, near the foot of the windmill below which, in 1860, Sir Moses Montefiore had established residences for indigent reli-gious Jews on land bequeathed by the New Orleans philanthropist Judah Touro. (The quarter known as Yemin Moshe remained part of Israel was renovated following their victory in the 1967 war.)

Reina would run to welcome her grandfather as he trudged up the winding road from Mount Zion, kiss his hand and receive his bless-ing, spoken in Ladino: *"Novia ki ti viamos con todos los kiridos."* ("May we soon see you a bride, together with all our dear ones.") As his grandfa-ther had in Salonika, Yitzhak spoke in Ladino to the women of the family and in Hebrew to his sons.

Aunt Simha's and Reina's memories of their father are much fuller. At eighty-seven, Reina's eyes still sparkle at the mention of Rabbi Aharon Haim Perera (my grandfather), the wise and lov-ing father who left them for Egypt when she was a young married woman and never returned. Simha writes: "My dear father I remember quite well. He was a wise student of Torah. He used to always wear *antiri,* a long, dark overcoat that he put on over his suit, and on his head he wore a special hat for wise Torah students, called the *toka* in Ladino.

"In contrast to my mother, Esther, who was short, my father was a tall man with an air of importance and dignity, very manly and full of life, as his name [Haim] implies. We the children were unbelievably in awe of Father. If Mother said, 'Be careful, I'll tell your father you're misbehaving,' we would all hide in the corners and quake with fear. When Father's footsteps sounded as he entered the house, an absolute silence would descend, as if there were no one else present. Mother would whisper our misdeeds in his ear, and Father would raise his voice: 'Where is the rascal who treated you badly? Avramiko?

Shlomiko? Who was it? Tell me.' Mother was afraid to tell him, because he would lift his hand to strike us, and we were all scared to
death. I don't remember an occasion when Father actually struck any of
the children, because it was enough for him to lift his hand as if he were
about to hit us, and we became frozen with fright. Father would then
tell Mother: 'That's the way it's going to be here. I will teach them fear
[*timor* in Ladino], and they'd better not engage in any mischief again,
because I will exact vengeance, and if I let my anger out on them, they
had better look out for themselves.' That threat usually lasted a long
time. The memory of those words and their effect on us were not soon
forgotten, and so for a long spell Mother had some peace and quiet in
the house."

A quarter of a century later in Guatemala City, when I was
nine, a similar scene was enacted on the day I called Mother *putana*.
Mother had flung that terrible word at a Virgin Mary in a gold crown
and blue-velvet gown she caught me spying on during the Holy Week
processions. My parents had expressly forbidden my sister Rebecca and
me to watch the Catholic saints that trooped past our window, floating
on clouds of incense to the discordant blaring of tubas and trumpets—
but the temptation had proved irresistible. Unlike my uncles and aunts,
I was to pay for my transgression with my hide.

It was my little sister who snitched on me and told Father I had
called Mother "a bad word." I was Mother's favorite, and she had been
reluctant to report my offense, knowing full well what the consequences
would be. On hearing I had called Mother a bad name, Father stiffened
and frowned menacingly, just as *his* father had frowned at him and his
siblings. The color rose and filled his cheeks until they looked as if they
would burst, and he shouted, "What did he call you!" repeating it
again and again until Mother mouthed *"putana"* with a faint smile on
her lips, a smile of complicity I knew intimately. But this time she was
an accomplice *against* me.

Father did not bother with threats or reprimands. He picked me
up by the scruff of the neck and dragged me to the hallway, removing
his belt. He had struck me a couple of times before for lesser offenses,
but they were as nothing compared with the lifelong rage he would vent
that afternoon on my frail shoulders, my back and my buttocks. I still
bear the scars from that strapping, the memory of which leaps across the
generations to connect me to a grandfather I never knew. Father was a
busy man, often distracted by the cares of running a business; that beat-

ing was one of our few interactions in which he took part in person, without resorting to surrogates. Nothing prepared me for the punish, ment: the cosmic detonation of the first lash, the burning in my skin that lasted for days, the longer-lasting burning humiliation. And yet I never questioned its appropriateness. If Father had not punished me after I called Mother a whore—even though she had provoked it—I would have thought that much less of him as a father, and that much less of him as a man. Over the years, that beating became one of the enduring bonds between us.

Although Grandfather's demeanor toward his children cor, roborated my assumptions about his patriarchal rigor and strictness, Aunt Simha's memoir reveals other sides of his character that came as a welcome surprise. Unlike my father, who tended toward solemnity, Aharon Haim Perera had a piquant sense of humor. He was a generous and resourceful provider and an incurable optimist. My grandfather's Achilles' heel was a wanderlust that would ultimately be his undoing. ("From my mother's stories I know that Father loved to travel," Simha writes with no hint of regret or accusation.) In common with other Torah students, my grandfather had traveled as a *sheliach* (religious envoy) to other cities of the Middle and Near East to raise money for the Sephardic yeshivas. Around 1908, shortly before Aunt Simha was born, my grandfather took a train to Bukhara, an Asian province of the former Soviet Union, which had a thriving Sephardic community.

"They needed a rabbi there and a teacher of Torah," Aunt Simha writes, "to teach Scripture to the children of the wealthy, be, cause the Bukharis were an ultrareligious and mitzvah-observing com, munity. Father traveled there intending to return several months after he completed his mission, which was to collect funds for Jerusalem's Sephardic communities [*kolelot*]. But the Bukharis were so pleased with him and with his tutoring of their children in the Torah that they per, suaded him to stay longer; they doubled his salary and showered him with gifts. Father decided to stay on, and we soon learned from Jews returning from Bukhara that they wanted him to live there permanently; they were even trying to persuade him to marry a Bukhari woman be, cause, after all, 'a man must not live alone.' "

The parallels between Aunt Simha's account and my mother's rueful memories of her father's sojourn in Samarkand are remarkable. Rabbi Shmuel Nissim had also traveled to Russia before World War I to teach Torah and raise funds for the yeshivas. As mentioned earlier, he had remarried there at the behest of his Samarkand congregation and raised a second family. But there was a key difference: Rabbi Shmuel Nissim had been stranded in Russia by the outbreak of the war, which prevented his return. He had pledged to return to Jerusalem as soon as the war ended—a pledge he kept, although he died on the way.

Aharon Haim was recalled from Bukhara by a different circum-stance altogether, as recorded in Aunt Simha's memoir: "Mother wept bitterly when she received this saddening message. Father left behind a large family—six children and a wife—who awaited his return daily, and so the message [from Bukhara] came as a thunderbolt in the middle of a sunny day. Immediately my grandfather Yitzhak Moshe Perera sent an angry letter to Bukhara. This letter had a quick effect: Father started packing. The pleas and supplications of his Bukhari hosts were in vain, and he was on his way."

Yitzhak Moshe died shortly after Aharon Haim's return, but not before he had written and notarized the testament forbidding his sons to travel outside of the Holy Land ever again, except under the re-strictions he spelled out in the document.

During Simha's childhood years Aharon Haim bowed to his father's wishes by staying put in Jerusalem; and he managed to provide for his family during the lean war years and the waning of Ottoman rule in the Holy Land. The family lived through the war in their small apartment below Montefiore's windmill. Simha depicts in loving detail the hillside neighborhood where she grew up, in plain view of Mount Zion and the ramparts of David's Tower: "The houses were prettier and more modern than those originally built by Moses Montefiore—the ones my mother's mother lived in. . . .

"Our apartment consisted of two small rooms on the ground floor of a two-story house. We had only one wide, iron-framed bed. We would arrange all the mattresses, pillows and slipcovers during the day, and cover everything with a pretty bedspread. At night, the mat-tresses were spread out across the entire bedroom. For a large family, it was quite a feat to sleep in a single bedroom, which was always filled with light and fresh air. Father had sold some of Mother's wedding jewelry to pay for this apartment, which he made himself from a wing of a two-bedroom house. It had a small kitchen and a large, beautiful courtyard. On the balcony there were pots with beautiful scented flowers that Mother tended to with a love and devotion that surprised us. She would say, 'Here lies my soul. I've always loved flowers, and in tending to them I find satisfaction and an easeful joy.'

"The view from the balcony was magnificent. It overlooked the distant train station, which was surrounded by greenery, many olive groves and fields. The owners of the fields were wheat farmers. It was a fabulous sight—a sea of wheat, tall as a person, covering the fields. In addition there were the olive groves, which always produced olives in season. The boys would collect the fruit that fell from the trees, fill their pockets and bring them to Mother. She would crush the olives, and soak them for a few days in salt water until they were edible."

"I was very little at the outbreak of the war, which lasted four years," Aunt Simha continues. "Those were years of hunger and depri- vation. No sugar was available, and Mother would boil us water in the morning with 'susy'—a vegetable which sweetened our tea a bit (the Arabs used to make lemonade out of it and sell it with ice on warm days). Many other items were unavailable: rice, oil, gasoline, biscuits and other goods. . . . I remember that in order to feed us Father would buy, with a few pennies that he saved, boxes of dried dates, from which we made jam and sold it secretly to the rich folk of Jerusalem."

Relative to other families, the Pereras were not so badly off dur- ing the war, according to Aunt Simha: "We were a family of eight— six children and two parents—but we had enough to eat, unlike others who went hungry. I once heard Mother praying quietly, 'Dear God, take care of these children, who are not at fault.' Mother would bake the family bread in the only bakery in the neighborhood. She would knead the dough early in the morning. She used a portion of the dough to bake nice round loaves of bread, and kept the remainder to make pita. She always saved one loaf of bread for the following week, and when it went sour, she used it as yeast—called *libadura* in Ladino."

The entire family joined in to prepare the bread. My grandfather would buy half a sack of wheat grains, which they would all sort and clean. Grandfather and Reina would place the grains in smaller sacks—Reina in the smaller one and Grandfather in the larger—and they would carry them to the flour mill, which was located in Me'ah Shearim (the Hasidic quarter). "When the flour came back," Aunt Simha writes, "it was Mother's and my older sister Margarita's task to knead the dough from a portion of the flour, which would last us the entire week. The last step was carrying the dough to Yosef Peretz's neighborhood oven, which baked the delicious white bread. . . .

"By word of mouth, the news got around that we had bread for sale, and one dark night a Turkish soldier knocked on our door and asked for *akmek*. Father let him in, but we were all scared. He started to take off his clothes, and finally took some money out of a pouch that hung by a string around his neck, over his worn-out undershirt. Until he took out one *beshlik* (the local currency then), we were very scared, especially since he was armed. During a conversation with Father, speaking in half-words, the soldier said he was buying the pita bread as provision for his journey. He was deserting, as were many other soldiers in the Turkish Army. 'The enemy is near,' he said, 'and we have been defeated.' And indeed, a little while later, we started hearing loud explosions and cannon fire close to the city. On Chanukah, the British soldiers marched singing into Jerusalem."

II

Simha's Jerusalem resonates with loud cries and laughter. She recalls all the hawkers' early-morning cries, among them *"Pan y pitika y franzilika"* ("Bread and pita and challah") from Eliyahu Zamiro the baker. Aunt Simha's more indelible memories are of the family's inventiveness in finding novel ways to survive during the war. In addition to teaching the Torah and conducting services in Montefiore, my grandfather was a *shohet*, or licensed ritual slaughterer. "During the war, Father had several sources of livelihood. He knew how to raise money *'min tachad el arad,'* as they say in Arabic—that is to say, from beneath the ground. He worked for several hours as a tutor in the 'Pereg' school, and he slaughtered cattle. Every morning he would rise early, take a quarter loaf of bread with salty cheese and eat it on his way. He was normally a healthy man. The slaughterhouse was on the Mount of Olives, and Father would pass by the windows of his father's courtyard apartment in the Old City. He would knock lightly at the window and inform him he was on his way to the slaughterhouse. On his return he would knock again on his father's window and announce that all was well. This was his custom day in and day out. The slaughterhouse paid Father for his work, and in addition he was given the internal organs of the animals he butchered, such as the liver, the lungs and so on. After several hours of work he would come home very tired, and Mother would make him a brimming plate of ricotta cheese—a very fat and savory cheese, not ground into powders as they are today—with crushed tomatoes. For him that was a gourmet dinner as well as a very inexpensive meal.

"Father would also attend for a few hours the Sephardic rab-binical court, where one could find Rabbi Ben Tzion Koinka and other *Chachamim,* or 'wise men.' Back then, everyone used to walk. There were special carriages harnessed to two horses which were called diligences, but those were only for rich people. In the rabbinical court Father would register couples applying to marry, write up their mar-riage contracts, and also arrange (God forbid) divorces. He also had some income from matchmaking and real-estate deals. For years Father was a *chazan,* or 'cantor,' in the Montefiore synagogue."

My grandfather Aharon Haim also prepared the family matzoth for Passover. Peretz's bakery was thoroughly swept and scrubbed to rid it of all traces of *chametz* (leaven). "Father with his own hands would bring the special flour set aside for the unleavened bread, and he would prepare the dough for the thin, round matzoth. He would bring the crisp flat-bread home wrapped in a clean white cloth, and every-one would pounce on it with a voracious appetite, because it was very tasty. . . .

"Father was also a *Stam* scribe—a writer of Torah and other scrolls. I remember when he used to sit in the large room, on a small stool—*benektika* in Ladino—leaning his back against the sofa, the white paper parchment on his knees, holding the tip of the pen, which he made himself from a reed stem sharpened like a pencil and dipped in black ink. When he wrote, the house was always silent. Woe to the child who made noise and disturbed his labors, because—God for-bid—he might make a mistake. All you could hear in the house was the sound of the reed pen scratching on the parchment. He would write in a graceful, special hand, composing each letter separately so it did not run into the others. Before he started writing, Father would recite: 'I am writing this for the holiness of the Torah Book.' "

Aunt Simha's memories of daily life in Montefiore brim with telling details: "Rachel my sister was born during the difficult years of the war. At that time the water was bought with rationing cards. We had several wells or cisterns in our neighborhood, which collected rain-

water. Every day the synagogue custodian Yosef Peretz would announce, 'Today we will open the well on this street.' Each street had a
deep, large cistern which was kept under lock, and the neighborhood
committee had the keys. During the summer they would scrub clean
the cisterns in order to collect fresh rainwater for the winter. In addition
to the cisterns, every house had a large clay pot—*minaza* in Ladino—to
collect rainwater for drinking and washing. There was also a spring
below, at the foot of Mount Zion. The Turkish government closed the
spring and doled out the water with rationing cards that could be purchased with a few *kuartikos*. Turkish currency consisted of paper lira,
copper coins called *mezidi,* and the smaller ones: *beshliks, kuartikos* and
kabaks. With one kabak that we might receive as a gift once in fifty
years, we could buy sweets called *bambalik* in the shop of Yehuda
Koinka, who was the son of Rabbi Ben Tzion Koinka."

When Simha was growing up, Sephardim were in the majority
in the Montefiore neighborhood. She lists the Sephardic families who
lived nearby, among them the Berachas, the Aroshes, the Zamiros and
many others. The Ashkenazic families lived separately, in the upper
quarters of Montefiore. Aunt Simha's mother, Esther, sent her there to
buy dates from an Eastern European housewife, who pressed them into
the paste they used in place of yeast for baking bread. Simha had a
number of schoolmates in the Ashkenazic neighborhood, and her father visited there often to offer his services.

The old Sephardic families and the arriving Ashkenazic Zionists coexisted peacefully in the Jerusalem of my aunts, although by and
large the two communities kept to themselves. Frictions emerged with
the influx of thousands of Eastern Europeans in flight from Hitler; these
frictions were compounded by the post-Independence mass migrations
of Oriental and Sephardic Jews from the Near East and North Africa.
And yet after Israel became a state, many of my cousins on both sides of
the family married Ashkenazim.

Aunt Simha vividly remembered the games favored by her
brothers and sisters, which mirror the games played by Sephardic children in Salonika, and before that in the *aljamas* of Spain and Portugal.
These games involved the recitation of magic refrains and doggerel in
Ladino while participants clapped hands, leap-frogged over one another or played a variant of jacks, odds or evens and hide-and-seek.
Like children everywhere, Simha and her siblings lusted after the sweets

in the sweetshops, although their fantasies of gorging on candy to their hearts' content became reality only once in a blue moon, during a rela-tive's *brit* or bar mitzvah, or a well-to-do neighbor's wedding.

Toys were even harder to come by. "Toys for children were un-heard of. Who had even a single toy? Some really lucky girls had one rag doll which their mother made for them, but I didn't. Mother didn't even have time to think about that. She had several live dolls she had to take care of, wash and feed—and that was plenty of work in itself, from sunrise until sunset."

Simha outgrew her early traumas and disappointments, and blossomed into the fairest of the four sisters, with green eyes and light brown hair—nearly blond—that her mother combed in two long braids as she sang a Ladino ballad about tresses that shine like gold *(brillas como oro)*.

"I remember one extraordinary event which made our family happy and rich, and that was the day my sister Reina found a wallet full of money when she went to the spring to buy water. When she brought the wallet home, Mother was lying in bed, because the week before she had given birth to Rachel. Grandmother was cooking a meal in the kitchen, and Grandfather was sitting on the couch reading the after-Sabbath prayers.

"Mother told Reina to pass the wallet to Grandfather so he could see what it contained. His eyes lit up when he opened it. There were thirty paper liras, nine mezidis and a few kuartikos and kabaks, as well as a soldier's birth certificate. Mother, with tears of happiness in her eyes, said God had sent us this fortune through Rachel. 'Rashel has brought good luck, for now we will have money to buy some milk and meat and soup for me, so that I will have enough milk to breast-feed this pretty baby.'

Aunt Simha's references to her mother, Esther, are oddly de-tached, as though she inhabited a place in the middle distance, analo-gous to the women's gallery in the rear of the synagogue. There is little doubt, however, that she was every bit as much the family's mainstay as her husband. Esther was the daughter of Rabbi David Rahamim Pi-zanty, a God-fearing wise man as well known for his *mitzvoth* (good deeds) as was Yitzhak Moshe Perera. David's father, the venerable Chacham Avraham Pizanty, had immigrated to Jerusalem from Salonika years ahead of the Pereras. Aunt Simha describes her mother as short of stature but "beautiful like all her sisters, with clear skin and green glowing eyes." (The blond hair and light eyes she took such pride in came from her mother.)

Aunt Simha's brightest memories of her mother are associated with her singing: "In the summer, Mother would install in our yard a swing made of ropes. She would lay me down on this swing and rock me, singing pretty lullabies until I fell asleep. I remember that with Rachel, when she was a baby, she would tie a rope to the swing and the other end to her toe so she could rock her and keep busy at the same time, sewing or sorting peas.

"I learned Mother's songs, and I sing them to this day. I learned them when she sang to Rachel to lull her to sleep. Mother told me that when she was young she loved to sing. When she got married and the children started coming every year and a half or so, she was over her head with chores and had no time for singing. But on occasion, when she was in a good mood and the house was peaceful, she would call some of her neighbors over to have some fun. And so my adopted aunts Buchara, Striya and Sultana would sit in our home to drink coffee, and they would sing together the Spanish *romanzas*. Each of them would teach a *romanza* she knew to the others, and Mother would accompany them and beat the earthen *darbuka* drum."

The singing of Ladino *romanzas* and medieval Spanish ballads was a tradition brought to Jerusalem from Turkey, Bosnia, Italy and other outposts of Sephardic culture. According to cultural historian Michael Molho, women's singing of *romanzas* was one of the few diversions enjoyed by my grandmother's forebears in Salonika. Sephardic housewives left their enclosed courtyards only to buy food and to attend *brits*, weddings and funerals; the rest of the time they stayed indoors or in the *cortijos*—as the enclosed courtyard tenements were known—washing clothes, baking bread, preparing meals and caring for their children. At all times, they wore a modest headdress and plain clothes to ward off the evil eye and the unwelcome attentions of strangers. All these customs were still observed in the Jerusalem of my grandmother's generation.

As in Salonika, coal was used to heat the house during the cold winters, as well as for cooking and ironing clothes with a coal iron. The day of coal delivery was particularly trying for Esther. The coal was brought in a bulky sack and had to be emptied into a large bin under the kitchen shelf. The entire kitchen would get covered with coal soot and dust, and afterward Esther had to clean all the cabinets and every corner of the house with a rag and soap.

Aunt Simha writes with special pride of Esther's father, David Pizanty, a *chacham* who founded the Haemtzahi, or "middle," syna^ gogue in the Old City, flanked by the Istanbuli and Yochanan ben Zakkai temples. She recalls the Passover seders her grandfather cele^ brated in his home, reading aloud each portion of the Passover Hag^ gadah with consummate care and illustrating it with Torah stories for the smaller children. He would then repeat the chief portions of the Haggadah in Ladino for the women. The seder would conclude with a rendition of Solomon's Song of Songs in a lilting melody Aunt Simha remembered to the end of her life. Rabbi Pizanty caught pneumonia and died after stubbornly trudging through the snow during the cold^ est winter in Simha's memory to conduct Sabbath services in the Old City.

In Simha's recollection, as in her older sister Reina's, their mother was nearly always pregnant. Although Simha and her sisters are effusive in praising their father, they are markedly reticent—almost grudging—in their appreciation of their mother, whose life in many ways was a good deal harder. Only toward the end of her memoir does Simha write of her mother's travails in delivering a new baby every year and a half: "Mother was weak and pale, and she worked very hard, with no help at all. Grandmother would help her only in the periods after she gave birth. There were no convalescent homes then, nor was there money to send her to relatives to recover from her difficult labors. Mother herself found a way to deal with her debility. When we came home from school and she wasn't there, we knew she was lying in the hospital with the new baby. She used to go to the doctor to complain that she had many children at home and lacked the strength to look after them; she would weep and complain that she could not go on like this, and the doctor would make an exception and allow her to remain in the hospital for several days. Grandmother would then come home to cook and look after us until Mother returned, refreshed from her rest and the care she received."

This is followed by Aunt Simha's tribute to her mother's skills as a pastry cook and her impeccable cleanliness, and then this: "On the eve of the Sabbath Mother used to visit the Western Wall to converse with God, pray and get some of the weight off her chest. On the Sab^ bath she would light a lamp and say blessings over it, whispering the prayers." A detailed description ensues of her mother's preparation of the oil and cotton wicks for the Sabbath lamps, which she lit and kept burning for the duration of the Sabbath week in and week out, even after they had electricity in the house. As in most Sephardic homes, the Sabbath was a joyous occasion: "On the Sabbath eve the table was covered with a white tablecloth, on which were placed two golden loaves of bread, some salt, a bread knife, pepper and wine for the blessing. Father would return from the synagogue with the boys, and they would remain on their feet to welcome the Sabbath with Hebrew and Ladino songs. Afterward Father would recite the blessing over the wine, and we would all kiss our parents' hands and receive their blessing. On the Sabbath day everyone was merry. Mother had made her traditional *hamin* (Sabbath stew)—called *cholent* by the Ashkenazim—with *kuklas* (physic nuts), eggs and a shank of beef, all cooked with dried white beans. The pleasant cooking smells would waft all over the house, and Father would eat and bless Mother, who had laughter on her lips and was filled with joy by Father's compliments. After the meal, we would all sing the lovely and unusual Sabbath melodies in Spanish."

Simha's closest friends for many years were the two daughters of her Aunt Flor, who gave birth to them after she had lost several children. In keeping with an ancient Hebrew custom, Aunt Flor had changed her daughters' names and "bought" them back from the rabbi to whom they were entrusted as a ruse to ward off the evil eye. They were both very spoiled, not only by the parents but by the entire family, including of course, Grandfather and Grandmother. They were guarded like valuable assets, and if one became sick, the family would immediately separate them and bring the healthy one to our house so she would not get infected. They were always dressed in the best of clothes, and got whatever their hearts desired."

Simha describes weddings and *brits* that might have leaped from the pages of Molho's chronicle of Sephardic customs in nineteenth-century Salonika: "The weddings of the old days didn't have the luxuries of today. In those days a proper wedding was one in which *simcha* [happiness] predominated, and not the fancifulness of the table settings and the ravenous devouring of victuals that mark a successful wedding today." The wedding was held in a large room cleared of all furniture, on which a small stage was erected and decorated with flowers for the bride and bridegroom. "The bride would leave her home and wend her way to the groom's house accompanied by musicians, including a violinist and a drummer. A song was customarily sung by the wedding party, whose words I recall: 'To the last drop of blood/ a young man stands guard with a sword and a plough/ with the plough he ploughed the earth/ our wishes have been fulfilled/ we came to the land of our ancestors to work our land/ here we shall live and here we shall die/ for our people and our freedom.' At the entrance to the groom's house sorbets and rose water would be served to the bride and her party by a neighbor. Inside the wedding chamber, creamy cakes would be served following the seven blessings. That was the only food served at weddings, whether the family was wealthy or poor. Of course, the rich families afterward threw a huge ball and a feast for the in-laws.

"Speaking about weddings, I'll mention the births. In those days, nearly all births took place at home. When the expectant mother was about to give birth the men would leave the house for a few hours, attend the synagogue for morning prayers or go to their place of business. Small children were sent to their neighbors' or relatives' homes. If the pregnant woman had a difficult labor, the women would tie a cord to the foot of her bed which led all the way to the synagogue, even if it was several blocks away. As a further precaution (to be doubly safe), they would place a prayer book under the pillow of the woman in labor to keep her from all evil."

III

The Palestinian Arab hovers on the edges of Aunt Simha's memoir. Apart from Turkish soldiers and Arab street vendors and fortune-tellers, the Palestinians were a shadowy and for the most part benign presence. When the family traveled north to Safed to attend the wedding of Esther's sister Mazal, an Arab guide led the wedding party on donkey back with crates full of Aunt Mazal's dowry, and found them shelter at nightfall in Arab villages along the way. "The Arabs were very hospitable," writes Aunt Simha, "and in those days there was friendship and fraternity between the Jews and Arabs who lived in Eretz Israel." Today when I ask Aunts Rachel and Reina as well as Uncle Moshe of their youthful contacts with Arabs, their responses are nearly identical: "Oh yes, we bought vegetables and fruits from the Arabs in the Old City, and we never felt any fear of them. Sometimes they gave us a sweet or a piece of fruit for free."

But there is condescension in Aunt Simha's repeated contrasting of their own standard of living with that of the Arabs: "We were all very clean, and so infectious diseases were unheard of among the Jews, as opposed to the Arabs." Simha's fascination with Arabs was laced with ambivalence, as was my aged mother's when she accused the Arab orderly who tucked her into bed at night of raping her room, mate's daughter. Sometimes an Arab provoked Simha's pity, like the boy who for one *bishlik* would jump stark naked into the Birket Ha, Sultan pool below Montefiore from a height of several meters, and re, main underwater for a heart-stopping sixty seconds before he emerged at the far end of the pool, gasping for breath.

Muslim and Christian Arabs were purveyors of all the good things to the neighborhood children: There was the ice-cream vendor, who hawked his merchandise in a mishmash of Hebrew and Arabic. Another carried a large chest on his back, decorated with bells, beads and photographs. "Cinema, *yala*, cinema!" he trumpeted to draw a crowd, and placed a stool in front of a glass aperture through which the viewer was treated to a kaleidoscope of fast-moving cartoon figures and cancan dancers as its owner assiduously cranked the handle.

The most eagerly awaited was the Arab who appeared with a monkey on his shoulder. "The neighborhood children were attracted to him as if by magic. He would stand in the middle of the street, and when a large audience had gathered, the show would begin: '*Inzey!*' he ordered the monkey in Arabic. The monkey would jump up on his shoulder. '*Urkod ya sa'adan,*' he would order him, and the monkey would skip and dance to the Arab's drumbeat. At the end of the per, formance people would toss a few kabaks or kuartikos into an old hat or a plate."

The boon-giver or magician and the pitiable figure were offset by the shadow Arab who spread infections, who might rob you or stab you when your back was turned. Although my aunts grew up free of the corrosive hatreds that divide Jews and Arabs in Israel today, a sense of "otherness" pervades Aunt Simha's memoir.

This is hardly surprising. The Perera women rarely traveled out, side their Montefiore neighborhood and the Old City, and they seldom saw the terraced vineyards or the thriving Arab towns and markets of the West Bank. To Aunt Simha, Hebron and Nablus were remote sat, ellites of Jerusalem, as removed from her day-to-day concerns as were Damascus or Alexandria.

My family no longer lived in Montefiore at the outbreak of the

1929 and 1936 Arab riots in Hebron and the West Bank that cost the lives of more than seventy Jewish residents. A premonition of the impending frictions between the two communities may partly account for my aunts' ambivalence toward the Arabs in their midst. But the sense of otherness that pervades Aunt Simha's memoir draws on far older prejudices and antagonisms rooted in the Old Testament.

Soon after the start of World War I, hardship descended on Aunt Simha's two eldest brothers—Uncle Alberto (Avram) and my father, Shlomo. The year my grandfather returned from Bukhara the Turks started looking for young men—boys, even—to conscript for their war against Britain and France. (To their misfortune, the Ottoman Turks sided with Germany. Their defeat led to the dissolution of the empire and the emergence of modern Turkey under Kemal Ataturk.)

Around 1912, Aharon Haim sent his firstborn son, Avram, to Bukhara to learn the diamond trade. When he returned, the sultan's gendarmes had begun picking up teenage boys and young men. "My parents were very worried," writes Simha, "and did not know what to do. Father repeatedly paid the officers ransoms, but when the soldiers began their house-to-house searches, Father decided to take drastic action. One morning he woke up very early, gave Avram a few clothes, some money and a warm blessing and sent him to the train station so he could make good his escape. 'But where to?' asked Avram, who was barely seventeen. 'To wherever your feet shall carry you,' Father answered. 'Just so long as they don't enlist you in the Turkish Army, because you will be miserable.' "

Avram climbed aboard a freight train, as did many other young men in flight from the Turkish conscripters. They had neither a passport nor a ticket, and simply went wherever the train took them, like hoboes. Avram traveled from city to city, from station to station, suffering hunger and thirst, until he arrived in Europe with a forged passport he had acquired en route. He made his way to Marseille, where he took up menial jobs for a few months, then caught a freighter to America. He was the first of our immediate family to reach the twentieth century's Promised Land. Through some Sephardic contacts he wangled his way into the diamond trade in Mexico and did not return to Jerusalem—and then only briefly—until the end of the war.

Aunt Rachel still recalls the extraordinary impression made by the dapper, bowler-hatted eldest brother whom she hardly knew, and who now called himself Alberto. He came laden with gifts and new-fangled contraptions, including the gramophone on which Uncle Albert played Caruso's arias to his dumbfounded younger siblings. The biggest shocker in my aunt's memoir is her story of what became of my father, who was barely fifteen at the start of the war. Her memoir states, matter-of-factly, "Shlomo was sent to Syria, dressed as a woman."

Had I read this far in the memoir years before, I would have kept after Aunt Simha for a fuller account of my father's escapade, which he had never mentioned to me while he was alive. I have learned since that many other young men resorted to Achilles' subterfuge to avoid military service with the Turks. In *Don Quixote,* Cervantes mentions a similar ruse to avoid induction into the sultan's army. Other members of my family, among them my great-uncle Ben Tzion Pizanty, went into hiding instead. His mother and sisters brought meals to him in the attic, where he stayed for the duration of the war, reading and praying all day like a precocious tzaddik.

"The war went on. The hunger worsened, the family grew; we needed warm clothes for winter, and Mother would mend the clothes and pass them down from one child to the next in order of birth. Once I saw Mother grieving for Avram and Shlomo, of whom we knew nothing. They left us without a letter or news of any sort. One day a stranger happened by and saw Mother in the yard with tears in her eyes. He held a string of beads in his hand and was dressed like an Arab sheikh. He said in Arabic, 'I am a fortune-teller.' He asked Mother why she was so sad and tearful. 'I can see the future,' he told her. 'Let me see your palm.' Neighbors who heard him gathered around and encouraged Mother to show him her palm. He examined her hand and told her, 'You have loved ones in distant lands, and that is why you are distressed. You should know that you will soon receive good news from them.'

"Several days passed, and indeed we did receive news from Avram, who was in America. The war was over by then, and soon after we received a telegram from Shlomo in Syria which stated: 'If you don't send me some money, dear parents, I will die here of hunger. I am lying in bed weak and exhausted, and eating three carob pods a day. That is what I live from, and I can no longer rise from my bed.' "

Reina recalls that the telegram arrived on the Sabbath. Aharon Haim was a religious man, but if he waited until Sunday to send the money, he would be risking his son's life. Therefore my grandfather invoked the rabbinic principle *"Pikuach nefesh docheh et ha-Shabbat,"* which means, freely translated, that Sabbath restrictions can be lifted when there is a threat to life and limb. Reina accompanied her father to the post office holding in her hands the Sabbath-desecrating money, which the clerk duly telegraphed to my father in Syria.

As soon as he received the money, my father set out on his journey home. He sent friends ahead to prepare the family for his arrival, fearing they might get a shock if he appeared without warning. Shortly before midnight the following Friday, my father arrived home.

"The reunion was very joyous," writes Aunt Simha, "but my parents were saddened by his poor health. They sat him down immediately and fed him dried chickpeas. Obviously a meal like that after several days of fasting upset Shlomo's stomach terribly."

Although Father had never mentioned any part of this story to his children, my mother had known all along. When we took a stroll in the park outside her Ramat Gan apartment one afternoon, she pointed to the stringy brown bean pods hanging from a carob tree: "See!" she exclaimed. "Those are what your father lived on when he was in Syria!" Stunned by the idea of Father surviving for a year on carob seeds, I still was not sufficiently intrigued to pursue the matter, and pushed it to the back of my mind. Like many other Sephardim of my generation, I had only a passing interest in these old family stories, which I found faintly embarrassing and démodé.

My father returned to his studies, and Aharon Haim gave him his post at the Talmud Torah Sepharadi so he could have some income. But his hard-scrabble year in Syria had evidently left its mark. When his younger brother Nissim (Isidoro) followed Alberto to the New World, Father was teaching at a Talmud Torah and studying law in the evenings with two of his friends. In 1922 Aharon Haim traveled to Alexandria as a religious emissary and remained there several months before he fell ill and died of an infected boil. It was Father who was called upon to travel to Egypt to recite the Kaddish over his father, eerily duplicating the ordeal of my mother's older brother Jacob, who had entrained to the Ukraine a few years earlier to say Kaddish over *his* father, buried in a common grave with hundreds of other victims of the plague.

When his brothers summoned him to Guatemala to be the bookkeeper of their newly opened department store, Father dropped his Torah instruction and his law studies and departed for America to

Salomon Perera with Talmud Torah students, Jerusalem, ca. 1920

make his fortune. He was one more immigrant among the hundreds of thousands of immigrants who landed on the shores of America after World War I in flight from the specter of hunger. Father went directly to Guatemala City, and did not return to the Holy Land until four months before his death.

IV

Aunt Simha's memoir goes on to describe the birth of Moshe, the youngest brother, who today lives on in Guatemala as the last surviving male Perera of his generation. As the last of Aharon Haim and Esther's children, and the one who benefited the least from his father's presence, Uncle Moshe merits only a single paragraph: "I remember when my brother Moshe studied the Sabbath prayers from our cousin Yehoshua, son of Aunt Malka. Every time he made a mistake he would get spanked, and the poor kid made mistakes quite often."

My uncle Moshe followed his older brothers to Guatemala in

1954, when he was thirty-four. He worked with Uncle Isidoro in the store for a time. After 1970, he struck out on his own and opened a shoe store.

At the start of the British mandate, economic conditions improved in Jerusalem, and the family moved out of Montefiore to a larger home in Shehunat Ruchama. Simha was only fourteen, but her memoir ends with her childhood years in Montefiore, where she had been happiest.

For me, the portraits that emerge of my great-grandfather and grandfather are a priceless boon, laden with insights: Given my grandfather's irrepressible yen for travel and the precedent of his near-defection to Bukhara as a young *shaliach,* the memoir provides a practical as well as a scriptural explanation for the sternness of Yitzhak Moshe's testament. The threat of excommunication had evidently been inserted for emphasis rather than from any cruel or sadistic intent. But even that extreme measure failed to achieve its purpose. Yitzhak Moshe's prohibition may have dampened my grandfather's wanderlust, but it failed to exorcise it. The genes for my own incurable wanderlust evidently swim in the DNA of both my paternal and maternal inheritance.

THE FAMILY'S irreparable sense of abandonment and loss had a devastating effect on the marriages of Simha and her sisters. Except for Reina, who married her dashing Albert before Aharon Haim left for Alexandria, the other Perera sisters—Margarita, Simha and Rachel—married poor, invalid or dependent husbands who died at an early age. The absent father died abroad without providing dowries *(ashugar)* for his daughters so they could fetch themselves proper husbands. His untimely death not only devalued his daughters in the marriage market but evidently damaged their self-esteem and addled their judgment. If they and their mother together could not hold on to a God-fearing, kind and providential husband and father like Aharon Haim, what hopes had they of finding and keeping halfway decent mates?

Simha's husband, Rahamim, who traded and repaired Oriental rugs, became an invalid in his fifties when he began losing his memory and could not keep track of where he had delivered his merchandise. He convalesced at home for the remainder of his life, while his wife and children became the breadwinners. It appears that Aunt Simha died without ever forgiving her mother for failing to keep her beloved father close to home. (Not once in her memoir does Simha blame her father directly for anything.) Aunt Simha's and my mother's shared bond of orphanhood would draw them together in their widowed years, forging a lasting friendship.

Of Aharon Haim's three sisters, Algerina and Rachel died of typhoid within a month of each other, and his two brothers are hardly mentioned. Rachel's daughter Sarina married a co-owner of the Edison movie theater in Jerusalem, and Algerina's only son, Nissim Alcalay, emigrated to New York, where I knew him as a smooth-talking moneylender and man-about-town. Nissim retired to Tel Aviv, where he embarked in his late sixties on a surreptitious courtship of my widowed mother—or so she insisted until the day she died. (For years, Mother badgered me to go after Nissim Alcalay's daughter Alegre, although we were both married.)

The only one of my grandfather's siblings to survive past middle age was Perla, the youngest, who married the future chief Sephardic rabbi of Haifa, Nissim Ohanna. "They say aunt Perla was a certified seamstress, and she dressed according to the best fashion of the time. She was tall and beautiful, and in her great self-confidence she turned down many marriage offers." Perla at first rejected the advances of Nissim Ohanna, a widower years older than herself who was set in his ways. In perhaps the most electrifying scene of her memoir, Simha describes Aharon Haim's reaction to Perla's obduracy: "My father used his influence with Grandfather Perera to persuade her to agree to the match. She kept refusing, and when his pleas had no result, he raised his hand and slapped her cheek. That offended Perla profoundly and she wept bitterly, but eventually with no other choice at hand she consented, and the date was set for the seven blessings of her wedding day."

Aunt Simha could not have witnessed this stark enactment of patriarchal authority, the only one of its kind in her memoir. But I find it altogether credible. For me, this scene marks the divide between the biblical world of my grandfathers and the twentieth century in which I grew up. Symbolically, that slap was the valedictory of generations of Pereras whose lives were premised on safeguarding family honor. When Aharon Haim traveled to Alexandria that millennial code was still in rigor, but his untimely death reduced it to a ritual observance. My father and his brothers would inherit the outer shell of the pa-

triarchs' precepts, and by the time I was born in Guatemala they had
become mere shadows. For the Pereras, a whole era came to an end
with that slap on the cheek of my proud great-aunt Perla.

Perla was an intelligent and resourceful woman who made the
most of her situation, as attested to by Simha: "Aunt Perla's life was
beautiful, and she did not lack for anything. She raised a large family,
and her husband was named rabbi, first of the Jewish community on
the island of Malta, and several years later of the community of Port
Said, which he served for many years. When they lived in Egypt, Aunt
Perla always had servants to do all the cleaning and housework. She
would travel to distant cities with her husband on the invitation of the
Jewish communities. They used to come often to Israel as well, and
people would throw parties for them."

When I first visited Israel in 1955 at the age of twenty-one, my
great-uncle Nissim Ohanna was the chief rabbi of Haifa. I was invited
to their spacious home, filled with mementos of their years in Egypt. I
recall my great-aunt Perla as a poised and attentive hostess with an air of
wistful melancholy who teased me about my skinny frame. After dinner I was seated in front of my venerable great-uncle, who delivered
himself of a long and sententious lecture on Zionism that did not make
much of an impression on me. I felt he was going through the motions
of admonishing me to make *aliyah* to Israel, not from conviction but
rather from a sense of obligation. I had put behind my Zionist youth in
Hechalutz Hatzair by the age of eighteen. My enthusiasm was roused
far more by European literature and Eastern religions than by the tenets
of kibbutz socialism or the prophecies of the Torah. What is more, I
soon learned that Nissim Ohanna and Perla's children had all chosen
secular careers in banking, the army and the private sector. They
showed even less interest in a religious vocation than I did, regarding
themselves as Israelis first and Jews second. The eldest son, Ellie
Ohanna, "a skinny bookworm" in Simha's words, was the manager of
a branch of Barclay's Discount Bank, where he granted me an interview whose substance has vanished from my memory.

The most vivid impression I have of that visit nearly forty years
ago is of Great-aunt Perla's poise and faded beauty, her witty repartee
and the aura of melancholy that enveloped her. Her despondency
sprang to mind when I visited Alexandria in 1980, and a doe-eyed,
septuagenarian beauty in the Jewish nursing home pronounced the
word "kismet" to describe her life's unfulfilled yearnings.

During that same visit to Israel I met my other great-uncle, Yehuda Burla, who gave me a Zionist lecture in his Carmel home. Although I found his summons to emigrate to Israel scarcely more inspiring than Rabbi Ohanna's, Burla had a compelling presence; I was mesmerized by the long row of his novels on the living room bookshelf, which were obligatory reading for a generation of Israeli schoolchildren. When I met him, Burla had already been pensioned by the state of Israel as one of its literary luminaries, on a par with S. Y. Agnon. But as none of his books had been translated into English or Spanish, they remained a mystery to me.

SIMHA'S MEMORIES NEVER stray far from her beloved father. She ends the memoir without mentioning his fateful departure for Alexandria in 1922, when she was in her early teens. Her writing, above all, was an attempt to fix her father in words—his medium— and keep him alive in memory. Her stories about him begin, "I remember" and go on, paragraph after paragraph, "I remember . . . I remember . . ." like a Passover litany. At times she free-associates, letting each word or phrase spark another until they create a Joycean flow of consciousness. Simha repeats the same stories over and over with slight variations, like musical leitmotifs, so that the narrative is circular rather than lineal. It is as if she hoped to snare her father inside her magic circle and hold him captive, the loving and provident paterfamilias preserved forever in his vigorous prime. Perhaps her most vivid memory is of accompanying her father when he performed the *kaparot* (rites of atonement) on the eve of Yom Kippur. (He also performed *kaparot* for sick or bedeviled persons, whom he cured by transferring their ailments to a sacrificial offering.)

"But let's return to my childhood memories. Since Father was a *shohet,* people from our neighborhood would bring him their poultry to be slaughtered. Father kept a limestone on which he would sharpen the knife before slaughtering the chicken, taking care that its blood spilled onto a large tin full of soil.

"On the night before Yom Kippur, Father would do the *kaparot* for us before dawn, while we were all asleep. He slaughtered the tender chickens, which he purchased in advance for each of the children. Of course, he would also do as much for Mother, and if she was pregnant two fowl were required for atonement, a cock and a hen. We would awake to the sound of the screeching birds as Father swung them around his head and they beat their wings while he recited the prayers of thanksgiving and atonement in a ringing voice. Afterward Father would take a lamp and a knife, and he would make the rounds of the neighborhood to perform the *kaparot* for whoever required them; for this service, he was compensated with a portion of the sacrifice. On many occasions I accompanied him in the darkness of the early dawn to hold the lamp for him while he slaughtered the chickens.

"Yom Kippur was a good day for us kids. For the parents it was a solemn holy day, which they spent in prayer from dawn to dusk at our temple. We dressed in holiday clothes, and I sat with Mother in the women's section. The women were dressed in their best finery and the scent of perfume filled the air. I would go without food for a short time, and then I would go home and eat *sivado*, a Yom Kippur specialty made of barley and grapes. Father would admonish me: 'Try to fast for a few more hours. God accepts that, as well.' "

CHAPTER VIII

THE OTHER ISRAEL I

IN OCTOBER 1973 I traveled to Israel to cover the aftermath of the Yom Kippur War for the *New York Times Magazine*. It was my first visit to the Holy Land since 1961, when I had sat shivah for my father in Haifa. In the aftermath of the Yom Kippur War I was to discover a new underclass composed of hundreds of thousands of Oriental and North African Jews who had emigrated to the Holy Land in the '50s and '60s in search of sanctuary and economic betterment. In my article for the *Times* I referred to these Sephardim and Oriental Jews as the "Other Israel," a phrase that raised the hackles of U.S. Zionist leaders. The opening paragraph read: "Israelis are seed-eaters: sunflower, pumpkin, watermelon, pistachio. They scatter shells everywhere they go. The sound of teeth cracking seeds follows me all over Israel, on the buses, in the cafes and cinemas and even into the lavatories. 'There is no time,' the Israelis seem to be saying. 'We cannot wait for them to flower and bear fruit. We must eat the seeds.' In the Taamon Cafe, in Jeru-salem, a friendly Trotskyist tells me, 'Israel carries the seeds of its dispersal.'"

I TOOK A ROOM IN THE marvelously posh yet inexpensive American Colony Hotel in East Jerusalem, where I had ready access to dissident Israelis and Sephardic Black Panthers, as well as to Pales-tinian spokespersons. The hotel manager, Mr. Vestner, was partial to foreign journalists and unstintingly generous with his high-level con-tacts on both sides of the Green Line. On the other hand, neither Mr. Vestner nor his impeccable wife and cohost was overly fond of Israelis, save for the writers and leftish politicians who frequented the American Colony for afternoon tea and the latest inside dope.

In West Jerusalem I had met with Dr. Eliyahu Eliachar, who would become my guide in exploring the origins of my family. At our first meeting in his book-lined study, Dr. Eliachar explained how the Israeli state had co-opted my great-uncles Yehuda Burla and Rabbi Nissim Ohanna and other members of the Sephardic elite.

Dr. Eliachar's references to Sephardic "Uncle Toms" who had

sold out to the state had shocked and galvanized me. I had never heard such straight talk from a Sephardic leader, and hardly expected it from a richly laureled, eighteenth-generation patrician Jerusalemite of eighty-two. And Eliachar was just warming up.

"Twenty-five years ago I foresaw that Ben-Gurion and other leaders of the Second Aliyah [Eastern European immigrants from the 30s and 40s] and their successors would try to divide and conquer the Sephardic community. Ben-Gurion himself had a profound ambivalence toward the Middle Eastern and North African immigrants, and feared they would undermine his plans for a European Zionist state. And so they began creating myths about the 'primitive' and 'backward' North African Jews, and set them apart from the rest of us.

"The truth is," Dr. Eliachar said, leaning forward in his seat, "that we, the so-called Sephardim Tahorim, or 'True Sephardim,' have indissoluble historical and cultural ties to the Jews of Tangier, Tetuán, Larache, Mogador, Safi; contrary to the Ashkenazic libel, these communities enjoyed the highest standards of education in North Africa. The intelligentsia, the professionals and the wealthier tradesmen emigrated to Paris, London and the Americas. Those who came here in the early fifties, to encounter wretched conditions in Negev settlement camps, were forced to become scavengers. They not only were denied educational opportunities but had to submerge their cultural distinctiveness in humiliating and menial pursuits. Only in recent years are young leaders emerging who have the pride and determination to cast off their shackles and assert their Sephardic identity."

At the end of our talk Dr. Eliachar counseled me to meet with Iraqi and Moroccan political leaders, including Black Panther activists, rather than limit myself to establishment Sephardim such as Yitzhak Navon and David Levy.

The Taamon Cafe, on King George Street, was a miniature Jerusalem where representatives of all factions met to sip arrack and espresso and air their political views. The Taamon was the favorite haunt not only of the Israeli Black Panthers but of Communist party leaders, Palestinian Arabs of various persuasions, lonely soldiers, delinquent kibbutz volunteers, Jesus freaks, junkies and foreign correspondents in search of local color. On my first visit there I was approached by Aviv, a paratrooper of Moroccan descent who confessed to having followed orders to kill Egyptian soldiers after they surrendered, because there were so many of them.

"I fought in the '67 war," remarked Aviv, whose brown eyes were so clear and unguarded I could feel his pain in my chest. "But this one was very different. The Egyptians fought harder and they had better weapons, such as the Soviet antitank missiles. But they were still no match for our weapons and training. Toward the end, they surrendered by the thousands. You could tell the Egyptians who had been in the '67 war and had learned all the tricks of giving themselves up. They would walk toward us with arms raised and their shoelaces untied, and they would present us their watches without being asked. But we couldn't take them. Write that," he said, pointing to my notebook. "Write that we weren't allowed to take prisoners. We had to shoot them. Tell them that Aviv said so, that he is very disappointed."

I interviewed a number of other Sephardic and Oriental soldiers who had distinguished themselves in Israel's wars—among them two relatives of mine—and whose faith in their leaders had been badly shaken by the Yom Kippur War and its aftermath. Only my cousin Oded, the same Oded who was killed on a volunteer mission in the Sinai and was regarded by those who knew him as "the best Israel had to offer," had never doubted or wavered and had marched to his death, in the words of Moshe, his father, "as if it were an important appointment."

Through a contact of Dr. Eliachar's, I met in the Taamon Cafe with Saadia Marciano and Charlie Bitton, two of the founders of the Israeli Black Panther party. The Black Panthers, whose support crested soon after the war at around 80,000 followers, readily admitted they had chosen their name with an eye to publicity.

"We sympathize very strongly with the Black Panthers in America," said Marciano, a light-skinned, boyishly handsome Moroccan immigrant in his late twenties who was number two in the party, "and we also sympathize with all the other oppressed minorities in the world; but the hard fact is that we represent an oppressed *majority* in Israel of North African, Middle Eastern and Asian Jews. We make up sixty percent of the grade-school enrollment in Israel, yet we are only fifteen percent of the university graduates. We are the first to die fighting in Israel's wars with the Arabs and the last to get decent housing, jobs and tax-free autos when we leave the army. These are reserved for newer immigrants from the Soviet Union. And why? Because there is a deliberate plan by the power structure, the old die-hard Eastern Europeans of the Second Aliyah and their successors—Golda Meir, Moshe Dayan,

Abba Eban—to keep the Oriental and Sephardic Jews at the bottom of Israeli society. They want us to provide cheap manpower for their wars and their industry without contaminating the European image they wish to project to the world."

"Let me tell him, let me tell him," burst in Charlie Bitton, a wiry Iraqi Jew with the unkempt, high-octane energy of a '60s-beat "barbarian." (Coincidentally, he bore a striking resemblance to Gregory Corso.) "They know that we Sephardim and the Arabs eat more rice, so they make the price of rice go up and up, while the prices of Ashkenazic foods remain the same. . . . In the prisons, whose population is ninety-eight percent Sephardim and Arabs, the jail guards are Sephardim and Orientals like us, but the bosses with the guns are all Ashkenazim. Do you understand? Shlomo Hillel, the chief of police, is Sephardic because criminals are Sephardic. He is put there to control us. The government buys out the big wheels of the Sephardic establishment—the Uncle Toms—and gives them high-paying jobs to put down the Panthers. That is how they rook us, by turning us against one another."

"In 1971," Marciano broke in, "we organized ourselves as the Black Panther movement and went into the streets. In May we held our first mass demonstration in Jerusalem. Molotov cocktails were thrown, guns were fired, and there were 170 arrests. Today we have 15,000 members in the labor federation—the Histadrut—and 300 Black Panther leaders throughout the country."

"Power comes from the barrel of a gun," interjected Bitton, citing Mao.

"Yes, and it also comes from the raised voices of the people," countered Marciano in a raised voice. "We will continue to work for more and better housing for all the poor—Jews, Arabs and Christians—for better education and economic opportunities, and for higher representation of Sephardim in government, in the Knesset and in the army hierarchy. We want the Jews of America to know where their money is going."

The following evening I met with Kochavi Shemesh, an Iraqi Jew of thirty who had come to Israel as a small boy. Shemesh is the sole leader of the Panthers' left wing, which had split off a year earlier on ideological grounds. "We are," he admitted, "a small minority within the Sephardic majority."

Like Charlie Bitton and other Panthers with prison records,

Shemesh took pride in his self-made reputation as a delinquent rebel. "I never completed the first grade," he boasted with a sly grin. "I became a thief. I steal from the rich to feed myself, my family and my friends."

With a bottle of arrack beside him, Shemesh made no attempt to disguise his scorn for Marciano and Bitton. "Saadia and Charlie are jokers," he said. "They have no ideology. They work to gain seats for themselves in the Knesset so they will have retirement pensions for the rest of their lives. I work to destroy the Knesset."

My interviews with Dr. Eliachar and the Panthers had intro-duced me to a new phenomenon on the Israeli landscape: the upstart, opportunistic Oriental Jew who refuses to buckle under to either the Sephardic or the Ashkenazic establishment. I sensed I was witnessing the dawn of a Sephardic renewal, marked by the sloughing off of gener-ations of taciturn, *ayin-hara*-haunted former Marranos who nurse their nostalgia for a faded Golden Age while stewing in envy of their more accomplished Ashkenazic brethren.

In the Sephardic slum neighborhoods of Katamon and Mus-rawa I would discover the nurseries of these resurgent Sephardim. Aviv, the disappointed Moroccan soldier, had invited me to meet his family in Katamon Tet, one of the blocks of tenements for new immi-grants that have mushroomed on the outskirts of Jerusalem. The Katamonim have a reputation for housing troublesome and backward *Pikudim,* the Israeli pejorative for unassimilated immigrants from Iraq and North Africa. Nearly all the children here had failed the admis-sions tests to Israeli public schools because they lacked a proper He-brew; in compensation, they were given special training by volunteer counselors, most of whom were foreigners who spoke little or no Hebrew.

After having tea with Aviv's mother and sister in a cramped but sunny apartment they share with another family, Aviv took me to meet the children in the courtyard, where they awaited the arrival of their counselors.

There were about two dozen of them, ranging in age from five to twelve or thirteen. The girls mostly huddled together in the corridor and chattered in shrill voices, while the boys played marbles on a small patch of earth at the far end of the courtyard.

These children reminded me of my own boyhood. They were energetic and warm, but lacked the keen competitive spirit typical of sa-bras. When I visited my ten-year-old nephew, Daniel, in Kibbutz Beit-

Oren, his playmates eyed me challengingly, as though estimating my military skills or how many sacks of cucumbers I could haul on my back. With these undersized, dark-skinned, functionally illiterate Sephardic children, the sort Ben-Gurion had in mind when he voiced concern about Israel's turning into "just another Levantine state," I relived my childhood in Guatemala as a misfit foreigner. I was also re-minded of my early teens in Brooklyn, when I languished in the retar-date section of junior high school because, as a native Spanish-speaker, I could not puzzle out the Stanford-Binet IQ tests.

In the courtyard I met with Simone, a very fair-skinned young volunteer from the Netherlands, who was engulfed by small girls eager to touch her Western dress and fondle her short blond hair.

"You learn a great deal about the other Israel, working with these children," Simone said in her slight Dutch accent. "I was told before I came here that these were slow, backward children and I would have to be very patient with them. So at first I did not trust my-self when I found them so outgoing and—you know—bright. It came to me gradually, of course, that they meant they were not intelligent by Israeli Ashkenazic standards. These children place more emphasis on close physical contacts and family activities than on competition and in-dividual accomplishment. The result is that they are made to feel in-ferior when they come to Ashkenazic schools, and they become timid and afraid to speak out. More than half of these children were born in Morocco, Yemen, Iraq, Tunis, but if you ask them they will all tell you they are sabras, because they are ashamed of their origins. They are ashamed that they have darker skin and don't have blond hair and blue eyes like the European Jewish children."

I would recall Simone's words the following week, when my cousin Malka enlightened me on the cultural abyss that separates Se-phardim Tahorim from the Orientals. As she escorted me around the Old City we talked about the trend toward intermarriage between the old Sephardic families and the Ashkenazic immigrants. Malka and two of her three siblings had married Ashkenazic sabras. "Will the same thing happen with the Oriental Jews?" I questioned.

"The North African and Middle Eastern immigrants are a spe-cial problem," she replied as we approached the Western Wall. "I do not consider them Sephardim. We call them *Pikudim,* 'primitives.' Most come from poor backgrounds and are lacking in ambition, especially the Moroccans. The educated and well-off Moroccans went to Paris and America, and the poor, the uneducated and the unwanted came to us. In many ways the problem is similar to that of the blacks in America. Many of the Moroccans who came here in the '50s are illiterate and so primitive that even the army could not make men out of them. These are the ones who call themselves Black Panthers. They complain the most and make propaganda that they do not get good housing or equal education with Ashkenazim, etcetera, etcetera. All of this exaggeration is only meant to call attention to themselves."

The Western Wall was lined with shawled and caftaned Ortho-dox worshippers and a few soldiers. They chanted aloud and brushed their foreheads rhythmically against the wall, each set apart from his neighbor, absorbed in private discourse with Elohim.

To the left, at the mouth of Wilson's Arch, a group of small, dark-skinned people conducted a ceremony that contrasted sharply with the introspective ritual of the Hasidim. The women, dressed in bright shawls and long, swirling skirts, whooped energetically and tossed sweets into the air. The men, spruced up in wedding suits, shuf-fled repeatedly between a brass tray with a decanter and the holy scroll against the wall, which they kissed and toasted with shot glasses of cognac.

After several more whoops, tossings of sweets and fervent toasts, the tray, decanter and glasses vanished into a cloth bag and the group itself dispersed in a single fluid movement.

"You see that?" Malka said, shaking her head. "That is a Moroccan family whose son has returned safely from the war. That is how they celebrate for him, in this place of mourning. They are a very primitive people, almost like children. But the army will make good Is-raelis out of the young generation. Normally it takes only three to four years to become assimilated here. Many of the Russian immigrants who are now arriving are already better Israelis than the majority of the *Pikudim.*"

She turned to the wall. "And look at the Hasidim, all day pray-ing and praying. For what? To me the Black Panthers and the ortho-dox of Mea Shearim are the same. They cry and complain all the time, and they contribute very little to the advancement of Israel. To survive, Israel will have to be very, very strong, without their help."

Within a year, Malka's son David, who had served with dis-tinction in the Sinai—not far from where his close friend and cousin Oded had fallen—had courted and married an Orthodox Moroccan

Jew. At first, Malka took pains to conceal her disappointment, then her daughter-in-law gave birth to a healthy and fair-skinned baby boy. Overnight, Malka had a change of heart and became a doting grand-mother.

IN 1973 I SPOKE FOR the first time with militant Jews who took pride in calling themselves reactionary, even fascist. Aharon Pick of the Tehiya party referred to Jewish bureaucrats and all Egyptians except Sadat as "human dust." Preying on the national longing for strong leadership, Israel's men on white horses—Generals Ariel "Arik" Sharon and Raphael "Rafu" Eitan, who once described West Bank Palestinians as "drunken cockroaches running around in a bottle"—were exalted by the right as messianic deliverers. Fearful that Israel was drifting toward a right-wing militarized state, I consulted dovish writers A. B. Yehoshua and Yehuda Amichai.

A.B.'s father, Ya'acob Yehoshua, was a respected Sephardic critic and editor who authored a memoir of early-twentieth-century Jerusalem that, for all the international celebrity achieved by his novelist son, remains untranslated into English. The younger Yehoshua, a strong advocate of the Jewish Right of Return, was also a strong supporter of a separate Palestinian state alongside Israel. Yehoshua spoke of the need to free ourselves of the double bind of "Never Again" and the biblical legacy of "chosenness":

"What is needed now is a profound change in our conception of ourselves as Jews. Our enslavement to history and to biblical precedent is so insidious that it prevents us from undertaking initiatives that could break our impasse with the Arabs. Our stiffneckedness and arrogance derive from a lack of confidence in the world. It's a terrible irony that our fears create our own traps. Masada, where the Jewish Zealots immolated themselves rather than be taken captive by the Romans, is far more today than just a national symbol. It is like a self-fulfilling metaphor that colors our everyday life. Every Israeli carries that hill around inside him, and the obsession only serves to bring the reality closer. The only way to shed our fatalism is to break our preoccupation with the past and learn to improvise. We must create a new Jew."

The poet Yehuda Amichai, a founder of the Peace Now movement who fought in four of Israel's wars, has infinitely sad eyes, without the defensive armor I had come to associate with Israelis, other than the returning soldiers. Amichai said he had known for a long time that a price would be paid sooner or later for Israel's hubris, its self-blinding pride. "We've been playing at Europe," he said. "We've mimicked the affluent society for short-term material gains and lost sight of our spiritual values. . . . But you know, when the crunch comes, tradition rears up in you, and there's no question of choosing sides. You become a menaced Jewish animal." (I mulled over this phrase many times in the coming weeks, each time underscoring a different word. When war breaks out, is the accent on "menaced," "Jewish" or "animal"?)

Amichai dismissed my apprehensions by saying Israelis are too independent and idiosyncratic to support a totalitarian ruler. "There is a rigidity in many people now, it is true. We are preparing ourselves for a shock. But there is more flexibility in this young country than appears on the surface. We will have no Masada here."

He then surprised me by advocating a Middle Eastern common market. "What we must begin to prepare ourselves for, in the long term, is a United States of the Middle East. We must work with the Arabs toward a mutual prosperity through an increased trade and exchange of ideas, instead of through war."

With the signing of the peace agreement between Israel and the PLO in September 1993, and the peace accord with Jordan in August 1994, Yehoshua's and Amichai's words have taken on the raiments of prophecy.

At the American Colony Hotel I interviewed Yitzhak Navon, the future president of Israel. As Mayor Kollek's deputy, he was already the highest-ranking Sephardi in government. Navon made short shrift of the issue of discrimination against Oriental and North African Jews with a single magic formula: intermarriage.

Within a generation, he assured me, half of the Orientals will have climbed out of their inferior station by intermarrying with Ashkenazim. "Look, for example, at the lovely Yemenite women," he said. "The Yekes [German Jews] are crazy about them. Take my word for it," he added, adjusting the horn-rimmed glasses on his gentle, owlish face. "The racial problem in Israel is a short-term phenomenon. The religious problem, on the other hand. . . ." He lifted his hand palm-up in the Ladino gesture for "what to do?" and abruptly changed the subject.

"Tell me, I'm curious. Are you of the same Perera family as Yitzhak Moshe and Aharon Haim?"

Caught off balance, I nodded assent. "They are my grandfather and great-grandfather."

Navon shook his head slowly. "What a burden," he said.

Two weeks later my aunt Reina informed me of the lasting ties between the Navons and the Pereras. Navon's paternal ancestors emigrated from Turkey in the seventeenth century, at around the same time as my relatives the Burlas, and Navon's father had been a friend and colleague of my grandfather Aharon Haim. Navon, who speaks perfect Arabic, has written popular folk dramas about the Ladino culture of Jerusalem's old Sephardic families. That same day my three aunts—Reina, Simha and Rachel—gathered around me in Reina's apartment to familiarize me with Yitzhak Moshe Perera's testament and initiate me into the family curse.

My "Letter From Israel" in the *Times* closed with an interview with Suhail Abu Nuwara, a Palestinian playwright whose work was produced in Beirut. On the day the Israeli war-casualty list was announced, everyone in the Taamon Cafe—Panthers, Palestinians, even Arye Bober, the Trotskyist writer—sat around grim-faced and silent.

"The next war," Abu Nuwara predicted, "will be started by Israeli Arabs, not because of loss of land or property, for they are still better off than many Jews, but because of a loss of identity. They care neither for the Jews nor the Jordanians, who have taken turns exploiting them.

"The next war," he said, "will be fought not from hatred or passion, or for protection of territory—all those reasons will have been exhausted. It will be fought from an instinct to kill based on the loss of all illusions. Right now you are seeing the death of the Zionist illusion, and next will be the illusion of the Chosen People for whom the Holy Land was singled out by God.

"The fact is that the Holy Land cannot be owned. It does not belong to anybody. It rejects all territorial claims based on the Torah, the New Testament or the Koran. This can never be a Palestinian state or a Christian state any more than it can be a Zionist one. These rocks are only for those who can love Jerusalem without the desire to possess her."

THE RESPONSE FROM Israelis to my "Letter From Israel" was tempered, and about evenly divided between praise and disapproval.

But in the week after the article appeared, the *New York Times Magazine* received the biggest barrage of hate mail in its history, most of it from U.S. Zionists and pro-Israel lobbyists. In these letters I was denounced, by turns, as a "self-hating Jew," a Nazi sympathizer and a secret collaborator with the Symbionese Liberation Army. (Two rabbis equated me with Patty Hearst as a traitor to my class.)

II

HEBRON

On the day my cousin Malka took me to the Istanbuli synagogue in the Old City, she reminded me that Yitzhak Moshe Perera and his father had lived in Hebron. "Your great-grandfather's father, Aharon Raphael Haim, held services in the Hebron synagogue, and when he died he was buried in the Jewish cemetery there. You will have to be careful if you go to Hebron, because the situation in the West Bank is still tense, but you may want to look for his grave and say the Kaddish over him."

Two days later I took the *servis* (Arab limousine shuttle) to Hebron. The redoubtable Mr. Vestner calmed my apprehensions by assuring me that I would be in no danger as long as I passed myself off as an American tourist. "But keep an eye out for the trigger-happy Israeli soldiers," he cautioned, with his British curled lip and raised brow.

My search for my great-great-grandfather's grave in the Jewish cemetery at the entrance to Hebron proved fruitless. Many of the stones had been rifled since the occupation, or had decayed to the point where they were no longer legible. I decided to recite the Kaddish in his memory outside the cave of the patriarchs, the Machpelah.

The streets of Hebron were empty of visitors, not surprisingly, considering the frequent clashes between Israeli settlers and Palestinians. As I made my way to the Machpelah, I passed a curious scene. The Hadassah hospital of Hebron, which is Arab-administered, had been taken over by Israeli women of Kiryat Arba, the new settlement on the hill overlooking the city. Miriam Levinger, wife of Moshe Levinger, the militant right-wing rabbi who founded Kiryat Arba, was screaming in her Brooklyn-accented Hebrew at the Palestinian police, who were—very politely—attempting to remove the women from the hospital grounds. In her Orthodox matron's wig and New York accent, Miriam Levinger cut a curious figure; she was adamant that Hebron belonged to the Jews as much as to the Arabs, and she had no intention of budging. The occupation of the Hadassah hospital would go on for months, as the settlers turned it into a bridgehead for the Jewish reset/ tling of Hebron.

The entrance to the mosque that guards the tombs of Abraham, Isaac, Jacob and their consorts was guarded by a garrison of Israeli sol/ diers with Uzi submachine guns. Inside, a crowd of kneeling Arabs paid homage before the giant tombs. The Jewish settlers worshipped in their own small prayer hall opposite the mausoleum, whence they glow/ ered at all passersby with undisguised hostility.

Across the street I struck up a conversation with the keeper of the tomb of Abner. He is a slight, shabbily dressed Muslim in his mid/thir/ ties, with large, liquid brown eyes. His name is Hasan al/Sharif, and his grandfather, he tells me, is a local sheikh and the religious head of Hebron.

In a colorful, idiosyncratic English he recites the story of Abner, Saul's captain, and of his treacherous end at Joab's hands within the gates of Hebron. Then he offers to show me the city.

"I am not a tourist guide," he assures me. "I like to show my city to visitors with a sincere interest." He squints at me, tilting his head to one side. "In your eyes I can see that you are looking for something. I think perhaps that you are open and a little sad, like me."

Hasan begins by showing me a small dark cave, annexed to the tomb, whose walls are lined with Arabic and English books. "When I am hurt or confused, I shut myself in this place for a week and write in my journal. I do not eat or sleep, so I come out thin like a skeleton and a little crazy, but my head will be clear."

Hasan escorts me around the tourists' quarter. We start out in the ceramics factory, then visit the leather worker's shop and the garru/ lous town potter, Ahmed, who spins out flawless identical tiny vessels as he traces his ancestry to the eighteenth and nineteenth generations, and finds potters in all of them. If his claims are valid, Ahmed's ances/ tors were already making pots in Hebron when the Eliachars settled in Jerusalem.

Hasan then leads me down the narrow, winding streets of the bazaar, which is larger than those I had visited in Jericho and Bethle/ hem, and more redolent of the Levant. In the butcher's stall I see my first skinned camel, and the falafel Hasan treats me to is spicier than any I've eaten before. Hasan appears to have friends everywhere in Hebron; we are invited to a smoke or a cup of tea at every other stall.

"Tourist shortage," I surmise. But when an Israeli police officer stops to converse with him and ask a favor, I realize that Hasan is a person of some importance.

As we wander through the maze of crowded stalls and shops Hasan tells me of his past life. He says he moved to Beirut at the age of seven and became an international spy when he was still a boy. He was, he says, a hotel manager, an actor. ("Acting," I soon catch on, is Hasan's synonym for wasteful or insincere behavior.)

After a visit to his uncle's glass factory at the other end of town, Hasan takes me to his favorite restaurant. The owner, who appears overwhelmed by our visit, leads us upstairs to a private stall. He brings us a delicious chickpea *teheena* salad and draws a curtain around our table. Hasan's mood turns serious. He shows me a photograph of his Arabic wife and three children, then another of himself with a blond Nordic woman a head taller than he is. "This is my Danish wife," he says. "We were married two years ago. Now she is in Copenhagen, and she is asking me for a divorce." Without further elaboration he shows me a letter from an American Catholic convent. "This letter is from Mary, a wife of the spirit only. We walked everywhere together. They are a part of me, these three women, and I am a part of them, but in my heart I have one wife only, and one God. My God is the God of the prophet Mohammed, but to me he is also Christ and Jehovah of the Hebrew prophets. They are all one God, and also my women are one. First comes God, who is One, and then my wives, who are one. In essence, I am monotheistic and I am monogamous. Can you try to understand this logic?"

I agree to try, in that curtained enclosure that lifts me above the everyday and invites me to suspend judgment. Hasan presses my hand. "We are now friends," he says. "You and I are the same case. I know this. You are to your people what I am to mine. We complete one another.

"Next time you come," he adds, "I will show you another Hebron. I will present you to my grandfather the sheikh, who is a very holy man."

As a foretaste of this other Hebron, Hasan takes me to a back alley of the bazaar, filled with piles of artillery shells salvaged from the

Sinai war. A metalworker flattens the brass casings on an anvil and reshapes them with saw and mallet into handsome lamps and ornamental trays.

"This is how we beat swords into ploughshares in Hebron," Hasan says.

Hasan accompanies me to Jerusalem so he can show me his favorite haunts in the Old City. As we approach Rachel's tomb, outside Bethlehem, he prepares me for the transition. "We are crossing the border. . . . One . . . two . . . three. . . . First the climate outside changes, then the one inside." And, indeed, as we leave behind the terraced vineyards of Arab Judea and begin the long ascent to Jerusalem the air turns sharply colder, the pace of traffic accelerates, the highrise apartment complexes and new hotels rear up to the left and right. They seem oddly frail and transitory, these soaring concrete structures, after the ageless clay and burlap hovels of Hebron's bazaar.

Hasan is watching me. "Now you begin to understand," he says, "why we are so careful of protecting our city."

We enter the Old City before dusk and climb to Hasan's favorite perch on the parapet above Damascus Gate. From here we look across Temple Mount and the gilt Dome of the Rock to the churches on Mount Gethsemane. We sit in silence as the sun fades behind us, bathing the limestone walls of the Old City in a vermilion glow. As the shadows lengthen over the domed roofs I have the sensation that this scene has been enacted before, that this is not the first silence Hasan and I have shared. I tell Hasan of my déjà vu, and he nods pensively. "You will see that when two people speak from the heart, time stands still. How long have we known each other? Two hours? Two years? Two centuries? Perhaps we knew one another in Spain."

I picture us in Granada, a Muslim and a Jew conversing about God in the gardens of the Alhambra.

"I like you, Hasan," I say sincerely, "but I cannot tell when you are making things up; and I find your manner didactic at times."

"Didactic? What is that?"

"Like a teacher. Sometimes you remind me of a *melamed* I had in Hebrew class before I was thirteen."

A long silence grows heavy between us, and I know I have wounded him.

"You will understand better," he says at last, "after you meet my grandfather. He also tells me I am didactic, but that is because he is a holy man. When I have a spirit like his I won't need to be didactic. I have to touch a person with all of myself, that is my way. Your way as a writer is like a dark bottle with rose petals inside. The scent of the petals can reach many people, even if they cannot see or touch them. I reach only one at a time.

"My grandfather also tells me that I give too much of myself to people. I don't know why I have this need. I think sometimes that we live in a dangerous time and the only way to save ourselves is to bare our throats to each other, like wolves. . . . I have given blood to my sisters and brothers, and sometimes it has been wasted."

He turns toward me and I feel the intensity in his eyes, although I can no longer see them.

Hasan touches my forehead. "When I touch you here," he says, "I know what is in your heart. You must care well, for I will feel it. We are now friends. If my grandfather accepts you, we will be brothers— you understand?—and then there is nothing I will not do for you."

"Yes," I say, as my heart thumps in my chest.

At the American Colony Hotel that evening I mention Hasan's name to the Arab headwaiter. "Al-Sharif? A very distinguished name. I believe there is a Sheikh al-Sharif who is head of a Muslim sect in Hebron." I speak of Hasan to Yehuda Amichai, and he is struck by the image of the dark bottle with rose petals inside, which reminds him of the Sufi poets. When I ask if he thinks Hasan is unusual, Amichai responds: "Unusual? I would say unique." I spend a week with my relatives in the joyless Sephardic neighborhoods of lower Haifa. "Arabs are always pretending to be your friends and cousins," says my aunt Viola, "so they can ask you for *baksheesh* afterward."

Two weeks after my first visit, I take the *servis* to Hebron. The atmosphere feels tense. There have been incidents of stone-throwing between Jewish settlers and Muslim residents, and the crowds in the *shuk* eye me with suspicion. But I feel guiltless and return their looks openly. I find the door to Abner's tomb barred shut. A vendor by the entrance tells me Hasan left only minutes before. I set out to look for him in the bazaar, leaving messages in the shops and tea stalls we had visited together. I pass a group of Jewish settlers reciting the Sabbath service in the heart of the *shuk,* next to stalls of hummus and skinned camels and Arab elders in *kaffiyehs* smoking hookah pipes, while Israeli soldiers in skullcaps stand guard nearby. It seems as if the settlers and the Arab res⁄ idents of Hebron occupy a wholly different dimension of time and space, and breathe a different air.

Everyone I meet has just seen Hasan, but no one has any idea where he was headed. The Palestinian police officer reports having seen him at his favorite restaurant, but when I get there Hasan is no longer there.

I stop next door for a cup of tea. A tall young man approaches my table. "I am not a tourist guide," he says with a warm, rehearsed smile. "I like to show my city to interested visitors. In your eyes I can see you are not a tourist."

I tell him I am looking for Hasan al⁄Sharif.

"Hasan?" His brown eyes widen. "Hasan is my teacher. Are you a friend of Hasan's?"

Without waiting for an answer he slips out of the restaurant. Five minutes later Hasan's disciple is back, and his teacher is with him. Hasan's eyes are bloodshot and the scruffy growth on his face is at least a week old.

"This man," Hasan says, smiling, "has interrupted my after⁄ noon coffee. He spills the cup on the floor and tells me I am looked for by a foreigner. 'He is one of us,' he tells me, so I know it must be you."

As we sit and drink coffee in silence I am overcome with affec⁄ tion and solicitude for this pale, slovenly figure with inflamed eyes and worn elbow patches on his sweater.

"Hasan, Hasan, you've been in your cave, haven't you? You look like a ghost."

He squints at me. "A short residence only. I have need to think of a new word I have learned, so I look for it in my dictionary. 'Didac⁄ tic,' it says in my dictionary, is a good word. A person who is didactic has high morals, and in Greece a didactic person is one who is skillful in teaching. So I feel very happy that my new friend gives me this com⁄ pliment and thinks me didactic. But farther down in my dictionary I see that when a didactic person moralizes too much he becomes pedan⁄ tic. A pedantic person, it says, is one who exhibits his learning ostenta⁄ tiously. And now I have to think of these new words, *didactic, pedantic, ostentatious*. And I ask myself, is my new friend saying I read too many books? Or is he saying I must read more books, and better books, so I can become a wise man?"

Moved by his vulnerability, I assure Hasan that his didacticism is the Greek kind, and he looks relieved.

"I think," he says, "it is time you meet my grandfather. I spoke to him of you and your writings, and he asked me many questions."

On the way to the mosque we visit the leather worker's shop, the potter and the metalworker. This time I am conscious of our descent into basement workshops, and of the quickness of the artisans' hands.

As we come out into the town square, the air fills with the muez-zin's call to prayer. The sounds are clear and resonant, without the background scratch you hear from Jerusalem's mosques, which use gramophones and tape recorders.

"My grandfather's voice is strong today," Hasan says. "It is a good day to visit him."

In a café nearby we stop to chat with two Arab policemen in green uniforms, who turn out to be Hasan's cousins. When Hasan tells them I am to meet his grandfather, they regard me with heightened in-terest. They smile tensely when Hasan says I am a Jew, and one of them asks if I believe in God. In the square three children are playing with hoops, as the afternoon sun creeps slowly up the walls of the houses. The desert breezes lift swirls of dust from the narrow, winding streets. I think of my walks in the Gibralfaro with Canon Bandeña, and of the first time he asked if I believed in God: his God, the Christ of forgive-ness and compassion, the Christ of the Holy Inquisition. . . . I am snapped back to the present by a glimpse of an armed Israeli soldier standing guard on a roof. His dark glasses catch the sun as he points his Uzi down at a funeral procession that has just turned the corner. About thirty men and women march dressed in white, two among them bear-ing a tiny bier on their shoulders. . . . Are deceased Arabs cremated, or is this only a child? In the stillness I hear the release of the Uzi's safety. The soldier's posture has tensed, but he will not shoot. I turn to peer into Hasan's eyes, which wear a look of eternity.

In a low voice I tell Hasan's cousin that I believe in godliness and that I believe it resides in living beings, for I cannot conceive of an all-powerful deity that exists independently of humankind. The police-men seem satisfied with this reply. Again I remember Hasan's words about time and feel myself slipping outside its flow and into a calm pool by its bank. I acknowledge within myself that I have a soul, of which I am the custodian.

Hasan touches my knee and I start up as if from a sleep. He is looking at me sternly. "Know this: You are not the first Jew that I have loved, but you are the first I can call my brother."

We stop one more time, at the baker's shop. Hasan opens a door and I peer into a deep cave with a large clay oven in the rear. A man in flour-dusted striped pajamas and a red cap is drawing four loaves of bread from the oven with a flat wooden paddle. The loaves are round and browned to perfection. As I bite into the bread the ripe yeasty smell and the sweet texture fill my senses, and I understand that the Hebron Hasan has been showing me is a community of craftsmen who depend on their hands for their livelihood, as it was in the beginning. I have been to communities like this before—in India, Guatemala, southern Spain—but at this moment Hasan persuades me that this is the first community, from which all the others derive.

As we walk back through the bazaar, I peel off the outer skins from every stall and tourist shop we pass and see a Hebronite in a cave, digging with his hands.

"How old do you think he is, my grandfather?" Hasan asks, peering at me, his head tilted.

I guess eighty. He laughs. "He is already 135. His present wife is seventy-five. She married him for his spirit only when he was already one hundred. The first two wives lived long lives and gave him many children."

I decide Hasan is exaggerating again, or reckoning by Old Testament norms; however, as we enter his grandfather's mosque, the perfect stillness in the courtyard makes my heart race.

"Yesterday, when I told my grandfather of you, he said he knew your name. He said your relatives lived here generations ago, and some of them converted to Islam. Their Arabic name is Brera."

Astonished, I ask Hasan, "And did he know my great-great-grandfather, Rabbi Aharon Raphael Haim Perera?"

"Wait here," Hasan says, ignoring my question, and slips inside the mosque to announce me. Through a window at the foot of the minaret I see the microphone the sheikh uses to call the faithful. I hear a grunting sound from within. My mouth is dry.

An eternity passes before Hasan returns and invites me inside. I walk down two stone steps into a dark room. I instruct myself to recall everything that is about to take place. All the light in the long, narrow chamber is drawn to two small squatting figures in the far corner. The sheikh's hands compel my attention: They are extended over a small white brazier whose bright red glow, I see on close inspection, is given off by an electric coil. The fingernails look cared for, the skin is white and paper-thin. The sheikh is blind and partly deaf. These long, translucent hands are his eyes and ears.

I sit on a cushion beside the sheikh and across from Hasan, who kisses his grandfather's hands and raises them to his forehead. As my eyes adjust, I see the gold embroidery on the sheikh's old-fashioned silver cap, or *toka,* the thick black Bedouin cape that encases his body except for the hands and the shrunken face. His complexion is ruddy, although most of his teeth are gone and his eyes are buried slits.

The sheikh clears his throat and turns to the round, bundled figure beside him, his wife. I am struck by the nacreous pallor of her skin—a mark of high birth—and the thickness of her hands compared with the slender delicacy of her husband's. He gestures to her that we are to have coffee. She does not say a word during our interview, but she smiles on occasion and nods her head.

In a firm voice the sheikh asks me through Hasan what I am besides American and what I do besides write. I tell him, and he grunts, nods and draws his hands inside his cape. We lapse into silence as we sip the sweet, thick coffee his wife has prepared.

When I turn to Hasan I see that the spasms in my spine are reflected in his, for he also squirms on his cushion. I know I am being scanned by this old man, and that he is seeking my center. I have no fears, only questions.

I finish my coffee and ask him through Hasan what he thinks will happen in the Middle East between Arabs and Jews. I tell him of the split I feel within myself, so that I am least whole with my own family.

He reaches for my hand and takes it in both of his, drawing them partway inside his cape. Just before I withdraw my hand I have the sensation that I am seeing through the sheikh's eyes. I visualize a horizontal band, curving at each end. All my questions and preoccupations, everything that crowds the center of my mind, is pulled to either end and diminishes in size. His reply to my questions is registered in this central space he has cleared for me.

He tells Hasan the war is God's way of correcting imbalances that are deeply rooted in past events. I should not allow my spirit to bog down in the present conflict but should take a longer perspective. He tells me I am a solitary who should find my way outside of my family.

After a time I cannot distinguish which words he is addressing only to me, which to Hasan, which to us both. And Hasan's transla-tion is more and more interwoven with his reactions to his grandfather's counsel. We speak of goodness, of the importance of staying with the flow of events and recording them faithfully, without distorting or becoming distorted by them. "It is more important to witness than to prophesy."

Many of the sheikh's words I have heard before, in other con-texts, or know already within myself. What makes them new is the presence of the man, the movement of his hands as he speaks, the timbre of his voice.

His last words to me are: "Be at peace with your connection to God, and He will find a way to heal your mind, body and soul."

In the silence that follows I learn that the soul can create its own order in this world, and erect the scaffolding to reach beyond it. I dis-cover that this and other important truths are available to me at any given moment but for my fear and neglect of them, and through fear and neglect I will forget many of them when I leave Hebron.

I bend down to kiss the sheikh's hands, and he recites a prayer with his palm on my forehead.

As we emerge from the mosque, I take two steps and stop, blinded by the sun, paralyzed, sundered in two. In the split second it takes to pull myself together, I see Hasan's face ahead, squinting at me.

"My brother stumbles in the sun," he says.

CHAPTER IX

THE OTHER ISRAEL II

Young tree, unburdened
By anything but your beautiful natural blossoms
And dew, the dark
Blood in my body drags me
Down with my brother.
—James Wright, "To a Blossoming Pear Tree"

MISHKENOT

I DID NOT SEE Hasan again for twelve years. Soon after my departure from Israel he flew to Copenhagen to be with his Danish wife,
leaving his first wife and children in the care of his mother. I received
two letters from Hasan; the first informed me that he had made up with
Katrin and decided to stay on with her in Copenhagen. He said the situation in Hebron had deteriorated: Clashes between settlers and Palestinians had grown frequent and bloody, and the Israeli military
command had resorted to deportations. The Arab mayor, Fahd Ka-
wasme, was among those deported to Jordan. Hasan wrote that these
events had negatively affected his grandfather, one of whose sons had
also been deported.

In his second letter Hasan wrote: "I don't know when I can go
back to Hebron. Knowing you makes me feel I can be a great man, like
my grandfather. But my life may not permit this."

IN THE MID-SEVENTIES I had renewed an acquaintance with
the forest-dwelling Lacandon Mayas of southern Mexico, five of whom
I had seen in a fairground in Guatemala City when I was a small boy.
The white-tunicked, long-haired Mayas were put on exhibit inside a
chicken-wire enclosure to ornament the sixth anniversary of President
Jorge Ubico's benevolent dictatorship. The Lacandones made an indelible impression on me, as they did on everyone else who saw them.

Early in 1979 I was living in the Lacandon rain-forest community of Nahá, 100 kilometers northwest of Palenque in Chiapas, when

I dreamed I was walking down Jaffa Road in Jerusalem. I was headed for the Municipality, where two men wearing thick glasses were expect-ing me. They rummaged through a thick folder to find my file, which they perused cursorily. "Well," one said to the other, "Perera writes too close to his hat; but he has strong recommendations, so we may have to approve him."

The following morning I was reproached by twenty-one-year-old K'ayum Ma'ax, a middle son of the Lacandon elder of Nahá, Chan K'in: "You and I climbed the hill together to have a talk, but when I turned around to look for you, you were gone." Lacandones habitually intermingle dreams and waking experiences in their conver-sation, as if they were strings from a single harp.

"Sorry, K'ayum," I replied. "I had an urgent appointment in Jerusalem."

K'ayum, the most widely traveled of Chan K'in's ten living sons, knew precisely where Jerusalem was, thanks to the Seventh-Day Adventists and other missionaries who had attempted to convert him. In later years K'ayum would travel to Europe to exhibit and sell his al-legorical paintings.

"Ah, you were far away," he said gravely, taking my "astral" visit to Jerusalem for granted. K'ayum traveled to near and far places in his dreams nearly every night, and loved to expound on the symbolic import of these journeys. "Perhaps," K'ayum added thoughtfully, "it is time you visit your family."

I had not been in the Holy Land for six years; on my return to the States I would find a letter from Mayor Teddy Kollek of Jerusalem inviting me to an eight-week residency at Mishkenot Sha'ananim. I had been recommended by Yehuda Amichai. That same week I dreamed of encountering two Hasidim in Jerusalem's Old City. "Who is that man?" they inquired, pointing behind me. I turned around to discover Chan K'in in a Hasid's caftan and fur hat, with dangling earlocks, grinning mischievously. "Bring him to our house," they said.

In the Lacandon jungle, synchronous and mirror-imaging dreams were commonplace. The nonagenarian Chan K'in, whose sto-ries and parables nurtured an unbroken 3,000-year-old tradition, served as a lightning rod for the "paranormal." One of Chan K'in's many functions as the to'ohil (guardian) of the Lacandon Maya tradition was interpreting dreams. From my dreams and encounters in the forest, he had deduced that my family totem, or *onen,* was the hummingbird.

I had connected magic with the Lacandones since the day I first spied on them behind the chicken-wire fence. More than a half century later, I can still summon up the aura of mystery that enveloped the five figures with shoulder-length matted hair and infinitely sad, beautiful eyes that made their sex a puzzle. Who were these people, and why were they being punished? Years later I would interview the adventurer who had lured them to Guatemala from their forest home in southern Mexico with the promise of a .22 shotgun.

My encounters with the Lacandones sprang to mind when I read of the Marrano adventurer Antonio de Montezinos, who in 1644 sought out a small group of Indians in the Peruvian rain forest who were known as "the holy people." When Montezinos finally located them and informed them of his Jewish origins, the Indians greeted him with a "Sh'ma Yisrael," and the announcement that they were descendants of the lost tribe of Reuben. On his return to Amsterdam, Montezinos, né Aaron Levi, reported his astonishing discovery to Rabbi Menasseh ben Israel, the same ben Israel who had been the tutor of my ancestor Abraham Israel Pereira. The rabbi accepted Montezinos's story on faith and used his printing press to spread the word throughout Europe and America. To the millenarian ben Israel, Montezinos's encounter was a confirmation of the Torah's prophecy that Israel's dispersed children would one day return to the Holy Land from the four corners of the earth, and bring to birth the Messianic Kingdom. Ben Israel's imprimatur on a centuries-old conjecture identifying indigenous Americans with Israel's lost tribes took the civilized world by storm. This New World gospel was avidly nurtured and propagated into our own century by—among other Christian traditions—the prophecies in the Book of Mormon.

That same sense of mystery returned in 1977, when I made my way to Chan K'in's thatch-roofed hut. The books of Robert D. Bruce, the Oklahoma-born linguist and anthropologist, had acquainted me with the Lacandon elder's stories and parables, which Bruce had been collecting for two decades. On my first visit to Nahá with Bruce, I would hear these parables firsthand: "What the men of the city do not realize is that the roots of all living things are tied together," Chan K'in exclaimed as we sat and smoked hand-rolled cigars in the thatch-

roofed, mahogany-sided "god house." "When a tree is felled in the forest, a star falls from the sky. That is why, before you cut down a mahog-
any, you must ask permission of the keeper of the forest, and you must
ask permission of the keeper of the stars."

On first reading the Zohar some years later, I was thrilled to discover the seeds of Chan K'in's wisdom in the words of Rabbis Abba
and Eleazar, who upon seeing two shooting stars intersect in the night
sky, embarked on a lengthy discourse on the relation between heavenly
bodies and the living beings below.

> All the stars in the firmament keep watch over this world;
> they are appointed to minister to every individual object in
> this world, to each object a star. Herbs and trees, grass and
> wild plants, cannot flourish and grow except for the influ-
> ences of the stars who stand above them and gaze upon them
> face to face, each according to his fashion. . . .

Rabbis Abba and Eleazar, speaking for the Zohar's putative author,
Shimeon Bar-Yohai, culminate their poetic discourse with a phrase that
in tone and syntax echoes uncannily Chan K'in's elegant proverb:
"And not the tiniest grass blade on earth but has its own appointed star
in heaven."

In the forest-dwelling, ninety-two-year-old storyteller I would
find a living link between his ancient spiritual tradition and the legacy
of my Kabbalist forebears. For nearly two decades, I have cleaved to
this wizened and durable Maya elder as if he were the grandfather I
never knew.

II

My Aunt Simha was seventy when I arrived in Israel in November
1979 for my two-month residence at Mishkenot Sha'ananim. Since her
gout prevented her from traveling to Jerusalem, she advised me to contact our cousin, Avshalom Levy, the only member of our family who
had moved back to Montefiore following the 1967 war. As a well-paid
attorney, Levy could afford the steep mortgages of gentrified Yemin
Moshe. (He had also bought the family's burial plot on the Mount of
Olives.) Levy lived with his wife, Leah, on Judah Touro Street, two
short blocks from my spacious apartment in Mishkenot.

By the time I contacted him I had done some homework on the history of the place. After Sir Moses Montefiore's last visit to Jerusalem in 1875, he commissioned British architect William Smith to erect a resi/ dence for religious Jews on the land bequeathed by the philanthrophist Touro. Completed in 1894, Mishkenot Sha'ananim ("Peaceful Dwell/ ings"), consisted of sixteen apartments, apportioned equally among Ashkenazic and Sephardic families, with synagogues at either end. Of the original Mishkenot, reclaimed from Jordan after the 1967 war, only two eucalyptus trees remained standing. Aunt Simha's detailed descrip/ tion of the Mishkenot of her childhood could have served as the blue/ print for its renovation: "The old houses were built in a single block and divided into rows, all according to the same plan: one large room, a smaller room and kitchen, and a continuous yard along each row of houses, through which you entered the apartments. The doors of the houses were thick and heavy, and the windows had iron bars. This was for security reasons, for fear of the robbers who always abounded, and in accordance with Moses Montefiore's orders, because the Jews of the Old City had not wanted to live outside the walls for fear of being attacked by the robbers. But gradually, as time passed many families got up the cour/ age to live in Mishkenot Sha'ananim and the neighborhood around it, which was known as Montefiore and later on Yemin Moshe. . . ."

When Mishkenot was renovated in 1973, the original thirty/two dwellings were converted into ten luxurious duplex apartments, which Mayor Kollek set aside for visiting artists and dignitaries.

During my first days at Mishkenot I spent hours walking the gardens, exploring the pool of Birket Sultan, the Hasmonaean tombs and other ancient landmarks, and watching the afternoons turn golden on the ramparts of David's citadel. The closest thing to a robber I en/ countered was a tourist guide who offered to sell me a Hasmonaean menorah for a bargain price.

After my first week there, Avshalom Levy led me on a tour of the old Montefiore, passing through the synagogue where my grandfa/ ther had worshipped. The tour ended with a knock on the door of the small house on Touro Street, two blocks north of Mishkenot, where our family had lived. The proprietors, a young couple, invited us inside to inspect the sunlit room where my father and his brothers and sisters were born; where Reina had handed the fat wallet to her grandfather Yitzhak Moshe, and where her father Aharon Haim had prepared *ka/ meot* and written the Torah scroll.

When I led Levy to my own apartment nearby, he exclaimed, "My God, you are living in the flat of my grandfather David Pizanty, the brother of your grandmother Esther. Do you realize," he added, sweeping his arm around the three large rooms, "that you are occupying a space that was used by a family of ten?"

That night my dreams were oppressed by the shades of accusing ancestors. In the morning I removed my belongings from the master bedroom and crept into the small alcove above. For the remainder of my stay, I seldom moved about the apartment without bumping into specters of great-uncles and great-aunts who bustled about the day's chores as the bearded patriarch, his face turned toward the Western Wall, intoned prayers to Elohim in a booming voice that could pierce the gates of heaven.

"You are sitting on a treasure," declared Yehuda Amichai when I visited him and his wife, Hannah, on neighboring Malki Street and recounted some of my family stories. Although I would not get around to setting these stories down for another decade, Amichai's words encouraged me and took some of the sting out of Navon's foreboding "what a burden."

AVSHALOM LEVY IS the most prosperous of my Jerusalem relatives, a fact he invariably touched upon while recounting anecdotes of his impoverished Montefiore childhood. As an attorney he represented powerful corporations and traveled widely in the Middle East and Europe on official business. During our dinners at his well-appointed home on Touro Street with his wife, Leah, and eldest daughter, Haggit, we often sparred over Israeli politics. The *New York Times Magazine* had assigned me to write an article on Peace Now, the antiwar movement started by 350 reservists in 1978. On the eve of Prime Minister Begin's departure for Camp David, Peace Now turned out 100,000 marchers in the streets of Jerusalem. The marchers called for an end to the West Bank settlements and the opening of negotiations with the Arabs. Levy, who had voted for Begin's right-wing Likud coalition, was not impressed. "I know what Shalom Achshav [Peace Now] is against, but what are they for?" he carped continually. "When are they going to form a legitimate political party? Let them dive into the rough-and-tumble of Israeli electoral politics, and then I will have some respect for them."

Levy, who prided himself on his sabra pragmatism, taunted me for brooding too much on Israel's problems.

"You remind me of the Talmudic scholar who was asked if he slept with his beard above the covers or beneath the covers. 'Beneath the covers,' he said, and reflected. 'Or is it above the covers?' and reflected again. 'No, it's beneath the covers.' He had completely forgotten, and was never able to get a good night's sleep again. Perhaps," Levy suggested with a chuckle, "it is time you shaved off your beard and accepted things as they are. As for myself, I sleep soundly every night, thank you very much."

Levy's unmarried eldest daughter, Haggit, who worked in a travel agency, often took mild exception to her father's conservative views. His youngest daughter had married a Lubavitcher Hasid and joined Teshuvah (Religious Return), a movement that had claimed many hundreds of sons and daughters of nonobservant middle-class families, both Sephardic and Ashkenazic.

One Friday evening she showed up unannounced in an unsightly wig with her small daughter and pale, burning husband in black caftan and dangling earlocks. She sat, hawk-eyed, waiting to pounce on the first deviation from Sabbath ritual or the laws of *kashrut*. As a rule, Levy wore his dereliction from religious observance lightly, like a badge of his worldly success. But his daughter's Sabbath vigil took the starch out of him. My wheeler-dealer cousin looked sheepishly contrite as he mumbled the *Kiddush* with wineglass held aloft, his skull-cap askew atop his gray, sparsely thatched scalp.

IN RAMAT GAN I stayed with my mother, who was seventy-three, and whose morale had not yet recovered from the October war and its aftershocks.

Mother rarely visited her older sister Rebecca, now aged seventy-six and in failing health, who lived three blocks away. When they did meet, they invariably talked about Oded, their favorite nephew, whose death in the Sinai seven years earlier had lost none of its immediacy. "Oded was one of a kind," the two old women chanted like a mantra as they shook their heads and clicked their tongues. They also spoke of Nehama, the proud German wife of their nephew Moshe, who visited her son's grave every day to lay fresh flowers on it. Even after Oded was killed, Mother and Aunt Rebecca had continued to criticize Nehama's

aloof, condescending manner. Now Nehama had finally gained acceptance. By grieving for six years with the dedication and constancy of a
proper Sephardi, she had become one of us.

When I visit Moshe and Nehama in their home, they are playing
bridge with a group of close friends. Moshe introduces me to them, all
Ashkenazim in their late forties and early fifties. They are an army captain, a nonreligious diamond dealer, a refrigeration specialist and a kindergarten supervisor. They sit around the card table in the middle of the
spacious living room, heatedly arguing politics as they munch pumpkin and sunflower seeds and assorted dried fruits. Although the stakes
of the game are low, their strident voices suggest parliamentarians at a
Knesset debate.

"In the past year we have all become bridge players," Nehama
explains. "I thought it would be a way to stop our arguing and fighting, but the way we play cards is like a small war. Our elbows get
bruised, our throats become hoarse and we get so mad we often will not
talk to one another after the game. Then we go home and forget all
about it."

My cousins' tastefully decorated house seems to have grown big-
ger since my last visit and is filled with echoes. The color photographs
of Oded appear shrunken against the bare expanse of white wall, but
his extraordinary black eyes return my gaze with the same vulnerable
intensity and challenge.

In the seven years since the death of Oded, Moshe had accom-
modated himself to the rise of secular and fundamentalist extremists and
to the sharp rightward shift in the government's domestic and foreign
policies. He had retired from a twenty-year-long army career in commu-
nications to sell sophisticated antimissile defense systems for a private
company jointly owned by Americans and Israelis. I sensed that coming to grips with the changes in Moshe and Nehama would help me
understand the direction Israel was taking.

"You come here every four or five years, stay a few weeks and
expect to understand what is happening to us?" Nehama challenges me
at once. "You talk to a few moderate Arabs and to leftists in Peace
Now, and that makes you an authority? I grew up with the Arabs, and
I can tell you that you can't trust them—not any of them. The only way
is to keep them down, control them; as soon as they feel any weakness
on your part, they will rise up and destroy you. That is how it is."

"This is a very different Israel we are living in," Moshe reflected, "from the one we knew before the '73 war with Egypt. Americans are the only allies we can trust. On all sides we are surrounded by enemies. The world has become a jungle, and everyone has to fend for himself. We have to sell arms for the foreign revenue, and also to renew our own arms stocks and keep them up to date. If Oded were alive, he would feel the same way."

"They all hate us," Nehama says bitterly, her anger undimmed at what she calls Israel's fair-weather friends. "We try our best to help the underdeveloped countries, and then, when the Arabs come along with their petrodollars, they throw us out and turn against us, like the Africans did. Well, let them go. Let them all go. We will get by, by being just like them—only smarter."

Moshe gets up abruptly to play a tape of an antiwar song written by their surviving son, Ofer. Following Oded's death he had moved to New York.

"Take us to a place where there is no war," sings a chorus of children against a background of synthesized music. "Take us to a place where there is no war, / and the guns don't open fire / And we can go out and all play ball, / We are not troops for hire."

"Ofer has started his own electronics firm," Moshe says while the tape plays on. "He has just returned from a trip to mainland China. He was invited by the government."

"To sell electronics?" I ask, taken aback.

"Yes, and other security-related products of his company," Nehama says, her head held high. "We are very proud of him."

But Nehama's voice lacks conviction. No one could measure up to the dreams she had nurtured for Oded. "I raised Oded to be perfect," she had said in 1973. "Not just good or very good, but perfect."

When I met with Ofer in New York some weeks later he spoke listlessly of his trip to China and showed me pictures of himself at the Great Wall, next to a Chinese functionary. Although he had been spared the close combat that claimed Oded, Ofer still looked haunted by the ghost of his "perfect" older brother, and by the contradictions that govern his own life. When I congratulated him on his antiwar songs, which had received some attention, Ofer shrugged his shoulders. "Oh, that's just a hobby," he said.

The bridge game is interrupted by another flare-up. The army captain, a burly, pink-faced fellow, launches a defense of the extreme right-wing policies of Arik Sharon—the firebrand general and agricul-

ture minister—against the attacks of the refrigeration expert and the pe-
tite, combative kindergarten supervisor.

"He is so fanatical, he scares all of us," says the balding refrigeration man, a veteran of five wars and a former kibbutznik. "He scares
even someone like me, who admired his bold strategy in the Sinai."

"Military strategy and peace strategy are two different things entirely," exclaims the kindergarten supervisor, waving her free hand
energetically as she cracks pumpkin seeds between her teeth. "What
may have seemed brilliant tactics in the battlefield becomes just plain
fascism when applied to domestic problems and the settlement policy."

"Look," says the gray-haired diamond dealer, a recent refugee
from Eastern Europe, "all of us here agree that we should have more
settlements in Judea and Samaria for reasons of security, but not if it
means hurling them in the teeth of world opinion. What's wrong with
a two-month moratorium?"

"Who gives a damn about world opinion?" the captain shouts,
slamming his palm on the card table. "When did world opinion prevent the Arabs from knifing us in the back? Better that the whole world
should turn against us, if we have defensible borders." He wheels on me
and demands gruffly, "What do you think about it?"

I breathe deeply. I had got so engrossed in the passions of the debate that I had lost sight of the issues. I want to say that there isn't
enough oxygen between arguments; that emotions, opinions and facts
get so entangled in Israel they can't be sorted out, and truth is more and
more difficult to arrive at.

I say instead, "I am against the new settlements in the West
Bank, both in their timing and in principle. On the other hand, I find
your arguments persuasive." This seems to disarm the captain, who
was poised to jump down my throat. "I also keep feeling that it is more
important with you Israelis to argue persuasively than to be right."

"That's true," Moshe puts in quickly to stave off another flare-
up. "That has always been the case with Jews, even in biblical times.
We are an argumentative people."

"Today," says Nehama with a strained smile, "we are having
an orgy of breast-beating. What other country will criticize itself as
we do?"

"In Israel," says Moshe, "there are up times and down times.
Now it is down."

Nehama will not let go. "The truth is, we are a country of masochists. We not only punish ourselves, we arrange it so that the rest of the world will punish us also."

"We are stiff-necked even with one another," the diamond dealer says.

The army captain returns to his defense of Sharon, who is Gush Emunim's current hero. "Listen to me. The fact is that we are isolated from the world. It is not a question of masochism, or of settlements now or settlements later. They all hate us simply because we are Jews. That is the reality. Sharon is right—we can trust only ourselves."

During a lull in the argument Nehama takes me aside and presses my arm. "You should realize that each one here has struggled a long time to get where they are. They grew up in the kibbutz, like the refrigeration specialist, or escaped persecution in Europe, like the dia-mond dealer, or they have come up through the army ranks, like the captain. Even the kindergarten supervisor had to fight hard to become an administrator, in competition with men less qualified than she is. Now they are middle-aged, they have children in the army or in the university, they have a house, good jobs, a little money in the bank— and they want to protect them."

I recall that at our last meeting, two weeks after Oded's death, Nehama had complained bitterly about the materialism that was over-taking the country and its leaders. Now, with Oded gone and Ofer only beginning to realize their modest expectations of him, Nehama and Moshe, like their Ashkenazic friends, are holding on to material comforts. Nothing will ever fill the void left by Oded. Nehama's pale face and clear blue eyes remain etched with grief.

"Forgive me, I do not yet know how to show grief. I will learn," Nehama had greeted me, stiff-backed and dry-eyed, six years earlier. Now she has learned. She and Moshe have become experts at mourn-ing, and throw themselves into keeping alive Oded's memory. Every part of the house is charged with some memory of Oded: his bedroom and studio, where his army regalia and decorations lie intact, along with his school diploma and perfect grade cards as well as the books he read and the records he liked to play. The house has become Oded's memorial, as much as the gravestone where Nehama brings flowers every day and the hillside in Arad, near Masada, where Moshe and other soldiers' fathers have erected a huge monument to all the boys of Oded's unit who fell in battle.

On an impulse, I remind Nehama of the prediction she had

made about the soldiers returning from the Yom Kippur War: "After peace is made this will be the main thrust of reform. The young soldiers who fought for this country will demand to be represented. When this happens, Oded's death will begin to have some meaning for me."

I ask her if the Peace Now movement, founded by battle-trained young officers and reservists of Oded's age, had given substance to her words.

"No." Nehama shakes her head emphatically. "They have gone too far to the left, and lost their influence with the rank and file. I don't think Oded would have had much patience with their naïve idealism. These are well-meaning but inexperienced young people who are look-ing for something." Her blue eyes narrow; she purses her lips. "They are not going to find it."

III

In mid-November I paid a visit to Eliyahu Eliachar and found him in failing health. His sharp patrician manner had mellowed and he argued with less vigor than previously; but he still sat erect in his chair when talking about Israel's Sephardim and the imperatives of peaceful coexis-tence with the Arabs. He had vigorously propounded this view in a re-cent book, *To Live with the Palestinians.*

Eliachar admitted that the status of the Sephardim had improved somewhat under Menachem Begin, who was swept into office in the 1977 elections on the strength of the Sephardic vote. "Everything has changed since Sadat's visit," Eliachar said. "Sephardim by the thou-sands lined the streets to cheer him, as if they had suddenly remembered their golden past in Arab lands. Now there are Sephardic actors, Sephardic musicians, Sephardic chefs and restaurant owners who are establishing a Middle Eastern cultural presence."

Eliachar approved of his good friend Yitzhak Navon, who had struck a moderate stance as Israel's new president, but he doubted the party bosses would ever permit him to be prime minister. Eliachar also lauded Sephardic chief rabbi Ovadia Yossef, who called for the evacu-ation of the West Bank and the start of peace negotiations with the Palestinians. On the political right, David Levy, Begin's housing min-ister, was a rising star as the first Sephardic politician of cabinet rank. "Levy's a wonderful boy who tends to see political realities through colored glasses, but he knows his constituency," Eliachar conceded. "I think he will go far with Likud."

Even before Sadat's visit in 1977, the Black Panthers had led the way in promoting a Sephardic rapprochement with the Arabs. Reflect- ing the views of their mentor Eliachar, they passed a resolution at their national convention which proclaimed: "A just peace is only possible on the basis of a mutual recognition of Israel and the Palestinians. . . . Each of them is entitled to an independent and sovereign state."

All of the Black Panthers I had interviewed six years before were prospering: Charlie Bitton was a Knesset minister from the Commu- nist party, Rakah; Marciano and Shemesh had become entrepreneurs and ran a popular café in Jerusalem and a Tel Aviv discotheque on Di- zengoff Road, respectively. But Marciano, Bitton and the other Pan- thers refused to join forces with Peace Now, whose ranks were predominantly Eastern European. "Our aims are similar," Marciano conceded when I tracked him down in his café, "but they are afraid we will contaminate them with our left-wing politics. Peace Now remains as lily-white as an Ashkenazic bride."

Yitzhak Navon's and my cousin Malka's predictions that Se- phardim would become assimilated through army service and intermar- riage have been partially borne out. At election time, however, Sephardim and Orientals voted as a solid bloc, suspicious of any politi- cian to the left of their anointed "king," Menachem Begin. In spite of the rising rate of intermarriage and the successes of individual members of the community, most Sephardim and Orientals still lived in shabby low-rent tenement housing like the Katamomim; as Eliachar had pointed out, they remained near the bottom in education and the job market, a notch above the poorest Palestinians who do most of Israel's manual labor. "These unrelieved disparities," Eliachar concluded, "represent a time bomb under Israel's foundations many times more powerful than any external Arab threat."

IV

After three weeks of tender care and nurturance from the staff at Mishkenot, I took the *servis* to Hebron, half hoping I might run into Hasan on a family visit. Ruth Cheshin, Mayor Kollek's personal assist- ant, who claimed descent from a Moshe Pereira who had been a rabbi in Hebron, admonished me to look up our common ancestor's grave; but I had no more luck finding his grave than I had locating my great-great-grandfather's burial site seven years earlier. Could it be they were one and the same?

IN SPITE OF Camp David and the recently signed peace with Egypt, the atmosphere in Hebron was a good deal tenser than on my first visit. Platoons of Israeli soldiers patrolled the streets, in part to pro-tect the settlers of Kiryat Arba and Hebron who insisted on conducting Shabbat services in the center of the city. After six settlers were shot by a Palestinian in the old Hadassah medical clinic that was now a Jewish enclave, Begin pledged to erect two Jewish schools in Hebron. Weeks after the murder of the six settlers, members of the Gush Emunim underground planted explosives in the cars of two West Bank mayors, injuring one and blowing off the legs of Nablus Mayor Bassam Shaka.

Abner's Tomb was unguarded and strewn with litter. In the *shuk* I was met with hostile glances from Arab passersby, who evidently questioned my presence in Hebron. On walking into a coffeehouse I had frequented with Hasan I was recognized by a youth, who ex-claimed "Hasan Denmark!" and offered to take me to Hasan's mother. As soon as we left the *shuk* and started climbing the hill to Hasan's fam-ily home, the atmosphere lightened. Children and adults greeted me with smiles, introducing themselves as cousins or nephews of Hasan and inviting me to their homes for coffee.

I met Hasan's mother in a sunny courtyard crisscrossed with clotheslines on which her niece was hanging the day's wash. She looked about seventy, with henna marks on her face and the Palestinian dashiki covering her thin, taut body. Her Arab daughter-in-law sat be-side her, dressed in white as though in mourning, and Hasan's two sons played nearby. I was introduced as "Uncle Victor" to the boys, who salaamed and shook my hand solemnly.

"Kalifa is sad that Hasan is away," her mother-in-law explained as we drank her thick sweet Turkish coffee. "She doesn't like that the children will grow up and not know their father. But"—she waved her hand—"the situation in Hebron is not good. For Hasan, there could be problems here now—perhaps it is just as well he is away."

This was only the second reference I had heard to Hasan's past career as a spy, and the problems it continued to cause him.

When I asked Hasan's mother if she knew of any Pereras in He-bron, she seemed mystified. But her nephew Khalil, who was serving as translator, offered to take me to someone who might know.

"My uncle Yousuf is a silversmith," Khalil explained. "We will go to him now."

Over another cup of thick sweet coffee in his small shop, Hasan's uncle Yousuf assured me that he personally knew a Brera who was a tradesman in silver and gold.

"I do not recall his first name, but he wears a *keffiyeh* as I do"— he pointed to his black checkered headdress—"and travels often to Nablus and Jordan. This man must be your cousin."

"Yes, but was he a Jew who converted?" I asked, growing wary. Hasan and his relatives seemed bent on linking me by hook or by crook to their extended family.

He raised both arms and grinned helplessly. "That I do not know. But my great-uncle Sheikh al-Sharif has lived in Hebron since"—he waved his hand to denote an eternity—"since the last cen-tury. Perhaps he can answer your questions. Come, I will take you to him."

Once again, my heart raced at the prospect of meeting with Sheikh al-Sharif. Our interview had sat in memory as a vial that re-leases its elixir in stages, as its recipient grows in merit and understand-ing. The truth is, I had been lazy and negligent, and feared submitting to the sheikh's laser scrutiny without the mediation of his grandson. How much of the magic of that first encounter had been the work of Hasan?

Yousuf led me through the winding streets of Hebron's *shuk,* stopping frequently for a quick business transaction or a more leisurely chat with a relative. I had to decline invitations to coffee each time my name was linked to Hasan's.

There was no aura of expectancy as we approached the mosque. And I heard no grunt of recognition as I waited outside the entrance for Yousuf to introduce me. I walked into a brightly lit room crowded with visitors. The sheikh sat on a carpet, small and shrunken, shouting to his guests at the top of his remarkably vigorous voice. As we waited by the entrance, Yousuf whispered that the visitors were travelers from

Jordan. "Sheikh al-Sharif's elder son is in Amman," Yousuf explained. "He is seventy-five and ailing, but the Israeli authorities will not give him an entry permit. That is why the sheikh is so upset."

Far from diminishing his holiness, the spectacle of the aged sheikh shaking his fists in a fury enhanced his legitimacy in my eyes. Holy man or not, Sheikh al-Sharif was flesh and blood, and as liable as any aggrieved mortal to lose sight of the long view when his progeny were threatened.

After the visitors left, Yousuf approached the sheikh and reintroduced me. His words drew a blank until the sheikh's wife, who recognized me, leaned over and whispered in his ear.

"Your friend Hasan is gone!" Sheikh al-Sharif said aloud. "He is living with an infidel in a northern country. If he does not return soon, he will lose his spirit, and there will be nothing I can do for him. You should go to him and bring him back."

Stunned, I promised the sheikh I would write Hasan a letter. A tense silence ensued, which Yousuf finally broke by relaying my request: Had the sheikh any recollection of a Rabbi Aharon or Moshe Perera?

"Brera?" the sheikh intoned. "Brera? The only Brera I knew was the milkman."

Evidently he had misheard my question. But repetition evinced no better reply, and Sheikh al-Sharif was losing patience. He gave me a perfunctory blessing and I walked out into the afternoon light. As the shock wore off, I was flooded by a sense of relief, as if a huge weight had slipped from my shoulders. For days after, I would be overtaken by giggling fits at the thought of my illustrious ancestor Brera, the milkman of Hebron.

(It would be several more years before I was able to verify, in the writings of Yitzhak Ben-Tzvi and elsewhere, that there had indeed been Pereiras who served as rabbis of Hebron. Ruth Cheshin's great-great-grandfather Moshe Bar Abraham Pereira had emigrated from Bosnia. As chief rabbi of Hebron, he had been involved in a dispute over the apportionment of funds collected by emissaries abroad for the community's yeshivas. Moshe Pereira died in 1865 and was buried in Hebron. Another Pereira, Mehoram, had also lived in Hebron in the 1860s, where he was known as a magician and wonder-worker who employed Kabbala to demonstrate the power of God. According to Ben-Tzvi, Rabbi Aharon Raphael Haim Moshe Pereira had made *aliyah* from Salonika, and settled in Jerusalem. He had been called a wise man of Kabbala and "Ash of Yitzhak"—a laudatory reference to his father, Yitzhak—which became the title of one of his three books of Kabbala. Another of his books was titled "Reflections on Peace" (*Divrei Shalom*), and he also composed a key to a book by Rabbi Chaim de la Rosa of Salonika. Like his son Yitzhak Moshe, my great-great-grandfather had written a testament to his sons, which has been lost. No mention is made of where Aharon Raphael Haim Pereira was buried, and there is no living member of the family left who knows.)

THE FOLLOWING WEEK I gave a slide presentation in Mishke-not on the Lacandon Mayas. The Lacandon jungle seemed the most remote place imaginable from the everyday concerns of Israelis, and yet I wanted to impart a sense of Chan K'in's wisdom and approach the Maya/Kabbala nexus from the opposite end. Mayor Kollek and Ruth Cheshin attended the talk, along with a half-dozen Eastern European artists who were guests at Mishkenot.

The audience sat with blank faces as I recounted the threats to the rain forest and to the Lacandon culture by the Mexican loggers and Pemex, the government oil monopoly, which had just started explora-tory drilling in the area of Nahá. But I captured their attention when I quoted Chan K'in's parable of the trees and the stars, and related it to Rabbis Abba and Eleazar and the *Zohar*.

Afterward Cheshin, relieved, judged my brief talk a success, based on her observation that Mayor Kollek had not dozed off, as he often did at public functions. The mayor later offered to escort me around the Maya wing of the Israel Museum, of which he was inordi-nately proud.

V

In December 1979 I visited a leader of the 300 Ethiopian Jews, known in the West as Falashas, who had made their way to the Holy Land in the past two decades. I had long been fascinated by this isolated com-munity of descendants from the tribe of Dan, who for centuries had lived according to the Five Books of Moses, convinced they were the last Jews on earth.

I found Abraham Yodai and his wife in Ashdod, "the Chicago of Israel," a fast-growing northern city dominated by its Moroccan and Oriental immigrants.

Yodai, a slender man in his early thirties with large, intense black eyes, had arrived in Israel on a tourist visa in 1970 after waiting for two years to obtain a passport. As we spoke his wife, Esther, a softly attractive young woman of twenty-six or twenty-seven who wore a well-groomed Afro and a floor-length flower-print dress, hovered nearby; she plied us with Ethiopian salads and sweets, 7-Ups and Cokes, while carrying in her free arm the smallest of their three children. The flat was decorated with garish bric-a-brac and plastic flowers, the ubiquitous Israeli kitsch; Esther's bright woven baskets, ceramic pots and other handiwork were crowded in one corner of the living room. In Ethiopia she had been an artisan, like most Falasha women, and had contributed to the family's livelihood with her ceramics and basket weaving. In Israel she did it as a hobby, she told us, for she would have considered it demeaning to accept money for her craft from fellow Jews.

"The Holy Land was always in our hearts and in our minds," Abraham Yodai said, "long before we learned of the Jewish state of Israel. There was never a time we did not dream of coming here. Now, with the persecution of Beta Yisrael [Falashas] in Ethiopia, further complicated by the droughts, famines and the terrible civil war, emigration to Israel has become a question of life and death for my brethren."

Abraham recalled bitterly that in 1956, when Emperor Haile Selassie agreed to allow fifty Falasha families to emigrate to Israel as a first contingent, Israeli leaders had balked. "They said to us, 'Let us wait and discuss it with our rabbis, and resolve the issue of your legitimacy before we allow you in.' It was not until 1971, when Sephardic chief rabbi Ovadia Yossef ruled favorably on our claim, that the question of our Jewishness was settled. By then, the Beta Yisrael community in Ethiopia had shrunk from half a million to about 30,000, cut down by terrible hardships and persecution by our Christian neighbors."

In 1971, the same year Ovadia Yossef recognized the Beta Yisrael as Jews, Interior Minister Yosef Burg issued an expulsion order for Abraham because his tourist visa had expired, and he was forced to go into hiding.

"They were saying I was not a Jew," Yodai recalled. "I, Abraham Yodai, who prayed every Sabbath in my village in Tigrai, kept all the Commandments and risked my life every day to keep the God of Israel alive among us—was accused of not being a Jew. . . . When I think of it, even now, tears spring to my eyes. . . ."

At that moment tears welled in Abraham Yodai's eyes and sprang out in a visible arc, like the tears of martyred saints in the paintings of medieval masters.

"Abraham," I asked, as tears welled in my own eyes, "what has happened to your religious customs since you arrived? Do you still keep the Sabbath?" I had read that the Falashas had no knowledge of the Talmud or the Commentaries, and practiced a Judaism that had remained virtually unchanged in more than 2,000 years.

Yodai took a deep breath and remained silent for a time. "We try to attend the synagogue every Sabbath, for the children's sake, but sometimes we are too tired. And there are other laws we are forgetting. In Ethiopia the tenth and fifteenth of every month was a holy day, which we observed faithfully. We calculated the observance of Yom Kippur by the cycles of the moon, because we had no calendar. . . . In their times of the moon, the women would leave our huts and live apart for eight days. Now we do not observe these customs, although I still do not sleep with my wife during her time. The old people, our teachers and wise men who know the customs—they are all in Ethiopia. We are only the young here, like children without their elders, and we are forgetting our laws."

"What can be done?" I ask Yodai. "How can we help?"

"Tell about us," he said. "Tell the Jews in America about our situation. If the Beta Yisrael do not leave Ethiopia in the next three to five years, there may be no one left to bring out, and their disappearance will be on the conscience of Jews everywhere—not only in Israel but all over the world. If our appeals are not heard here, if our fellow Jews cannot or will not help us, we will raise our voices to the heavens until they reach the ears of Elohim, may he have mercy on all of us. . . ."

None of my encounters with Jews from far corners of the globe—nor any of my readings in Spinoza, the *Zohar* or the Torah—had touched my Jewish core as had Abraham Yodai's testimony. If this man's claim was denied by self-appointed white-skinned Eastern European judges, what right had I to call myself a Jew?

Four years after that interview Israel brought the few thousand remaining Jews out of Ethiopia in a well-executed, highly publicized airlift code-named Operation Moses, which had been negotiated by two U.S. Middle Eastern experts. By then many of Abraham Yodai's elders who taught the ancient laws and traditions had fallen victim to famine, disease and old age. Just as Yodai feared, the Israelis waited until the Ethiopian Falasha community was reduced to a manageable size before they accepted them as fellow Jews and airlifted them with self-congratulatory fanfare to Israel.

VI

In the 1980s, as my now-aged mother came to need constant care, my sister's son Daniel and I visited Israel more frequently. Even in her weakened condition, Mother found ways to drive a wedge between us, altering her will from week to week to favor one or the other of us. (Her final testament divided her dwindling inheritance from Father among my sister, Rebecca, Daniel and myself in about equal portions.)

In 1985 *Mother Jones* magazine sent me to Israel to do a piece on Israel's role as arms trader to the Third World. Earlier I had spoken on that subject at the Institute for Policy Studies in Washington. A year later I gave the same talk in the West Bank, at the invitation of a Palestinian journalist with Bir Zeit University. A photographer for the Guatemalan Embassy took my picture at the first lecture, and some weeks later a letter was sent to Rabbi Marc Tanenbaum of the American Jewish Committee by Rabbi Morton M. Rosenthal, the director of Latin American Affairs for the B'nai B'rith Anti-Defamation League. He included letters from the vice president of the Guatemalan Jewish community, who, among other things, accused me of belonging to "a leftist organization subsidized by the Soviets"—an apparent reference to the Institute of Policy Studies, where I had occasionally lectured.

The noose hung on my neck by the pro-Israel lobby after my "Letter From Israel" appeared in *The New York Times* was drawn tighter by imperceptible degrees until the day, in 1987, when my agent told me I was now "brown listed" by national publications I had formerly contributed to and was unlikely to write for them again.

I did continue to write for *Present Tense* on issues bridging the Middle East with my renewed interest in Guatemala. On my increasingly frequent visits to Israel, I stayed at the American Colony Hotel, where I came to know the emerging Palestinian moderate leaders, among them Hanna Siniora, Saib Arakat and Faisal al-Husseini.

After *Present Tense* closed down following its exposé of the pro-Israel lobby, I was unable to publish any of my articles on Israeli-Palestinian issues, including my reports on the crucial role played by Faisal al-Hus-seini and other moderates in bringing Arafat to the peace table.

IN THE SUMMER OF 1985 I at last made contact with Hasan al-Sharif, when he visited his family in Hebron. He looked spectrally thin and suffered from angina, but the spark still burned in his eyes and his mind was as sharp as ever. Hasan took me for a walk around Abra-ham's Oak, where he told me for the first time of the lasting effects on his health of the torture he had undergone years before at the hands of Israeli agents. There was no trace of bitterness in his voice as he spoke of his brief career in espionage, which he looked back on as a youthful in-discretion. But Hasan would neither confirm nor deny my surmise that he had been a double agent.

In the afternoon Hasan took me to visit the mosque of his grand-father, who had died two years before, "filled with grace and sadness," in Hasan's words. Sheikh al-Sharif's widow, younger than her hus-band by nearly half a century, was devoting the rest of her life to keeping his memory alive.

In the afternoon Hasan took me to Deheisha, the Palestinian ref-ugee camp outside of Bethlehem, where he wanted me to meet Rad-wan, a journalist friend of his who was under house arrest. We were stopped at the entrance by Israeli soldiers, who checked my journalistic credentials. After some haggling, the soldiers allowed Hasan into the camp as my assistant. His journalist friend came across as Hasan de-scribed him—an even-handed, un-ideological observer; Radwan saw both the PLO and the Israeli positions with a lucid impartiality that was a kind of gift all its own. The journalist's responsibility to this gift had cost him dearly, as the hard-line Palestinians accused him of be-traying his Fatah comrades and the Israelis censored his writings and confined him to his home.

Two other images endure from that visit to Deheisha: the village *mukhtar*, stripped by the Israelis of his authority, spent his day playing *shesh-besh* (backgammon) in the sun outside his home. The eyes of Radwan's ten-year-old daughter flared when she told us she was a fol-lower of George Habash—the head of the extremist Palestine Libera-tion Front—and would fight with bare fists to free her people from the

Israeli yoke. When I asked her what else she planned to do when she grew up, her eyes softened and she said in a small voice, "I want to be a schoolteacher."

Hasan, ever the teacher, watched the tears rise to my eyes and said, "Here in this girl you see how my people have learned to live in two worlds, two realities at the same time: the world of their dreams and the world of their rage."

Outside Deheisha we ran into the white van occupied by Rabbi Moshe Levinger, which had been parked there for several weeks. On an impulse we knocked on his door. Hasan introduced himself as a friend of the rabbi's son—which happened to be true—whereas I lied and said I was acquainted with his wife, Miriam, whom I had set eyes on only once, when she and other settlers took over the Hadassah medi⁄cal clinic in Hebron.

After some warm⁄up conversation about the Kabbala and my great⁄great⁄grandfather, I asked Levinger why he had parked his van outside Deheisha. For the first time, he showed pale gums and dark brown teeth in a grimace, as his voice rose several decibels.

"I am here," he said, "to make certain these people receive their punishment."

I assumed he meant the militant dissidents and the stone⁄throw⁄ers, but when I asked him why they should be punished, Rabbi Lev⁄inger answered, "Because of who they are."

"Palestinians, you mean?"

Hasan touched my shoulder with a look of profound sadness. "Rabbi Levinger means we are to be punished because we are the chil⁄dren of Ishmael, the outcast son of Abraham—isn't that so, Rabbi Levinger?"

"That is correct," Rabbi Levinger said, fixing his eyes on Hasan for the first time. "And who are you?"

"I, Rabbi Levinger, am one of those children of Ishmael, and I have already been punished."

"So you are one of *them?*" the Brooklyn⁄born rabbi exploded, pointing up the hill with one arm. He gazed on Hasan with mingled disdain and pity, and ushered us out without another word. As we stepped down from the van, I got a whiff of decay from Rabbi Lev⁄inger's breath.

In May 1988, three years after our meeting, Rabbi Levinger stormed into an Arab home in Hebron after his daughter accused

members of the Samooch family of having harassed her. Levinger as-
saulted the mother, her son and her seven-year-old daughter before he
was stopped by an Israeli policeman, whom Levinger spat upon and
called "a PLO agent." The soldier brought charges against Levinger,
and he was sentenced to ten weeks' imprisonment for trespass and as-
sault and insulting an Israeli policeman. Four months later, Levinger
opened fire on a crowd of thirty Palestinians he claimed had been ston-
ing his car. A forty-two-year-old merchant was shot in the back and
died at the scene. In June 1990, Rabbi Levinger was tried for man-
slaughter in a courtroom filled with his vociferous supporters from
Gush Emunim and the militant Kach party. Under a plea bargain,
Rabbi Levinger received a one-year prison sentence with seven months
suspended—a fraction of the time spent in jail by Palestinian stone-
throwers. Levinger served only ten weeks of his sentence; the day he was
released he boasted publicly, "Next time I will take greater care not to
miss my target."

BEFORE DAWN ON the morning of February 25, 1994, during
the Jewish celebration of Purim and the Muslim observances of Rama-
dan, Doctor Baruch Goldstein of Kiryat Arba opened fire on Muslim
worshippers in the Mosque of Abraham with his Galil automatic rifle.
Before Goldstein was subdued and killed by enraged survivors, he mur-
dered at least twenty-nine and wounded at least ninety Muslim worshippers. Goldstein, a Brooklyn-born immigrant and a surgeon who
had treated fellow settlers wounded in clashes with Palestinians, had
been a close associate of Rabbi Meir Kahane, the founder of Kach. The
Kach party and its affiliate Kahane Chai, founded by Kahane's son
Benjamin, joined Gush Emunim in calling for the Jewish reclamation
of the biblical lands of Israel by expelling all Arabs from the West
Bank.

The day after the massacre in the Mosque of Abraham I attempted to reach Hasan to express my grief and sense of shame. I could
not locate him at the Copenhagen address where he had lived for years
with his Danish wife. The outbreak of the Intifada and the rising violence in Hebron had driven a wedge between us, and I had not seen
Hasan or heard from him in several years.

In Kiryat Arba the exultation was palpable for several days after
the shooting. Baruch Goldstein was eulogized as a saint and martyr

who had sanctified God's name by killing Arabs in a redemptive act of self-sacrifice. As it happened, two of his intellectual accomplices in the Hebron massacre—Rabbis Kahane and Levinger—were born and raised in Brooklyn, as was Baruch—né Benjamin—Goldstein. I grew up in Bensonhurst, a few blocks from Goldstein's birthplace, after emigrating to the States from Guatemala at age twelve. We frequented the same Jewish community center on Bay Parkway—over a decade apart—and attended Zionist kaffeeklatsches in the same Bensonhurst and East Flatbush neighborhoods.

In the fifties and sixties, these neighborhoods had a reputation for being cradles of Zionist extremists of both right and left. As a teenager I belonged to Hechalutz Hatzair, a Zionist group linked with Israel's socialist movement. I recall discussions at our weekly meetings where issues of moral equivalency arose that were identical to those espoused by Kahane's and Levinger's followers. How many Arabs are worth the life of a single Jew? As the tally climbed into the hundreds, we remained oblivious to the irony that we were mimicking grotesquely Goebbels's doctrine on Germans and Jews.

Our weekly gatherings were often crashed by doctrinaire Stalinists as well as Orthodox zealots—precursors of Kahane and Levinger—who harangued us in the poisonous vocabulary of ethnic cleansing, calling among other outrages for the expulsion of all Arabs from the young state of Israel. These zealots identified the Palestinians with Amalek, Esau's son and the personification of the Jews' biblical enemy, who must be wiped off the face of the earth. I was not surprised to hear that Goldstein frequently referred to the Palestinians as "Nazis," since the Kahanists believe that Amalek reappears in a different guise in each generation. In our Zionist summer camp in the Catskills, we recapitulated the ancient disputes between the followers of Judah Halevi and Maimonides, as many of us prepared our predestined return—or *aliyah*—to Israel.

The proto-Kahanists and -Levingerites championed Halevi as their prophet and embraced his implicit rejection of Ishmael as Abraham's "bad seed." Today's settler rabbis are intimately acquainted with Halevi's admonition to the king of the Khazars that the Law of Moses was given to the Jews alone when he led them out of Egypt, because "we are the elect of mankind. . . ."

The rabbis of Kiryat Arba, Yamit, Kfar Tapuach and other West Bank settlements who see themselves as the cutting edge of God's elect and harbingers of the Messiah, draw on Halevi's arguments and the Old Testament exhortations against Amalek to justify the expulsion of Arabs from the West Bank.

The air breathed by the Jewish settlers *is* different; it is a purer, biblical air from an eternal past when Jews lived in God's radiance and all others lived in their shadow as enemies, servants or outcasts. Spurred on by the approaching end of the millennium, which Jewish tradition associates with miracles and portents, the Kahanist and Gush Emunim rabbis believe that only when the last square foot of Judea and Samaria is reclaimed from Amalek's descendants—or Ishmael's impure seed— will the Messiah enter Jerusalem through the Golden Gate.

Rabbi Yaacov Perrin spoke literally when he declared at Goldstein's funeral that a million Arabs are not worth a Jew's fingernail. And Miriam Goldstein, of the postwar generation of Bensonhurst zealots, drew on the Book of Esther, which Goldstein had been reading the day before the massacre, when she praised her son as a hero who prevented a planned massacre of Jews by Hebron's Arabs. "He did what he did," the settlers repeat in the Old Testament litany, as if Goldstein were Queen Esther.

I have wondered what my great-great-grandfather would have made of the zealots from both sides who have taken over Hebron. In his time, decades before the riots of 1929, Jews and Arabs coexisted peacefully, as they had by and large for centuries. As a mystic and healer, Aharon Raphael Haim Perera was absorbed with the same issues of redemption and the Messiah's arrival that troubled Baruch Goldstein mightily, and obsess the rabbis in Hebron and Kiryat Arba. But the books of practical Kabbala my great-great-grandfather published in the 1870s invoke ancient formulas of Abulafia, Moses Cordovero and other Kabbalists mainly to invite God's favor and ward off the evil eye.

Sheikh al-Sharif died a decade ago and was thus spared having to witness the massacre of a number of his followers in the Mosque of Abraham. But Sheikh Mohammed Kafrawi may have spoken for him when he asked, at the end of a prayer service in Al Aqsa Mosque to honor the victims, "How can the Palestinians find security when there is more than one Baruch?" And, he might have added, more than one Moshe.

In the days following the massacre, while Prime Minister Yitzhak Rabin cast out Baruch Goldstein from Abraham's fold in the biblical language of excommunication, Levinger's and Kahane's lieutenants agitated to have his remains interred in the Jewish cemetery where Rabbi Moshe Bar Abraham Pereira and others of my ancestors lie uncommemorated, beside Hebron's sages and holy men. Instead Goldstein was buried in a park next to Meir Kahane Square. His grave has become a shrine visited by fundamentalist Jews who are intent on raising Goldstein to the ranks of martyred saints.

Three weeks after the shooting in the Mosque of Abraham, Rabbi Levinger was called to Jerusalem's Magistrate Court to answer relatively minor charges of having defied an army order in June 1992 to leave a closed military area. A trial date was set for April 12. Rabbi Levinger remained silent on the massacre, but his daughter Rachel Levinger, fifteen, spoke for him when she declared, "Now the Arabs know their place and they see that the Jews are in charge." Echoing her father and mother she warned, ominously, "We'll only leave here in coffins."

CHAPTER X

EGYPT

IN LATE DECEMBER 1979 I traveled to the Sinai en route to upper Egypt and Cairo. Aunt Simha had enjoined me to visit my grandfather's grave in Alexandria and recite the Kaddish, an observance the family had neglected since 1923, when Father last visited Grandfather's grave.

"How do I locate it?" I asked, reminding her of my failure to find any trace of my greatgreatgrandfather's remains in Hebron, or of Abraham Pereira's yeshiva for that matter.

"Just go to the synagogue. I'm sure his name will be in the registry. And inquire among the older Jews. Someone is bound to remember where he is buried."

Aunt Simha herself had never traveled outside the Holy Land. To help me in my quest she produced a calling card of her father's she had found with his belongings. It pictured a hand with index finger pointing eastward and the word *sheliah* (envoy) below Grandfather's name.

On Christmas Day 1979 I boarded a bus for Eilat, planning to connect with a group touring the Sinai. When I first visited Santa Katerina Monastery at the foot of Mount Sinai in 1973, I engaged the Greek Orthodox patriarch in a lengthy conversation on Middle Eastern religions; to my surprise, he invited me to return on a retreat so I could pursue my studies in the monastery library. Now, as a result of the Camp David agreements, Sinai was being returned to Egypt, and I was curious to find out if the patriarch's invitation still stood.

Santa Katerina, or Saint Catherine, is a religious fortress erected by order of Queen Helena in the fourth century A.D. to house the burning bush, from which God spoke to Moses. (The monks claim the roots of the original bush lie under the altar in St. Helena's chapel.) With its thirtyfoothigh granite walls, Santa Katerina reminded me of the soaring, nearly inaccessible Byzantine monasteries of Meteora, high on the pinnacles above Greece's Thessalian plain. But Santa Katerina sits on an outcropping at the bottom of a desert wadi the monks have coaxed into bloom with lush flower and vegetable gardens. Santa Katerina's basilica is encircled by redandblack gran ite peaks where giants once walked in Elohim's shadow, and where Moses received the commandments that became bedrock for three of the world's great religions.

An Israeli tour guide dropped me at the entrance to the monas, tery, which is open to visitors only during morning hours. I approached the first monk I saw and asked to speak with the patriarch. When I gave his name the monk informed me that the patriarch had been reas, signed to Greece. Could he be of any assistance?

I congratulated the black-robed, woolen-capped monk on his excellent English, and he introduced himself as Brother Michael of Pittsburgh, Pennsylvania. Flustered, I informed him of my seven-year, old invitation and handed him my calling card. Brother Michael perused the card from behind thick horn-rimmed glasses, withdrew and reappeared fifteen minutes later to ask if I might consider staying in the Santa Katerina hostel, outside the monastery walls.

"I would prefer a room inside the monastery," I said, reminding him of the patriarch's invitation. "I have need of reflection."

"Very well then," Brother Michael said in his plainspoken man, ner. "You may stay for three nights in one of our guest rooms. Our other guest at present is Professor Oshi of Osaka University, who is a specialist in Byzantine architecture."

That evening I attended the vespers service in the basilica, and sat in awe of the massive chandeliers with pendant ostrich eggs, flanked by soaring Byzantine columns and arches. On the cupola of the adjoin, ing iconostasis I glimpsed the Pantocrator Christ, surrounded by kneel, ing Disciples. The gilt mosaic seemed to glow with an eerie light from within. The *Kyrie Eleisons* ("Lord have mercy") of the assembled monks rose and fell like ocean waves, crashing against the thick chapel walls with a sonority that reverberated inside my chest. So this, then, was the power Aunt Simha attributed to my great-grandfather—the booming voices of unshakable belief that could pierce the vaults of heaven and reach the guardian stars. Tears flowed as my chest heaved with spasms of release, sorrow and a regret that had no boundaries. My soul could not fathom the generations I had been in exile from my ori, gins. I felt a hand on my shoulder and turned to see Brother Michael peering at me solicitously from behind thick glasses.

The following day I arose before dawn to attend the matins. A three-quarter moon shone on the parapet, spreading a patina on the walls and glass windows of the chapel. I walked to the west end of the citadel, where I had been told the burning bush was kept out of view of the tourists. The "public" raspberry bush, said to be the only one of its kind in the Sinai, shone in the moonlight as though it had caught fire; its slender branches burned without becoming consumed by the lamb bent silver flames.

I attended morning and evening prayers each of my three days in Santa Katerina, without anyone suspecting that I was a Jew—least of all Professor Oshi, who had been told I was a California University scholar completing a book on Middle Eastern religions.

"Ah, how very interesting," Professor Oshi said, bowing from the waist when Brother Michael introduced me. "We must take a walk together so you can acquaint me with this very interesting subject. I my/ self am making drawings of every architectural feature of this monastery. It is a life work. I have completed similar studies in Mount Athos and Meteora, and this work will conclude my labor."

On the morning of New Year's Eve I accompanied Professor Oshi on a walk on Jebel Musa, or Mount Sinai. It was his first excur/ sion outside the walls in the three weeks he had been there. As we turned a corner, we came upon a riveting sight: three Bedouin shepherd girls squatting atop a teardrop/shaped granite boulder. They were veiled, and the middle one played a delicate flute melody to the sheep and goats gathered at her feet.

"How beautiful!" the professor exclaimed, raising his camera. But the shepherd girls quickly averted their kohl/lined eyes, refusing to be photographed. I offered the flutist a small vial of ground/up carda/ mom, or *hell*, which is highly prized by Bedouins as a condiment for their coffee. The shepherd girls relented, and the professor snapped his picture.

"How beautiful!" the professor exclaimed intermittently the re/ mainder of the day, reliving the encounter in memory.

On New Year's Day, while conversing with Brother Michael about insensitive and abusive Israelis, I confessed to him that I was a Jew. He had been telling me about Israeli officers who talked down to the patriarch and to the Bedouin *mukhtars,* ordering them around as if they were prisoners of war.

"I suspected you were a Jew," Brother Michael said with a gleam in his eye that was magnified by his bifocals. "I noticed how you shied away from the illuminated manuscripts in the library. And your emotional response to the services." My unmasking by Brother Michael recalled with a pang the inquisitory *proceso* I had undergone with Canon Bandeña a quarter of a century earlier. But the present circum/stances were different in at least one important respect: The monks had not inquired into my religion as a precondition for inviting me.

"You should know," Brother Michael went on with an air of complicity, "that the brothers get skittish about Jewish guests inside the monastery. And no wonder, since most of them live in a time capsule. Fifteen of the sixteen monks here besides myself are Greeks from Mount Athos. Konstantinos, who cooks our meals and tends the gardens, grew up on an Aegean island and had not even seen a Jew until two years ago. His experience with the Israeli occupiers confirmed many of his apprehensions, I regret to say."

Dropping his guard, Brother Michael confessed to his growing apprehensions regarding the monastic life. He was a serious student of religion with some experience of the world, and he found no one in the monastery to converse with. "I am a quester like you," he said. "And like you I am a fish out of water in hermetic institutions like this one, which regard intellectual curiosity as deviant behavior."

During the course of the day each of the brothers approached me to assure me of my welcome in the monastery, and the patriarch person/ally invited me to return at some future date. But I was not permitted inside the library again. Professor Oshi seemed most surprised of all by my confession.

"You are Jewish? I did not know that you are Jewish. I am Bud/dhist, and am so happy to meet a fellow non/Christian in this remark/able and so beautiful place."

I spent my last hours in Santa Katerina walking the magnificent gardens, pausing by the well where Moses met Zippora, Jethro's daughter. But it was the charnel house that compelled my attention. The ossuary contained layers upon layers of monks' skeletons piled up since the fourth century. Except for the remains of a former guardian named Stephanos, which still conserved his vestments, the thousands of other skeletons had decayed into mounds of dust. I wondered, with a sense of foreboding, if this was all I would ever find of my grandfather.

II

After a week of sightseeing in Upper Egypt I reached Cairo by road and visited the Ben Ezra Synagogue, one of the oldest in the world, which was erected on the spot where Moses is said to have prayed prior to the Exodus. I also met with a handful of Karaite Jews, who dress in the floor-length djellabas of the Egyptian peasant and jealously guard an ancient holy scroll they can no longer read.

I had briefly attended the summit in Aswan between Sadat and Menachem Begin, which produced nothing of lasting significance, apart from its symbolism. The huge blisters on my lips—a gift of the Sinai Desert—made me self-conscious about hobnobbing with the dig-nitaries in attendance. I did, however, deliver a message from a mutual friend to Mrs. Leah Boutros-Ghali, wife of the UN Secretary General, a red-headed Egyptian Jew and candy butcher's daughter. True to her reputation, Mrs. Boutros-Ghali was sensuous and sharp-witted, and poked fun at my attempts to cover my unsightly blisters; they caused me such discomfort that I could barely speak coherently, and I never asked Mrs. Boutros-Ghali if she had known Lawrence Durrell.

In Cairo a few days later I interviewed her husband, who was then Sadat's foreign minister. As one of the architects of Camp David and the peace with Israel, Boutros Boutros-Ghali gave the impression of being a skillful if cagey negotiator; my clearest recollection from that in-terview is the way he paled and fell silent when I asked him about the Muslim Brotherhood, the fanatical fundamentalists who were threaten-ing to topple Sadat. "They are not to be taken lightly," he said pen-sively, and changed the subject. Sadat was assassinated by Muslim fanatics the following year.

Arriving in Alexandria on a blustery January day, I checked in at the rundown but vestigially elegant Cecil Hotel, a few steps from the Mediterranean. My senses still hummed with images of Santa Katerina, Karnak, Abu Simbel, the fabulous tombs of Ramses and Tutankha-men in the Valley of Kings. In Alexandria's wintry streets I felt as if I had left Egypt and arrived at a Greek or Balkan city. The women were tall and almond-eyed, showing traces of their Hellenic and Roman an-cestry. Horse carriages and wagons were still common in the city streets, one of the lingering touches of a Durrellesque *vieux monde*. Slender Ara-bian steeds—their hind legs splinted to carry heavier loads—were harnessed to heavy carts and forced to haul burdens that a dray horse would have balked at. Several times I saw cart drivers viciously lashing them on.

After dark the center of downtown Alexandria was filled with restless young men in tight bell-bottom jeans, crowding the cheap discotheques and the tape and record shops, while their elders sipped tea in dingy, dim-lit coffeehouses. The film *Cleopatra*, banned for years because of Elizabeth Taylor's conversion to Judaism, had belatedly reached Alexandria, and played to packed houses under a peeling billboard that displayed the recumbent star as a gaudily dressed butterball from some Hindi film.

The next morning I stopped at the tourist office to ask for directions to the Eliyahu Hanavi Synagogue. The clerk, a slender woman with large green Levantine eyes, opened a city map and pointed to Shari Nabi Daniel.

"Just walk down this street to Building 60 and look for a small wall on your right. That will be the synagogue—but I doubt you'll find anyone—there are only a few old people left, you know."

"Yes, I know," I said, although I hadn't known.

At Nabi Daniel Street I soon came to Building 60 and approached the huge, rusted iron portal, chained shut. Inside rose an imposing building with a classic facade and a Magen David above the lintel.

I called to a man in a black beret, who shuffled slowly toward the gate. "Ah, Monsieur Perera, we have been expecting you," he said in French. "I am the *gabbai* [synagogue official]. Please come around to the side. We no longer use this entrance."

I turned into the side street and Menahem Mori, as he introduced himself, opened a small metal door and escorted me into the courtyard, which was awash in bright sunlight.

"Our president, Monsieur Setton, received your letter and told us you'd be coming," said Mori, a short, stocky man of about seventy who moved with the unhurried, rolling gait of caretakers, night watchmen and synagogue officials. "I understand your grandfather is buried in Alexandria?"

"That is correct. His name is Aharon Haim Perera."

"A very notable name," said Mori as he ushered me up an elegant staircase and turned right into the vestibule, past a bulletin board

with the words "Communauté Israélite d'Alexandrie" above yellow-
ing announcements of long-outdated events, including a fund-raising
ball and an excursion to Upper Egypt. (I was to discover that most of
Alexandria's aging Jews had never been to Luxor or Abu Simbel, and
they rarely traveled as far south as Cairo.)

"This is Monsieur Perera," Mori announced to a small white-
haired man in his eighties sitting behind an enormous bare desk. "Our
chancellor, Monsieur Rafael Bilboul."

A stern portrait of President Sadat stared down from the rear
wall of the chancellor's office. Along the side walls hung faded portraits
and color lithographs of Alexandria's illustrious rabbis—Ventura,
Prato, Pergola—each more hallowed and severe of countenance than
his successor. The history of Alexandria's Jews went back even farther
than Salonika's, having originated during the time of Alexander the
Great. Following the destruction of the Temple in Jerusalem in 72
A.D., seventy Alexandrine wise men had translated the Torah into
Greek—the Septuagint—for the exiles who sought refuge in the city.
Over the centuries, Alexandria had birthed generations of Talmudists
and wonder-working rabbis, enough of both to rival Baghdad and
Salonika. Anti-Semitism in Alexandria is equally ancient, and more
virulent than that affecting most other Jewish communities; and yet Bil-
boul seemed untouched by this dark legacy as he greeted me with a
sparkling smile.

"Ah yes, yes, we've been awaiting you—*nous vous attendions.*"
Bilboul rose and offered me a seat in front of his vast, empty desk.
When he sank back into his chair, only his small, gnomish head and
neck remained visible. "Since the normalization began, we are getting
many visitors from abroad," he said, sinking lower in his seat until his
bespectacled eyes peered at me across the top of his desk like a pair of
lively oysters. "But it is not every day someone comes to look for a relative's grave. Your grandfather, was it?" he inquired with an incongru-
ous chuckle.

"Yes. Aharon Haim Perera. I thought perhaps you might have
known him."

"A familiar name," he said. "Very notable. In cotton, was he?
Or was it shipping?"

"No, he was a religious man, a *shohet* and Torah scribe. He performed services and special rituals, such as the *kaparot.*" I could see by

his blank stare that the Hebrew words had gone over Bilboul's head. I indicated that my grandfather had only been in Alexandria a short time before he died.

Monsieur Bilboul nodded, raised himself up and clasped his hands above the desk. *"Eh bien,* I knew a Perera in cotton, but he left years ago, after the troubles of '48."

"A distant relation, perhaps," I said, without suspecting that the "Perera in cotton" would turn out to be my uncle Alberto's disowned firstborn son, Victor Perera, of whose existence I was entirely ignorant at the time.

"Ah, here she is," Bilboul said, rising and welcoming Madame Lina, a small, birdlike woman of about sixty-five. "Madame Lina, this young man is looking for his deceased grandfather—could you please fetch the registry?"

"Right away, Monsieur Bilboul," said Lina in a twittery voice.

"Madame Lina is the secretary of the community," Bilboul explained. "She's been working here since her husband died earlier this year—not for money, you understand, as she is fairly well off. It gives her something to do. Truth to tell"—again he emitted his soft chuckle—"we are all past retirement age, but what would we do with ourselves, a collection of antique widows and widowers, our children and grandchildren all abroad? So we do our best to cheer one another up—isn't that so, Madame Lina?" he called to the secretary, who had returned with a thick, leather-bound ledger.

"Absolutely, Monsieur Bilboul," she said in her birdlike inflection, crossing her stockinged legs provocatively.

"I was telling Monsieur Perera we have to cheer one another up, and keep an active life. Otherwise we might as well retire to the nursing home—isn't that so, Madame Lina?"

"Ah, Monsieur Bilboul." She had sat down on a large wicker chair, which lowered her nearly to his eye level. "You will never end up in a nursing home. You are too witty and lively. *Et alors,* what would the community do without you?"

"There—" Bilboul rose in his seat and swept an arm over the empty desk. "Isn't she enchanting? I don't know what I would do without her. My wife, who died six years ago, was an angel, and angels are not easily replaced, especially in Egypt. . . ."

"Have you no other family?" I asked Bilboul.

"Ah yes, I have a son in Israel and another in Oxford—a writer like you—married to an Anglican woman who converted to Judaism. And I have a daughter here who married a Lebanese Christian, a Maronite, so that their two children could have the privileges of Egyptian citizenship. Her husband owns a prosperous produce business and is very pro-Semitic. He loves Jews." He snorted cheerily. "You could say I'm doing my bit for religious tolerance, eh? A Christian son-in-law and daughter and a Jewish son and daughter-in-law. If I had another daughter I would marry her to a Muslim, and then the picture would be complete. What do you think, Madame Lina?"

"Why, then President Sadat would decorate you personally, Monsieur Bilboul."

I joined in their frivolous laughter but could not shake the feeling that they were dancing on the edge of an abyss. I asked Bilboul why he did not leave for England or Israel to live with his sons.

"What, and leave Madame Lina?" He pressed her arm, and she responded with a coquettish tilt of the head. "And who would guard the community? I may not be a very religious man—few of us are any more—but I do assist the cantor with his duties at the synagogue. We are the last guardians of the Jewish heritage in Alexandria. And this is our home, after all. We were born here, and Egypt has been good to us." The twinkle in his eyes dimmed for the first time. "It is true that we've had some troubles; in 1967 they interned my son for several months. But that was true of other young men as well, and not only Jews. The government has treated me personally with consummate respect, and they extended me their protection during the troubles. Now, since the peace treaty, we can travel to Israel, and our sons and daughters can visit more often. I may even decide to go back into business. Commerce is in my blood, and I was quite a success at it, if I say so myself—eh, Madame Lina?"

"Monsieur Bilboul was the director of a halvah factory," explained Madame Lina. "It was very prosperous, too, until the government took it over. Now it is almost bankrupt."

"Yes, yes"—he was not smiling now—"but they nationalized many other businesses—Italian and Greek ones included. No, we are safe and tranquil here. We have no complaints. Have you looked at the registry, Madame Lina? I am sure we must have fatigued Monsieur Perera with our little stories."

Madame Lina opened the ledger and thumbed through the 1920s: Pergola, Perez, Picciotto, Pinhas. More than ninety percent seemed to be Sephardic names, interspersed with a few Perlmans and Koslovskis. At last we found my grandfather's entry.

"*Aharon Chaim Perera, fils d'Isaac Moshe Perera. Décedé 22 Janvier 1923 à l'hôpital Israélite d'Alexandrie.*" Below it was the Hebrew date, "*Shevat, 5683.*"

"It does not say where he is buried," pondered Bilboul. "To judge from the date, he should be in Cemetery Number 1. We have three, you know, each more stately than the last. Your grandfather, I am afraid, is most likely buried in the oldest and humblest one."

Bilboul summoned Mori and asked him to accompany me to the cemetery. "The cemetery is some distance away," Bilboul whispered in my ear. "Afterward, you may want to give him something."

As we came out of the vestibule I almost bumped into a distin-guished-looking elder gentleman, who turned out to be the Jewish council president, Clement Setton, arriving at his office an hour late.

"Ah, I suspect you won't find your grandfather," he said when Bilboul explained our mission. "It is a terrible jumble down there. But you should at least try."

Setton invited me into his study for a brief interview. "To most Alexandrians we are the invisible Jews," he observed, under the very visible and ubiquitous Sadat portrait. An aristocratic man of seventy-five with thick arching eyebrows, the chairman was dressed in a gray pinstripe suit and vest, and his English was as smooth as wine. He said his family originally came from Syria and Morocco, an inconvenience that denies him Egyptian citizenship. "Our enemies have long wished us to be gone from this city together with our families. But we have stayed on, and so rather than accept us as fellow Egyptians with full rights and privileges, they have chosen to pretend we don't exist. But the reports of our demise, to paraphrase your Monsieur Mark Twain, are grossly exaggerated.

"Egypt used to be a land of golden opportunity," Setton said with a sigh. "In the second half of the nineteenth century foreigners could come here, start a business or industry and remain immune from Egyptian taxes and lawsuits simply by retaining their original citizen-ship. Even we stateless Jews, who could not boast such privileges, were able to get along on our wits. As a result, many businesses and proper-ties fell into Jewish hands, and we fared so well that we incurred the envy of the Egyptian managerial class that rose to power in the 1930s. Still, we continued to prosper under King Farouk, making large profits in cotton, sugar, textiles and the stock market and rising to the top in many leading professions. Why, we had respected members of Parliament, and one of King Farouk's trusted royal advisers was a Jew.

"But in 1947 a company law was passed which provided that ninety percent of the workforce of a joint-stock company and half the directors must be native Egyptians—which is to say, mostly Christian Copts and Muslims. This led to the massive dismissal of foreign entrepreneurs, not only Jews but Englishmen, Greeks, Italians and Frenchmen. After the establishment of Israel in 1948, thousands of Alexandria's Jews left for the Holy Land and Europe. It was the beginning of the end of our prosperity. In 1955, under President Nasser, a parliamentary decree abolished consular and religious courts, and put an end to our diplomatic immunity."

Setton adjusted his dark glasses and folded his manicured hands. "And, as you know, after the Six-Day War in 1967, most of our men between the ages of eighteen and fifty were placed in detention camps for reasons of security. After they were released, all but a few of these younger people had to waive all legal and property rights before they could leave the country. We are the survivors. Before 1948 we were 40,000. Today we are less than 400 practicing Jews in both Cairo and Alexandria, and our average age is somewhere in the high sixties or low seventies. Rather nice as a golf score," he added, arching an eyebrow, "but not the best average for maintaining a healthy, growing community."

I asked him, "Would any of the young people—your nephews, cousins, sons and daughters—return to Alexandria at some point in the future?"

"Very unlikely. Those Jews who leave Egypt seldom return. That has been the tradition here since the time of the Pharaohs. In truth, I've stayed on to look after a younger brother who is rather depressed and quite disinclined to travel. Our mother died just five years ago, you see—she was well into her nineties—and left him in my care. But you must be careful what you write about this; he is very sensitive, and reads all the foreign periodicals, including the ones you write for."

Setton donned his hat and signaled to the waiting Mori to open the doors of the synagogue.

The mid-nineteenth-century naves and vaulted ceiling, the classically proportioned marble Doric columns, were impressive beyond all my expectations. They testified to the past opulence of the Alexandria

Jewish community—remarked on as early as the twelfth century by the legendary traveler Benjamin de Tudela, as well as by more recent wan-derers—rather than to their religious piety, in spite of all their famous and lesser known rabbis.

Setton nodded sadly when I exclaimed over the magnificent Torah scroll, with its dazzling damask-silk covers and gold-embossed shields.

"Many before you have been similarly moved. Monsieur Begin was struck with admiration when he visited us here several months ago and led the prayer services. You see, we have no rabbi. The *hazan* [can-tor] officiates on Sabbaths and the High Holidays when his health per-mits. He is almost ninety years old."

"Ninety!"

"Yes, we don't like to trouble him unless we can raise a quorum of ten. I don't think you'd like our services too well," he remarked with a sigh. "They are a bit *triste,* except when we have distinguished visitors like Menachem Begin. . . .

"This is the largest and richest of our synagogues," Setton said, completing our tour. "We had ten of them; all but three have been razed, and the land was sold for revenue. Our hospital is gone as well, and our famous Hatikvah Club; our school building next door is leased to the Egyptian Department of Education. We have liquidated all our community property except for this square block, the nursing home—oh yes, and the three cemeteries, of course."

I shook Setton's hand warmly. *"Lehitraot,"* I said. To my sur-prise Setton asked, "What is that?"

"Why, it means 'until we meet again,' in Hebrew."

He nodded his head. *"Inshallah*—Allah willing. And best of luck in finding your grandfather."

MORI DECIDED TO make a detour via the Foyer, or nursing home, on the off chance we might find someone there who remembered my grandfather.

We were met at the entrance by the home's director, Victor Mair Balassiano, a tall, heavyset man of forty-three with a club foot, who turned out to be the youngest living Jewish male in Alexandria. Balas-siano, who has a young wife and a six-month-old daughter, used to be the community's schoolteacher. He took over the nursing home after all his pupils decamped. He remained a vigorous, paternalistic presence and was hugged warmly by each of the fourteen residents of the Foyer as he escorted me from ward to ward.

Balassiano explained that there had been many more residents, but they had died off. The home now loses three or four for every new resident it admits. The halls and wards were large and gloomy, the only decor provided by old pastoral scenes on yellowed walls and crude crayon drawings of menorahs, Sabbath candles, Hanukkah tops and other holiday symbols sent by Jewish children from Houston, Texas. "Thanks, kids—the Foyer" read a scrawled inscription tacked up next to the drawings. Small wonder Balassiano seemed so at home. The re-tirement home of Alexandria's once-proud Jewish gerontocracy resem-bled a lugubrious kindergarten.

The residents, in fact, seemed only marginally older than the working members of the community I had met. They sat playing cards on oversize tables, or loitered on the edges of beds in their striped paja-mas in dark, empty wards, with hands clasped between their thighs. Balassiano explained that each resident had a disabling illness or infir-mity, or was prey to an incapacitating "sadness." The director patted his aged pupils on the back and said "bravo" when anyone showed a spark of life by delivering a coherent sentence. "Bravo," he said when I suggested that the drama of Alexandria's Jews was worthy of a novel or a play. "Yes, our story is rich, sad, complicated."

In the largest ward two men—a professor and a former engineer, each about eighty years old—sat at the edge of their beds, unspeaking, while a third man in his seventies extended both hands for alms.

"His mind has slipped, poor man," Balassiano said. "He used to be a well-known industrialist. After his wife died his grown children all fled, and the solitude was too much for him. Now he begs scraps of food from the other residents and from visitors, although he is well off and we give him more than enough to eat."

"And how are you today, Professor Moran?" he asked one of the eighty-year-olds, a bearded man with rheumy eyes who lifted his head slowly and asked for a cup of tea.

"Bravo, that's the spirit," the director said, patting him on the shoulder. "I'll ask the maid to bring you some."

In another ward I met Madame Kuperman, a full-bodied, faded beauty in her late sixties who strikingly resembled my aunt Rebecca. Coincidentally, Kuperman recalled playing poker with Rebecca in the

1930s, shortly after my aunt and her Egyptian husband moved to Alexandria from Cairo. None of the residents had any recollection of my grandfather, although most would have been adults when he was here. Evidently he had not had time to establish himself in Alexandria before his boil became infected and did him in.

Kuperman was upset because her companion, Monsieur Cohen, a wizened former tradesman half her size, had suffered a heart attack two days before and had nearly slipped away. The director had saved him with a shot of adrenalin and a chest massage.

"*Mon Dieu,* if I had lost Monsieur Cohen I would have no one in this world to live for," she said, holding fast to Cohen's arm. He had the faraway, slightly clownish look of a man with one foot in the grave.

"But you still have your sister, Madame Kuperman," Monsieur Balassiano reminded her.

"Yes, but she lives halfway around the world in Brooklyn."

"Well, I'm sure Monsieur Perera here knows Brooklyn. Don't you, Monsieur Perera?"

"Yes," I said. "I lived my adolescent years there."

"Bravo," said the director, patting my back as if I had made a bon mot, or asked for a cup of tea. "Perhaps you can deliver a message to Madame Kuperman's sister, eh Monsieur Perera?"

"I shall be delighted to," I assured Kuperman, who took my hand and squeezed it thankfully.

I took down her sister's address, and she said, "Tell her I am very, very tired, but I would like to see her and the children before I die." She heaved a great, shuddering sigh. "But what can one do? One cannot run ahead of one's kismet. It will always catch up with you, and take you where you have to go. I don't think I shall be permitted to see my sister again. . . .

"May you have a good kismet," she called as I got up to leave. "And may your grandfather's soul rest in peace."

We rode a taxi across town to the cemetery, which lay behind an unlatched iron gate. Inside, a chaotic array of gravestones and larger monuments spread to distant walls.

"We will have to locate Ibrahim, the caretaker," Mori said, pushing back his beret and scratching his bald head. "Otherwise we will be here for hours."

"Ibrahim!" he called as we started down the first row of gravestones. "Ibrahim!" he called again in a strangled voice, as if he were wary of rousing unhelpful specters.

The only response came from a band of dogs, who growled and yelped at us from several rows away without revealing themselves.

"Those are Ibrahim's guard dogs," Mori explained. "Stay close behind me and they won't bite you." He toddled along slowly, his hands clasped behind his bulky overcoat. He explained that Ibrahim, a Muslim, had been caretaker of the cemetery for more than fifty years and may already have been here when my grandfather was buried. "But Ibrahim is a very old man now, and his memory is slipping." Again he called out "Ibrahim!" in a louder voice. The dogs responded with a sustained howl but remained as invisible as their master.

The rows of headstones seemed to follow no chronological order, or any other logical progression. A family group from the 1920s was followed by large oval tablets from the 1940s, incised with cupped hands and forget-me-nots. Many of the gravestones betrayed the same disregard for Elohim's injunction against graven images as the tomb-stones of Amsterdam Jews in Ouderkerk.

Italian inscriptions *("a mia cara")* lay next to French *("à ma chère")* and Hebrew devotions. Clusters of gravestones dedicated to short-lived occupants hinted at plagues and wars, but these were not specified. (Even in death, Jews seemed loath to divulge their calamities to strangers.) All the stones dated before 1930 were carved in Hebrew letters; most were cracked or disfigured by lichen and the weather.

My hopes sank, but I trudged on behind Mori, falling into his unhurried, toddling gait. We came to the east wall and turned right, toward the remote section where most of the older Hebrew gravestones lay. Once I stopped over a cracked stone with the name "Haim" barely legible on one side. Mori brushed off the dust and lichen until a letter of the second name was exposed.

"No, it's not Perera," he said. "It begins with a *taf.*"

We could find no evidence of the caretaker or his dogs, whose barks we continued to hear intermittently. I was growing giddy from the heat of the sun and the profusion of legends and names, none of them my grandfather's. The afternoon was unfolding with the desultory unreality of a dream.

I had not brought a prayer book, and repeated in my head the opening phrases of the Kaddish—*Yitgadal veyitkadash*—whenever I surmised that my grandfather's grave might be nearby. I imagined him in his last hours of life, confined to his quarters with an infected boil he could not afford medicine for. What had become of the prodigal survivor in Aunt Simha's memoir who turned whatever he touched into gold? How had an intelligent, resourceful man like Aharon Haim Perera fallen into such a desperate quandary? Who was my grandfather, and why was I led on this unending quest, seeking him out everywhere I went, glimpsing him only in shadows or in surrogates who embodied his imagined virtues and defects? Was my grandfather truly the last Perera to incarnate my ancestors' unshakable faith in Elohim? Or was he, in his last moments of desolation and despair, one more descendant of the Marrano Pereras, doomed through all eternity to wander in search of legitimacy and redemption, clutching at every illusory manifestation of God's divine radiance and finding only their sad, earthbound reflections peering back at them? One thing alone felt certain: My grandfather's untimely death in Alexandria had orphaned two generations of his descendants.

After another hour, it no longer mattered so much whether I found the gravestone. Beneath the ground, the dust and ashes all mingled in a common decay. My prayers would seep below and eventually reach their objective, or they would not.

I knelt down to scrutinize a Hebrew inscription with a 1923 date, and a puppy tumbled out and began yapping at my heels.

"Take us to my grandfather," I said to the puppy, as if it were an infant Cerberus guarding the entrance to Hades; but it yipped and chewed on my trouser cuffs until I stepped on its paws. The puppy's piercing whine brought not only its incensed, piebald mother but three other snarling mongrels. Circling us with snapping jaws, they kept up a howling din that finally roused the old caretaker from the shack where he had been snoozing, to judge from his glazed eyes, rumpled cap and unbuttoned fly.

"Ah, there you are, Ibrahim." Mori placed a hand on the old watchman's shoulder and described my grandfather's death and burial, embellished with fanciful details of the distinguished cortege that would have attended the funeral of someone of my grandfather's importance.

- Ibrahim nodded his large head and grunted, his toothless mouth agape. Finally he mumbled a few questions with his eyes half closed, casting about for some long-forgotten memory.

"Yes, of course he was a Jew," Mori replied patiently. "Didn't I just tell you? He was a religious man from Jerusalem, widely known and respected in Alexandria."

I knew then that my search would be fruitless, but I was beyond regret. The events of the past hour had taken the place of the unsaid Kaddish so far as I was concerned.

"Ibrahim's memory is not very clear today," Mori explained as we headed for the exit. "All he can remember is that your grandfather's headstone is in Hebrew. It would take days to find it."

I handed Mori a five-pound note for his trouble. He pocketed it without a glance, but his face lit up. "Next week I will come back, and Ibrahim's memory may have cleared up. I will take a photograph of your grandfather's grave and send it to you."

"If you wish," I said, not caring all that much one way or the other. My obligation to my family was now discharged. For the first time since my father had burdened me with his father's name and legacy, I felt at peace with my grandfather's memory.

CHAPTER XI

GUATEMALA I

AHARON HAIM PERERA sat for a family portrait shortly before he departed for Alexandria. It is the only likeness of my grandfather I have found, and it is a revealing one. He fills the center of the frame, seated a foot or more in front of my grandmother, to his right, as he clasps the hand of two-year-old Moshe, the baby of the family. To his left sits his eldest daughter, Margarita, a full-bloomed beauty of nineteen, with seven-year-old Rachel by her side, looking characteristically glum. Standing in back are a pubescent Simha with her waist-length blond tresses, a glowing prenuptial Reina and my father, age twenty-four, who was teaching the Talmud Torah by day and studying law in the evenings. Conspicuously absent is Father's younger brother Nissim (Isidoro), who had already joined Alberto, the eldest brother, in Guatemala.

In his wise Torah-student's *toka,* beard and black caftan, thick arching eyebrows and stubby fingers resting on his knees, Grandfather dominates the picture, as befits the patriarch. The photographer approached his subject like a court painter; he positioned Grandfather so that the ambient light in the studio concentrates on his face, and his family is relegated to the shadows. There is another idiosyncrasy: While everyone else looks straight ahead at the camera lens, Aharon Haim Perera's eyes slant several degrees to the left and slightly upward. My grandfather wasn't about to let the fast-talking shyster with the large box camera out of his sight, not for one moment.

Within a year after the photograph was taken, Aunt Reina had married in Jerusalem and my grandfather had died in Alexandria. Shortly after that, Father and Aunt Margo followed their brothers to the New World.

When I was three, I likewise took the measure of a photographer—probably a visiting gringo—who deigned to snap a picture of me pedaling my toy car in Guatemala City's Parque Central. Aharon Haim Perera had been dead for nearly fifteen years; apart from our physical resemblance and the fact that I bear his name, the two photographic images—Grandfather's and mine—are linked by their aura of alert self-sufficiency.

Aharon Haim Perera and family (Salomon Perera standing), ca. 1922

In my first years of life in Guatemala I was known as a cocky kid. I was cosseted and spoiled by my mother, by my seventeen-year-old Indian nanny, Chata, by two housemaids and all fifteen salesgirls in Father's department store. As Mother's firstborn, I was dressed to look the part of her *machito* in outlandish mariachi outfits and sailor suits. My *china* (nanny), Chata, a Catholic Maya from a highland village of Cobán, was determined to save my Jewish soul from perdition; she often sneaked me into the cathedral, where she had me kneel at the foot of the crucified Christ and recite the Ave Maria. My senses reeled from the mingled scents of incense and Chata's blouse as she pressed her firm breasts against the back of my neck; this was her way of allaying my fright of the terrifying naked figure on the cross. At night she would tuck me into bed and tell me stories of bogeys and spooks, while she lightly stroked my groin. Chata was a spirited young woman who still haunts my dreams in her long black tresses and wraparound Maya skirt and white blouse. In the afternoons, when she took me to the park, men were drawn to her like dogs to a bitch in heat. Chata had many *novios,* most of whom she kept on tenterhooks with her teasing ways. At bottom I did not mind these rivals because I knew that I was her favorite.

Apart from being outrageously spoiled, I was also precocious. I had an ear for adult phony talk and looked with suspicion not only on the shutterbugs who snapped my picture without asking permission but on the grown-up world as a whole. Mother was fond of recalling that when her Hadassah group gathered at our home for their weekly game of bridge or poker, I would tell them to quit their nattering gossip and watch me tap-dance. I even took in stride the birth of my baby sister, Becky, secure in the knowledge that I would always be Mama's boy.

Father, who thought me a spoiled namby-pamby and lazy to boot, conspired with the Sephardic community's new rabbi to assure that my boyhood hubris was short-lived.

When I wrote the following paragraphs in 1967, I knew nothing of my great-grandfather's testament or the circumstances surrounding Grandfather's death in Alexandria.

"I was not quite six when I was circumcised for the second time because the first job, performed by a gentile doctor, was pronounced unclean by our new rabbi. My mother tells me that a small flap of foreskin survived the first operation, so that I hung by this integument for six years between Baal and the shield of David, a part-heathen. The ceremonial tableau has lodged in my memory, held there in trust for my understanding to ripen and draw out its full significance.

"Rabbi Isaac Musan, summoned from Turkey to be the first pastor of our growing Jewish community, was a man of Gothic appearance. In height scarcely above a dwarf, Rabbi Musan bore on his back a sizable hump, but lightly, as if he was vain of it. He had raven eyes and thick brows. A black homburg perched on his large head, never a skullcap. From inside his beaked nose wiry hairs radiated like an insect's antennae.

"His nose is the last thing I remember as he leaned over me, whispering unintelligible blandishments in fifteenth-century Spanish. The rest was howls, astonishing pain, the bitter, sinking knowledge that I would never again be whole."

Before the end of my fifth year, two other calamities befell me that would alter the course of my life forever.

When I entered kindergarten in 1939, Kristallnacht had already taken place. The Gestapo was rounding up all Jews in Germany and forcing them to wear yellow badges.

During recess one morning, two Catholic boys accused me of having killed Christ. When I could not answer their questions about my Jewish culpability, Friedrich, a blond German boy a head taller than I, said his mother had told him all Jews were the devil. He called over the other boys in the patio, and they all fell on me and stripped me naked to look for my cloven hooves and tail. All they found was my tender Jewish feet and bare butt and my twice-harrowed member, which they gloatingly dubbed *paloma pelada* (bald pigeon).

The only boy to come to my aid was Michel, who spoke with a foreign accent. When he offered me his beret to cover myself, the boys snatched it away and stamped on it, one by one, chanting slurs on his French nationality. Although my chest ached from holding back tears, I did not break down and cry until Grace Saavedra, an occasional playmate who had long, glossy black hair and violet eyes, stared at my exposed genitals and said, "I hate you." Most disconcerting of all was the reaction of our North American kindergarten teacher, a tall, un-smiling woman named Miss Good. When she found me cowering naked against the fountain, she offered no sympathy whatever; in her stern North American voice, she ordered the boys and girls out of the patio and told me to get dressed.

The following year I was left back in kindergarten. Miss Good and my parents agreed that I was too tender for first grade.

Years later, Friedrich and I became casual friends. We stayed in touch after he returned from medical studies abroad and became a re-spected cardiac surgeon. In 1989 he died of the heart condition that had been his specialty, and that he alone in Guatemala was qualified to treat.

One of Chata's lovers shadowed us one morning when she took me to school. I remember Chata staring straight ahead and warning me not to turn around. (Like other women accustomed to attracting men, Chata had eyes in the back of her head.) After she dropped me off, her jealous *novio* waylaid her two blocks from the school and knifed her to death.

I waited in the school's hallway for what seemed an eternity until Father picked me up after closing the store and declared, "Chata has gone away. We will get you another *china.*" Later that day I wormed the truth out of our cook, María, who said Chata's *novio* had given her "seven knife stabs in the very heart" *(Siete puñaladas en el mero corazón.)* This happened to be the title and refrain of a popular song. I chanted the phrase energetically for several days, while stamping my boots on the tiled floor of our corridor. But Chata's death did not sink in until her older sister Elvira took her place as my *china*. Elvira was neither as spir-ited nor as pretty as Chata, and her blouse and skirts did not smell half as sweet.

My brief career as precocious mama's boy came to an abrupt end. By the time I encountered the five Lacandones at the national fair, I had confirmed Father's dim opinion of me by growing acutely timid and dull-witted in all my school subjects except English. Without my realizing it, the sad-eyed figures in the long white tunics and shoulder-length hair became my secret sharers; I could make no more sense of their incarceration behind the chicken-wire enclosure than I could fathom the calamities and humiliations that had descended on my head.

II

Father was twenty-five when he arrived in Guatemala to be the book-keeper for Mi Casa, the Perera brothers' department store. Neither Al-berto nor Isidoro had a head for figures, and it soon became apparent that without Father's sharp eye on the ledgers, the business would never have gotten off the ground. ("Your father was the only Perera with a head on his shoulders," Mother never tired of reminding me. "The other brothers were pumpkins.")

It may have been Uncle Alberto's visit to Jerusalem with his phonograph player that first piqued Father's curiosity about the New World. His year of penury in Damascus, where he very nearly starved to death, stoked his resolution never to sink into abject poverty again. After Aharon Haim died in Alexandria, my uncles had no trouble persuading Father to abandon his Torah teaching and law studies and join them in America to pick the gold from the paving stones. (Uncle Alberto, of course, already knew better; in Mexico he barely got by dealing not in gold but in diamonds.)

On the same visit to Jerusalem, Uncle Alberto persuaded Grandmother Esther to pack her bags and accompany them to Amer-ica. As Aunt Rachel remembers, Albert casually let drop that he and Isidoro no longer kept kosher, and opened the store for business on the Sabbath.

"You work on Shabbat?" Grandmother exclaimed, incredu-lous. "From here I do not budge!" Grandmother Esther unpacked

Author in sailor suit and family, 1940

her bags and sent Father and Uncle Alberto on their way without another word. She died in Jerusalem a few years later wearing the black
dress she had put on the day she learned of Grandfather's death in
Alexandria.

The seed of the patriarch's curse that my father and his brothers carried with them to the New World was watered by my
grandmother's tears when she mourned her sons as if they had
banished themselves to the valley of death where her husband lay
buried.

III

My uncles were not the first Pereras to arrive in the New World, nor
were they the first to set foot in Guatemala. The record shows that a
number of Pereiras—Marranos among them—accompanied the conquistadores to what is today Mexico and Guatemala. In 1711, Simón
Pereira Berdugo, a descendant of conquistadores and great-grandson of

Mi Casa, the Perera brothers' department store, Guatemala City, ca. 1934

a Guatemalan governor, solicited a pension from the Crown on the strength of his hidalgo blood. Another Pereira applied for the liquor concession in Guatemala. After the Inquisition reached the Spanish colonies in the seventeenth century, two Pereiras were accused and tried by the Holy Office's tribunals in Mexico. Nunes Pereira, of Portuguese extraction, was sent to Spain from Guadalajara, Mexico, on charges of blaspheming against San Felipe de Jesús, a Mexican saint. He was sentenced to 200 lashes and imprisonment for life. In 1595 another Nunes Pereira, a university student in Guatemala charged with Judaizing and apostasy, was burned at the stake in an auto-da-fé in Mexico City.

On the south coast of Guatemala I encountered Pereiras who bridled at my suggestion that they might be descended from Portuguese Marranos. Most of these Pereiras are dark-skinned Ladinos descended of Iberian colonists who interbred with Mayas.

In Guatemala and elsewhere in Central America I have also encountered Catholic Bendanas and Avendaños who retained distinct European characteristics; these distant relatives tend to be ambassadors, lawyers, Jesuit priests, and one Avendaño was briefly a Guatemalan president. Most of the Bendanas and Avendaños I met recognized the Jewish origins of their name and seemed not at all put out by the possibility that we shared a common ancestor. (None of them were moved to pursue the matter further, however; nor, for that matter, was I.)

In 1993 I visited the New York branch of the famous Mormon family archive and looked up our names in their computers. I was surprised to discover that the Mormons' files contained many more Abendanas than Pereras. I already knew of the Rodrigues Pereiras, who sailed to the British colonies in the wake of the *Mayflower* and whose descendants became members in good standing of New England's Jewish community. In the Mormon archive for the first time I found Abendanas with Jewish first names who lived in the United States. But these distant relations play no part in this chronicle.

The Pereiras and Abendanas whose forebears emigrated to the New World in the sixteenth and seventeenth centuries are of a separate lineage from the Pere(i)ras who arrived in Mexico and Central America after World War I. These Pere(i)ras, my direct ancestors among them, were driven from the Balkans and the Middle East by desperate economic need. The earlier arrival in Guatemala of Turkish and Syrian families such as the Mishaans, the Picciottos, the Sassons, the Sabbajs and the Kaires provided a welcoming climate for the new arrivals, and persuaded them to remain. Like most of their coreligionists, Uncles Alberto and Isidoro—and for a brief period, Father as well—worked in Guatemala as ambulant pedlars, selling bolts of colored gingham to urban and rural Ladinos and better-off Indians.

I have written elsewhere of Father's courtship of Mother by transatlantic mail, so that their pledged passions had months to cool on each crossing. Uncle Alberto brokered the marital contract between these second cousins, and also falsified Mother's passport—as he had earlier forged Uncle Isidoro's and Father's—to claim Salonika as their birthplace. Apart from the legal advantages of Greek nationality, my parents hoped to avoid the stigma of being lumped with immigrant "Turks." They need not have bothered. In Guatemala, they soon discovered, there were only two kinds of Jews: *turcos y polacos* (Turks and Polacks). In our family, only my little sister was fair enough to pass for an Eastern European.

Despite the modest success of the Perera brothers' department store, ill luck would shadow my family's ventures in the New World from beginning to end. As soon as the store opened, Uncles Alberto and Isidoro began quarrelling bitterly over finances and the day-to-day management of the store. The mediating influence expected of Father when he arrived from Jerusalem proved to be short-lived.

Uncle Alberto had discontents of his own. His marriage to a spirited Egyptian Jew he had brought from Alexandria turned sour almost from the start. According to family lore, Alberto decided to divorce Lina Carazo after he discovered her in bed with another man. When she gave birth to a boy, Alberto refused to acknowledge him, scorning Lina's assurances that the boy was his. He gave Lina and her infant son passage back to Cairo and returned to Mexico shortly afterward.

I met Uncle Alberto only once, during a brief visit he made to Guatemala when I was five. He was living the unattached bachelor's life in Mexico City and wore a fine blue suit—probably imported silk—and a bowler hat. I remember a heady whiff of cologne when he leaned down to present me with a gold ring. In the afternoon he took me to see *Snow White and the Seven Dwarfs,* which had just opened in Guatemala. Save for some Betty Boop cartoons, this was my very first movie. I was spellbound by the dwarfs and enchanted with Snow

White, but I ducked under the seat whenever the wicked stepmother appeared on screen. In later years I would be reminded of her by my beautiful and cold aunt Lottie.

I wore Uncle Alberto's ring for about a year, until it began to turn green and no longer fit comfortably, not even on my little finger. I lost the ring while playing a silly game with a schoolmate, the trick of which was to hop on both legs with the ring clamped between our but-tocks. I won the competition, and lost the ring in high grass. I spent hours looking in vain for that ring, under the darkening cloud that set-tles over a boy's head when he thinks he has committed the ultimate misdeed.

This was not the only time I lost a family heirloom. On my eighth birthday Father ceremoniously presented me with a gold-plated fob watch that had belonged to his father. I was so overwhelmed by the gift that I promptly mislaid it. When the cleaning maid found it under my bed several days later, Father scolded me for my carelessness and re-placed the watch in his safe box. I never saw the watch again, except in a dream I had several years after Father passed away. In my dream Fa-ther removed the watch from an underground locker and presented it to me with the words, "Here—you're old enough to have it now." I often wonder what became of that watch in the waking world.

Shortly after Uncle Alberto's Guatemalan visit, he met and married a Turkish Sephardi living in Mexico, Aida, who presented him with a daughter. I did not meet my cousin Esther until she was thirty-five. She was living in straitened circumstances with her wid-owed mother in Mexico City, divorced, despondent and working her-self to the bone to pay off the debts Uncle Alberto had piled up during a long life of extravagance.

In July 1994 I looked up my cousin Esther in Mexico City. She told me her mother had died in 1985. In her mid-forties, Cousin Esther was at last coming into her own. She was astounded that I had been in communication, if only indirectly, with her half brother, Victor, of whom she had heard only in family gossip.

"My father never mentioned him or his mother," Esther said. "To him, they were as good as dead."

Although Father and Uncle Isidoro would remain business partners for more than three decades, their family ties became strained in the early forties, after Uncle Isidoro returned from Mexico with a tall,

Author and family, 1944

blond Bukharan bride, my elegant aunt Lottie. In a lightly fictionalized boyhood memoir I published,* I devoted several chapters to Uncle Isidoro and Aunt Lottie, and to my unhappy relationship with their two sons, my younger cousins Jaime and David Perera.

The ill star Mother complained of practically from the day she arrived in Guatemala would shadow three generations of Pereras. I was too small to recall who fired off the first salvo when my aunt Lottie, college-bred and exquisitely refined, was introduced to her short, earthy and tart-tongued sister-in-law, my mother. Among my early memories is Mother's incessant bitching about Aunt Lottie, whom she accused of scheming with Uncle Isidoro to steal the store from Father and usurp his high standing in the Jewish community. I gave scant credence to Mother's accusations until one afternoon many years later, when Aunt Lottie pointed to Father's face in the family photograph that hung on her living-room wall. "Here is your uncle Isidoro," she declared in a hard-edged voice. I was so stunned I took leave of my wits and failed to point out to Aunt Lottie that Uncle Isidoro had been long gone from the Holy Land when that photograph was taken.

*Rites: A Guatemalan Boyhood. New York: Harcourt Brace Jovanovich, 1986. Mercury House, 1994.

I was nine when the quarrels broke out in our living room between Father and Uncle Isidoro. He and Aunt Lottie stayed with us
their first year in Guatemala while they looked for a house in the upscale
neighborhood of La Reforma. There was a nasty edge to their accusations and counteraccusations—most of them having to do with
money—which kept me awake late into the night. In the morning,
when I mentioned the flare-ups to Father, he would insist that it had
been just a friendly discussion. If this was "discussion," I wondered,
what would a real quarrel be like? I pictured mangled bodies in the living room.

My sister Rebecca was blond and fair as a child, and heartbreak-
ingly pretty. I remember looking down into her crib in Parque Central
and tweaking her nose when Chata wasn't looking. When she
frowned and was on the verge of crying, I stroked her cheek and made
soothing noises. This ambivalence toward my little sister sharpened as
we grew older and our family loyalties split cleanly down the middle;
Becky was Father's favorite from the start, while Mother and I, the
swarthy ones, were natural allies. Our legacy divided us in other ways
as well. If as a small boy I bore the brunt of my family's dark star,
Becky got the worst of it as we grew older.

I was ten and Becky seven when the quarrels between Father and
Uncle Isidoro intensified to such a pitch that they could no longer manage the business together. After months of bickering and negotiating
they agreed that Father would move to New York to do the buying for
the store while Uncle Isidoro stayed behind to run the business. (In this
decision Aunt Lottie no doubt played a persuasive role.)

Father and Mother departed for New York to look for a place to
live and left us with Aunt Lottie, whose firstborn, Jaime, was barely
two years old. The week before my parents left, Becky played the princess in a school pageant, and they gave her a seventh-birthday piñata
party. I harbor a memory of her surrounded by well-wishers, radiant
with happiness in her royal pink taffeta dress set off by her long blond
curls. In a family photograph taken that same week, she smiles seduc-
tively in her princess dress as she drapes herself around Father's shoulder. I would not see that radiance in Becky's face again.

Becky and Aunt Lottie clashed from the first day. For all the
huge disparities in their age and authority, both were strong-willed and
set in their ways. One of their quarrels erupted after Becky painted one
trouser leg of a clown in her coloring book purple and the other green.

"This will not do, Becky," Aunt Lottie said firmly. "You can't color one trouser leg purple and the other green." "But this is *my* clown!" Becky retorted. "I can color it any way I want to."

On another occasion Aunt Lottie disciplined Becky when she came home distraught after biting into a small finger she found in her cornmeal *tamal*. We had bought the *tamal* in the park from an Indian vendor who had stuffed it with a dead infant's pinky. Instead of comforting Becky, who cried inconsolably, Aunt Lottie sent us both to bed early for buying food from street vendors without her permission.

From my disengaged vantage, I could see the cards were stacked against my little sister, but there wasn't much I could do. Becky and I hardly played together anymore. For a boy of eleven, it was considered sissy by his peers to be seen consorting with a kid sister. Shortly after the *tamal* incident, I overheard Becky talking at night with an imaginary playmate. And she started bringing home stray cats and dogs that Aunt Lottie invariably turned out.

By the time we moved to Brooklyn a year later, Becky's personality appeared to be already formed, while mine remained frozen in time, like a frog in aspic. She was outstanding in school and went out for tournament sports like basketball and softball, while I was still smacking a pink Spalding ball against our stoop and playing Chinese handball with the neighborhood toughs.

Becky remained devoted to Father, and to his authoritarian ways, with a constancy that recalled a Sephardic daughter from Salonika or Jerusalem. When I turned thirteen, I was subjected to a humiliating bar mitzvah in the Kastoriali synagogue, made all the more painful by my stunted growth and choir boy's soprano. "You had better stay with the books," my perspicacious aunt Perla advised me in Ladino after witnessing my dispirited performance. "They'll swallow you whole on Canal Street." She was referring to Father's declared intention to put me to work in his partner's import-export firm on the day I graduated from high school.

After the bar mitzvah I turned my back on religion and sent away for Charles Atlas's bodybuilders' kit, determined never to have sand kicked in my face at the beach. I began to quarrel frequently with Becky, mostly about my intransigence toward my parents and teachers. Becky was a far more accomplished student in school than I was, so her reproaches carried weight, but not enough to alter my behavior. In the Bensonhurst of my adolescence you gained status by flouting adult authority, the more conspicuously the better. In my eagerness to be ac-cepted by my peers, and avoid getting labeled a "spic faggot," I memo-rized every Brooklyn Dodger pitcher's earned-run average like a Kabbala student memorizing his gematria, and picked fights with my Italian and Syrian neighbors.

Unlike Becky, who made the Special Progress section of her class, I was put in the dummies' seventh grade because of my dismal performance on the Stanford-Binet test. The test had been administered to me without explanation on my first day in school, in a language I barely spoke. On my second day in the dummies' class I was sent to the blackboard to multiply 7 × 35. As the 7 was not crossed, I balked at doing the simple multiplication, suspecting it was another trick. This satisfied Miss Mannes that I belonged in her class. In my senior year at Seth Low Junior High, I made the Junior Golden Gloves elimination round and was named captain of the cafeteria monitors, which meant I got to beat up on smaller kids. The yearbook editors, at a loss for any-thing more constructive to say, dubbed me "class babyface" and "the answer to a French teacher's prayer."

After graduating from Seth Low, Becky and I got to attend Abraham Lincoln High, a few blocks from Coney Island on Ocean Parkway, where we could take Hebrew classes. On my first day at Lin-coln I got into a lively discussion on Zionism with Al Ivry, a school standout who did not know that I had graduated from the dim section of ninth grade. For the first time since I was five, I felt moved to speak my mind. For a brief spell, a dormant spark in my brain spontaneously reignited. My conversation with Al marked the start of a long, painful reawakening from a twelve-year-long hibernation.

A few days later I was walking with Father along the Coney Is-land boardwalk as he delivered his post–bar mitzvah lecture about the importance of upholding our ancient Jewish heritage.

Without thinking twice, I blurted out, "Just because we have been Jews for 4,000 years, does that make it good?"

Father stopped dead in his tracks, as if struck by lightning. We were nearly the same height, so I got a good look at his astonished ex-pression. "My God!" he gasped. "You're intelligent!"

In high school my IQ jumped from eighty-seven to well over a hundred in two years, and my scholastic performance improved to the point where I was admitted to Brooklyn College as one of a handful of tuition-free foreign students. Most unexpectedly of all, I sprouted five inches after my seventeenth birthday, which made me as tall as Uncle Isidoro and a head taller than Father.

With her superior grades, my sister got a scholarship to Barnard College after graduating from high school. Becky and I were driven farther and farther apart by our contrasting temperaments. To avoid quarreling, we rarely spoke about anything of substance. This distance would come back to haunt me three years later, when she suffered a severe nervous breakdown.

I was in Ann Arbor working on a master's in writing and American literature when I got a disturbing note from Becky's academic counselor saying that she was in urgent need of psychiatric attention. Becky was then starting her junior year, having just returned from a summer in Guatemala.

When I telephoned my parents, who were staying in a hotel on Broadway, Mother told me that Becky had fallen in love with Alberto Mishaan, the youngest member of a large Syrian Sephardic family, one of the wealthiest in Guatemala. Becky and Alberto had become engaged, but when the time came for discussing marital arrangements, Father, Uncle Isidoro and Samuel Mishaan could not agree on the size of the dowry we were to pay.

Mother described the scene in Ladino, the only language in which the byzantine marital negotiations between two twentieth-century Sephardic families made any sense. It was painfully obvious that neither Becky nor Alberto, who as the youngest Mishaan occupied the bottom of the totem pole, had the gumption or the resources to defy their families and go off on their own. The engagement was broken off, and Becky, deeply despondent, returned to a cold, uncaring New York City.

Before seeing Rebecca, I met with her counselor, who told me bluntly that she was in a state of acute depression, and if she did not get immediate psychiatric help, she was liable to jump into the Hudson River.

It took me a whole day to track down my sister. Her roommate told me she had stopped studying and spent her days roaming from one coffee shop to another. I walked south on Broadway from 116th Street to 96th, crossed east to Amsterdam Avenue and walked north, looking for a lone, bulky figure in a trench coat. After hours of searching, I found Becky sitting in a dark corner of a coffee shop across from the

Cathedral of St. John the Divine, gesticulating with both hands as she talked back to her voices at the top of her lungs.

"Christ doesn't let me study anymore," she said on seeing me approach. "He and my mother have taken away my initiative."

I recalled, faintly, that Becky had once told me of Elvira sneak-ing her inside the cathedral to pray to the same crucifix Chata and I had knelt in front of.

Father, who had had a heart attack several months before, fol-lowing on his massive stroke of a decade earlier, refused to pay for a psy-chiatrist for Becky, insisting that her problem was spiritual rather than medical; he wanted her to consult a rabbi. But I told him that Becky would not hear of it, as she had decided to convert to Christianity. Frustrated in my attempts to mediate between my sister and my parents, I returned to my graduate studies in Ann Arbor.

Several days later Becky disappeared and could not be found in any of her usual haunts. The police finally contacted my parents to in-form them that they had found her wandering in Greenwich Village, stark naked and raving. A friend of Father's persuaded him to commit her to a mental hospital.

That winter I visited Becky in the Long Island Home, a private institution in Amityville where she had been interned for several weeks. Her doctor diagnosed her as a paranoid schizophrenic and recom-mended a regimen of electric-shock therapy.

When I took Becky out for a short walk she said, "Take me out of here, I don't like this place. Instead of a fish out of water, I feel like a fish in wine, or Coca-Cola."

Once again, like the time Becky had found the baby finger in her *tamal,* I was overwhelmed by hopelessness. Five years of college had pro-vided me with no explanation for the calamities that continued to stalk the family. By degrees, I had come to believe in the *malocchio* I had im-bibed with my mother's milk, one more indication of our unlucky star. When I pleaded with my parents to take Becky out of the hospital, Mother reminded me that Becky had attacked her with flailing fists dur-ing their last visit, and she was now terrified of her own daughter. Fa-ther shook his head and became abstracted, his eyes gray and distant, as they often were since his heart attack.

In later years I would joust with my sister's demons, under the illusion that I could spear her schizophrenia as Saint George had smote the dragon, or wrestle it to the ground as Jacob had wrestled with his angel. At the outset, however, the enormity of her descent into mad/ness paralyzed me just as it did Father, and I tuned out to escape the contagion.

In the late fifties, patients in private as well as state/run psychiat/ric hospitals were given electroshock and insulin therapy as a matter of course, whether they suffered from schizophrenia or chronic depression. During the two decades of my sister's confinement I would come to know many of these private and public institutions from the inside, ward by ward, not only in New York and Long Island but in Israel and Guatemala as well. In the decade before the advent of Thorazine, Haldol, Clozapine and other state/of/the/art psychotropic drugs, Becky and her fellow mental patients were used as guinea pigs for an inventory of psychiatric therapies that ranged from crude chemical tranquilizers with horrendous side effects to prefrontal lobotomy. Becky became con/vinced that we had abandoned her, a conviction she would carry out of the hospitals and into a succession of halfway houses.

I came to see Becky's schizophrenia as a metaphor for the fractur/ing of our family by a dark legacy of ancestral sins. According to this demonology, I was the one the curse was intended for, but I had managed to divert it to my younger sister, who lacked my survival in/stincts. In actuality, Becky became a victim twice over—first as the fam/ily's scapegoat and later as guinea pig for an era of psychiatric care that now seems medieval by comparison, although it was neither more nor less cold/hearted than the present age of miracle drugs.

When I visited Becky in Pilgrim State Hospital in upstate New York, and later in a Haifa mental institution after my parents moved back to Israel, I would often find her defending me against voices on her radio who accused me of betrayal. My own survivor's guilt testified against me in these extended court trials inside my sister's head.

Becky was twenty/four when her son, Daniel, was born in New York, the product of a liaison with a poet who had been hospitalized briefly for depression. Father had died the year before in Haifa, sad/dened by his daughter's condition but refreshed by four months in the Holy Land, where he experienced a resurgence of his ancestors' reli/gious faith. Uncle Isidoro had insisted that Becky be given a psychiatric abortion, a proposal I supported—but Mother was dead set against it. She insisted that giving birth would prove therapeutic for Becky and "straighten her out."

Mother had ulterior motives in having her daughter deliver the baby. When Daniel was two, Becky was hospitalized briefly for attacking Mother in Central Park after accusing her of plotting to take Daniel away from her. "Daniel will be my salvation," Mother announced a week before she returned to Haifa with her grandson. When Becky was released from the hospital, she seemed resigned; during a remission she remarked that Israel might be a better place for Daniel to grow up in, as she could not care for him properly in New York. But I felt her pain and loss, and her renewed sense of betrayal.

Mother's absconding with Daniel drew me closer to Becky, and led to my final break with Mother; our relationship had already been severely strained when I married a Brahmin writer in India without consulting my parents. The one time Father met Padma he was so charmed by her that he all but forgave my apostasy on the spot. Mother, who had once confided that she wanted me to have many love affairs and live the grand passion that had been denied her, turned to stone and never forgave. Her last word on the subject was pronounced the last time I saw her alive, in December 1990: "I had nothing personally against your Indian bride, but keep in mind—my father was a *shohet!*" It was the closest we ever came to a reconciliation.

As Mother and I drifted apart, Becky and I became close for the first time, bonded by our sense of victimization by a legacy we only dimly understood and felt powerless to change.

In 1975, two years after I moved to California on the heels of my divorce, I made the single hardest decision of my life: I took Becky out of her ratinfested Broadway hotel room and moved her to Santa Cruz, acting as her selfappointed trustee. The one person who had kept an eye on her, a Guatemalan psychiatric social worker, had died of cancer. I knew Becky would not survive by herself in New York City, and I would have to bear the responsibility for her disintegration the rest of my life.

I set her up in an apartment in the seaside village of Capitola. I paid her rent out of my own pocket, as her Social Security check covered only basic necessities. (Becky spent about half of her monthly check on cigarettes.)

In time, she worked out rituals of attachment to coffee shops and restaurants that tolerated her presence, and she made friends among her New Age Capitola neighbors. Several times she cleaned out the joint bank account I had opened for her, saddling me with a rash of rubber

checks. But in some ways she appeared to be on the mend, and I nur/
tured the hope that in time I could have my sister back as I had once
known her.

At times she became downright oracular. One afternoon I took
Becky to meet Katya, a student counselor at the Santa Cruz college
where I taught. Katya, who is Greek/Mexican and something of a psy/
chic, had two schizophrenic brothers in the hospital. In response to a
probing question from Katya, Becky said, "My mother says it will al/
ways be hard for my brother, but he will be all right in the end." "And
what about my brothers?" Katya cried out, like a supplicant before the
Pythian Oracle. "Speak, Rebecca!" But Becky fell silent and was soon
lost in conversation with her voices.

During Becky's years in California, a window in her inner cell
would occasionally open a crack and shed light on her affliction. Once
she told me she lacked a specific chemical—she had a name for it that I
have forgotten—that enabled people to function in stressful situations.
"Other people get —— from their food, from the air, but I can't pro/
cess it, so I have no aggression," she insisted. "I don't know how to
compete." I reminded her of the time she pummeled Father in Haifa,
and of the aggressive incidents that had led to her expulsion from several
halfway houses and welfare hotels. "Those weren't me," she replied.

Becky has an internal clock that was set the day she received
her first electric shock. The experience scrambled her perceptions
and obliterated—only temporarily, as it turned out—her childhood
memories.

"Becky, look up at those lovely stars," I cry out on a cloudless
Santa Cruz autumn evening. Becky glances up obliquely and replies,
"I haven't seen the stars in twenty/seven years."

"You let them give me the electric shocks," she reproaches me
even today. "You didn't take me out."

Becky's improvement dates from the day Daniel came for a visit
with Mother in 1979. I was returning from New Mexico when they
barged unannounced into her apartment in Capitola. Becky and
Mother had not seen each other in nearly a decade. That night Becky
left her bathtub tap running, and the water poured down the walls and
spoiled $2,000 worth of clothes in the shop below. When the shop
owner threatened to sue, Mother and I divided the cost between us.

A year later, Daniel came to California to stay.

Today Becky's medicines thicken her tongue so she is hardly in/

telligible at times. But her son's presence has helped her express long,
buried feelings and restored her childhood memories, which are intact.
When the three of us are together, I get glimpses of the person she
would have become if she had not fallen ill. She is as stubborn as ever
about her likes and dislikes, and conservative in her politics like most of
my relatives. Although she calls herself a Christian, she never attends
church. She admires authority figures and supports the sitting president
of either party, in the same way she favors Christ over Elohim.

On our outings we have long conversations in which she dem,
onstrates sharp insight on a range of issues and a skewed judgment on
others. I search continually for a pattern or congruence between her nu,
minous perceptions and her monumental blind spots. She likes me to
take her to the movies, but walks out after the first scene of violence or
tenderness, exclaiming, "The hospital does not let me stay and watch."

After Father died in 1961, Becky refused to accept his death, and
frequently asked me if I had heard from him. When our mother died
thirty years later, she took the loss in her stride, as though it had taken
place long before.

During our first meeting after Mother's death, Becky spoke again
of their competition when she was a small girl, and of how Mother had
taken away her aggressiveness. "Mother made us all sick," she said once
when the three of us were together. "We will have to go to the hospital
and have shock therapy to get well." She bears no ill will toward Aunt
Lottie and asks after her regularly, although Lottie refused to receive her
in Guatemala.

Even on her best days, Becky still has her voices. Most of her
conversations are with Richard Nixon, whom she supported unflag,
gingly through Watergate, his resignation and all his earlier and later
travails.

"Nixon again?" I ask when she starts yelling out the window at
him because, she tells me, "he does not understand." We sit in my car
by the Pacific on East Cliff Drive, as Becky smokes with the window
open and her Walkman tuned to her favorite rock,and,roll station.

"That's right." Since she started her conversations with Nixon,
she has put on thirty pounds. Her face is deeply creased and her blond
hair has grayed. But her eyes still sparkle whenever Nixon says some,
thing clever.

"How long have you been talking with him now?"

"Twenty years," she says unhesitatingly, dragging deep on her cigarette. Nicotine, a Canadian therapist discovered, has a calming effect on schizophrenics.

"Whew," I whistle. "Isn't it time to let go of him?" I have the sudden conviction that Becky is keeping Nixon alive, along with God knows how many other schizophrenics who are invested in making him understand, at long last.

She nods and then smiles knowingly. "But you have to understand, Richard Nixon and I have been through a hell of a lot together." I turn to face her, stunned, and she looks back at me and bursts into laughter. I join in, and the waves of robust, real laughter wash over us and drown out, for a moment, the voices of all the saints, villains and U.S. presidents who have haggled, bickered, cajoled, tormented and traded jokes with my sister for the better part of three decades.

(*Postscript:* Conversation with my sister the week after Richard Nixon died:

"Nixon died."

"I know. I can't talk about it."

"But you can still talk to him."

Long pause.

"What do you mean, I can still talk to him? He's dead, isn't he?"

Becky's new companion and sparring partner is a Hollywood agent from the '40s, when we were children in Guatemala.)

CHAPTER XII

GUATEMALA II

"MY SON IS crazier than you!" Uncle Isidoro welcomed me when I returned to Guatemala in 1971, following the death of his eldest son, Jaime, who had died in a freak fishing accident on the Pacific coast. I thought the loss of his firstborn had unhinged his mind at last. But he meant David, his second son, who had become a hippie in Europe and led a guerrilla-theater group in the streets of Guatemala.

At age thirty David had returned from London, where he had written and performed plays in the manner of Antonin Artaud. David had grown his curly black hair down to his shoulders and wore sandals and Moroccan silk tunics. His guerrilla theater group reenacted in broad pantomime the overthrow of Jacobo Arbenz by Colonel Castillo Armas, with the collusion of the U.S. C.I.A. and the United Fruit Company. After the group had performed it several times in front of the National Palace, two of the actors were arrested and thrown into prison. David himself had been spared, probably because of his elder brother's connections when he worked for President Arana Osorio.

"My son is crazier than you!" and an open-handed slap on the counter. Unhinged or not, the gesture was quintessentially Uncle Isidoro's, and it instantly reasserted his patriarchal authority. (After he learned of my marriage in India, Uncle Isidoro sent word he would stop me at customs if I attempted to enter the country with my wife.) His thick head of hair was spun white, his eyes were glazed and sunk into their sockets, the loose folds of skin under his chin shook from the impact of the slap. At age seventy-one, and over the brink of senility, he was struck down with grief, like a great oak whose roots had dried up, but the presence was still there. More than any of his brothers, Uncle Isidoro projected the larger-than-life aura Aharon Haim impressed on his near kin and descendants. Now the senseless death of his eldest son and the alienation of his youngest, and favorite, had raised Uncle Isidoro in my eyes to the realm of Greek tragedy.

When I visited Guatemala again in 1981, David had shorn his long curls; he had also given up drugs and his theater career, and taken charge of the family business. Since the death of Jaime, Uncle Isidoro's heart condition had worsened, and he was in need of constant care.

David had sold the department store and invested the revenue in ware/
houses. At age thirty/five, to the great relief of his parents, David had
come around and decided to follow in the footsteps of his elder brother.
His instincts for self/preservation caused him to move toward the politi/
cal center, together with most of his friends and associates.

On that visit, to my lasting sorrow and regret, I became ac/
quainted with *mala saña,* a fury in the marrow that went far beyond the
mala sangre (revenge killings) of the previous decade. Nothing in my ed/
ucation or my years in Europe and India had prepared me for this level
of violence, which turned neighbor against neighbor, friend against
friend, and provoked respectable heads of family to hire contract killers
to rid themselves of an offending relative over a petty argument or politi/
cal disagreement. In the highlands, the army's war of counterinsurgency
against three guerrilla organizations had cost the lives of more than
40,000 Guatemalans, the great majority of them Indians of Mayan de/
scent. Hundreds of thousands more had fled across the border into
Mexico or were hiding out in the mountains.

David had married a Colombian woman, Luz María, who
gave him two sons. Uncle Isidoro, who had been so adamant in
opposition to my marriage in India and to his eldest son's affair with
a Gentile, weathered David's marriage to a Catholic diplomat's
twenty/four/year/old daughter surprisingly well. The birth of Henry,
who looks the spitting image of his grandfather, right down to the
prominent Levantine nose, melted any lingering resistance, and Luz
María was welcome at the Sabbath table in spite of her decision not to
convert.

Nearly a decade after the death of Jaime, Aunt Lottie remained
beyond consolation. Like my proud Israeli cousin Nehama, she had
made a vocation of mourning for her firstborn and favorite son. "Luz
María is a fine daughter/in/law," Aunt Lottie said softly, her eyes small
and distant across the Sabbath table. "And little Henry has brought the
first sunlight into our lives since the tragedy. But too much of my life
ended with Jaime's passing and your uncle's heart condition, which re/
quires my constant attention, day in and day out. Nothing can rekindle
the light that went out the day Jaime died."

Uncle Isidoro sat every morning in his son's office, shaking his
full head of silver hair over the atrocities he found in the Guatemalan
papers. The kidnapping and murder of several Jewish businessmen ag/
gravated Uncle Isidoro's symptoms of senile dementia. Every morning

he asked his driver to take him to "the house by the windmill," where he was born.

On his eighty-fifth birthday Uncle Isidoro's three sisters sent him a cassette tape crammed with old Ladino and Hebrew songs and pungent reminiscences of their impoverished youth in Jerusalem. "*Ti ricordras* [do you remember] *Nissimico,*" Reina the eldest asks in Ladino, "how cold it was that winter, and you ran barefoot through the snow to cure your blisters?" She then reminds him of the date jam they prepared with their father to sell to the neighbors, and of the raising of the tabernacle on Succoth. "Do you still raise a *succah,* Nissimico?" Rachel the youngest follows with a gentle rebuke, punctuated with sighs. "All is forgiven, older brother. You are the only one left to us, and we pray every Sabbath that you will return home soon to receive your blessing." Simha adds pointedly, "You know your place is here in the family grave site on the Mount of Olives. Think what a pity it will be, Nissimico, if the Messiah's arrival finds you buried on foreign soil."

The voices of my three aunts are as melodious and sturdy as on the evening they read me Yitzhak Moshe's testament in Aunt Reina's apartment.

Uncle Isidoro plays the tape again and again, singing along with his younger sisters, nodding his head and talking back at them, as his eyes fill with tears.

On my previous visit to Guatemala, when Uncle Isidoro was still lucid, I had shown him my great-grandfather's testament, which he had not looked at in more than fifty years. "There are things in this life," he had said, shaking his head, "that we can never comprehend."

II

In March 1993 I tracked down Uncle Moshe to his shoe store in one of the bustling, high-crime quarters of Guatemala City, sealed off by a brown pall of diesel fumes and the nerve-racking din of bus and truck traffic. At seventy-three, Moshe is the last surviving male Perera of his generation. I found him bowed over his desk, his graying head buried in his father's prayer book, which he had brought with him from Jerusalem in 1955. Although we had not seen each other in nearly two decades, Uncle Moshe recognized me at once, and appeared not at all put out by my unannounced visit. It was as if he had been expecting me. I was relieved to discover that, despite Aunt Simha's poor opinion of him as a Torah student, Uncle Moshe was coherent and in full possession of his wits, and his childhood memories were nearly intact.

Not a single customer entered the store during our hour-long interview as he recollected in detail his early years in Montefiore, more than a generation after my father was born. Uncle Moshe drew me a map of Mishkenot Sha'ananim with the windmill, Yosef Peretz's bakery and communal cistern, the Montefiore synagogue and the Pizanty and Perera homes nearby, including the small apartment where he and his brothers and sisters were born. He even drew me a *lonchera* (lunch container) in which his father carried chickpeas, rice, meat and vegetables when the family visited the Old City. Aharon Haim had left for Alexandria when Moshe was two, and his memories of him are few and fragmentary. He remembers a large trunk his father kept under the bed, from which he would draw prayer books and *tallithim,* his father's amulets and other religious accoutrements.

Moshe said that of the original Montefiore only the windmill and a huge old eucalyptus tree still stand, but he praised Teddy Kollek for having restored the neighborhood to its original understated grandeur, save for the missing cistern and Peretz's bakery.

Moshe informed me that he had donated all his father's and grandfather's manuscripts and books to Hebrew University in 1954, except for the wine-stained prayer book he kept always by his side. Inside the front cover Aharon Haim had inscribed family births, marriages, and deaths in old Hebrew, to which Uncle Moshe had appended, in modern Hebrew, the dates and places of more recent family events, including the births and marriages of his two sons. Moshe had inherited his elder sister Simha's vocation as family chronicler.

Uncle Moshe confirmed that my father and mother had traveled to the New World with Greek passports arranged by his brother Alberto.

"I traveled here on an Israeli passport in 1955," Uncle Moshe recalled, "and was called a Turk even though Israel had already been a state for several years. I worked with your cousin Jaime in a *kenaf* plant we started, to produce burlap sacks for coffee and other export crops. After Jaime died in 1972, the plant closed down and I bought this shoe store."

When I invited Uncle Moshe to lunch to continue our interview, he turned me down cold. "Oh no, I have to be here in the store. I go out for only a half hour at midday." I turned toward the salesgirls, who had stood idly by the shoe-stocked counters for the past hour, puzzling over our conversation. With no clients to attend to, their chief function appeared to be decorative.

When I passed the store an hour later I caught a glimpse of Uncle Moshe at his second-floor desk, bowed over his father's prayer book. At seventy-three, amid the din and distraction of Guatemala City, Uncle Moshe was still working on his Torah lessons.

III

All the important events in my life eventually circle back to the scene of my second circumcision, when my father looked on as Rabbi Musan lifted his *mohel*'s knife to remove the flap of foreskin that had survived the gentile Doctor Quevedo's bungled job, may his name and memory be erased. Mother informed me years later that this had been his first circumcision and that he had performed it with a book open by his side.

"I pleaded with your father that he should wait until you were older, that the *brit* could scar you for life, but he would not listen. After Rabbi Musan spoke to him, his heart turned to stone. It had become a question of law—Halakhah—and you must remember how many generations of your father's family—"

"And yours?" I interjected.

"Yes, my family too—had lived and died by the Torah and Talmud."

I did not believe in Mother's protestations. She was after all a fatalist, a creature of the *ayin hara*. I did not doubt they had both conspired in my second mutilation.

Father died before I had a chance to question his motives. Was it Halakhah, or was it a working out of the guilt he bore on his shoulders for having defied his grandfather's testament? I know from Mother that when he arrived in Guatemala, Father had made a big to-do over turning a new leaf and putting behind him centuries of what he called Kabbalistic superstition. As proof of his modernity, Father chose to flout the custom of sending for a *mohel* from Mexico when a boy was born to a member of the Sephardic community.

. . .

IN 1981 I had a chance encounter with one of Father's former Talmud students. Marcos Cohen, who had followed Father to Guatemala,
opened a store in the southern coastal town of Mazatenango. I remembered him as a cheerful sort who sang the old Sephardic *romanzas* with
flair when he accompanied us to the seashore. He was also an accomplished raconteur whose eyes always moistened with remembrance
when he told stories of his Jerusalem youth.

There was another side to this story, as I learned from the family
gossip mill. Shortly after he arrived in Guatemala he fell in love with
and married a gentile woman from the coast. Rather than move to the
capital and risk the Sephardic community's censure, Cohen had decided to open a business in Mazatenango and raise his family there.

I was traveling the countryside with a friend when we passed
Cohen's store. Although I had not seen him in nearly thirty years, he
recognized me and invited me inside for a Coke.

"In Jerusalem, I was your father's student at the Talmud
Torah," he said, matter-of-factly. "Your father was a good teacher, and
he imbued us with a love of Torah. He was also a Zionist who lectured
us on the importance of building a strong Eretz Israel."

"Then why did he leave?" I asked him. "Why did you?"

"You have to remember the times," Cohen said. "There was
terrible poverty. Your father nearly starved when he escaped to Syria
to evade the Turkish draft, and that was something he never forgot.

Marcos Cohen and the author, 1981 (Jean Marie Simon)

After your uncles left for America, I think he became envious of their success, of all the money they were making; or he thought they were making. The reality was different, as he soon found out." Cohen shrugged his shoulders mournfully, surrounded by stacks of yard goods in the only Jewish-owned business on the coast. "As we all found out."

After marrying a Gentile, Cohen had the last word. Not only did he prosper in this remote, unpromising coastal outpost; he did well enough to send his two sons and a daughter to college in the States, where they embarked on successful careers in government and international relations.

"So you think my father felt guilty for leaving the Holy Land?" I asked Cohen.

"I have no doubt he did," he said. "After all he was a teacher of Talmud and a Zionist. He taught us all about our prophetic destiny in Eretz Israel, and then he got up and left."

WITH THE HINDSIGHT of over half a century, I swoop down again on the scene of the second circumcision. What thoughts went through my father's head as Rabbi Musan raised his blade? Was he moved by the look of terror in my tender eyes, or by my astonished howls of pain? Or had he turned to stone, as Mother claimed? What dark memory of tribal sacrifice stirred deep in Father's heart? For all his stated intention to shed superstition and embrace modernity, was he capable of offering up my manhood at the altar of his ancestors' God? Or was his heart so twisted by his grandfather's excommunication of his father that he wanted to put an end to the Perera line by castrating, symbolically, the first fruit of his loins?

Today I know Father was ultimately relieved that I had survived my early childhood years and the dark family dramas he acted out on them. The last time we met was in Ann Arbor, where he, Becky and Mother had visited me shortly before they left for Israel. I took them to a lakefront beach outside of town, where we conversed about my plans to study for a doctorate in English and Spanish literature. I also told Father, outside of Mother's hearing, that I was in love with Padma, the Indian writer he had met briefly in New York and been enchanted by. Suddenly Father moved close and placed his head on my groin. He heaved a deep sigh.

"*Ya mi hize viejo,*" he said in Ladino, which he rarely spoke. "I am old. It is your time now. Look after your mother and sister."

Five months later he died in Haifa.

My father's legacy weighed so heavily on my shoulders, I made a decision in my twenties not to father children, for fear they would inherit the family curse my sister and I have had to grapple with and which I only dimly understood at the time. By remaining childless, I have internalized my father's unarticulated desires to end the Perera line, and paid the penalty exacted by my great-grandfather. Just as Rabbi Levinger would punish Hasan for having been born of the seed of Ishmael, I have done penance for my father's transgression in having sired me in a foreign land. I am the last of the Pereras. But it does not end there.

I am the first of the Pereras.

EPILOGUE

IN THE SPRING of 1992 I received a telephone call from Alan Berliner, a young filmmaker who was showing *Intimate Stranger*, his prize-winning portrayal of his grandfather Joseph Cassuto, at the Sephardic Film Festival in New York City. He said he had found among his grandfather's papers a letter postdated June 8, 1949, in Alexandria, Egypt. "The letter," Alan Berliner said, "has your letterhead and signature, and I have been waiting for years to meet you so I can return it to you."

Bewildered, I asked Berliner to read the letter on the phone. It turned out to be an application to Guatemala's minister of the interior for a passport so the letter writer could travel to Guatemala to be with his father, Alberto Perera, who had divorced his mother in 1939.

"I was not in Alexandria in 1949," I said to Berliner. "I was a junior high school student in Brooklyn. And Alberto Perera is my uncle, not my father."

"I also have your birth certificate," Berliner said, and read out the place and date on the document: Guatemala City 1932, two years before I was born.

I decided this was one of Uncle Alberto's scams. He had evidently used my name without my knowing it to get someone a false passport. Just like him!

We made arrangements to meet at the film festival the following day.

Before meeting with Berliner I saw his film. In a brilliant montage of interviews, family and archival footage and photographs, Berliner traces the story of his grandfather, a cotton trader from Alexandria who struck up a relationship with Japanese importers prior to World War II. In the early forties Cassuto had moved with his family to America, as had many of his coreligionists, and they settled for a time in Brooklyn. Cassuto is pictured as a vain, dapper businessman and an indifferent father and provider who loved to dress in white and managed to hog the center in every family and business photograph. After the war, Joseph Cassuto reestablished ties with his old Japanese friends at the Nichimen Corporation. He was brought to Japan, where he was hosted extravagantly as an old friend and supporter of the postwar Japanese recovery. The film shows images of Joseph Cassuto in a kimono, surrounded by geishas who wait on him hand and foot. He is a father figure to Japanese junior/level managers, who seek his counsel and shower him with favors.

In the meantime, his family in Brooklyn hardly ever sees him. Joseph Cassuto discourages his daughter Regina—Alan's mother—from attending college and pursuing her longed/for career in the theater. She becomes a travel agent instead, and Cassuto nearly disowns her after she marries an Ashkenazi he considers beneath her. Some of the best and funniest voice/overs in the film are Berliner's father's earthy put/downs of his father/in/law, played against Cassuto's extravagant receptions in Tokyo.

Before I meet Alan and his mother, Regina, I know we will be friends. A capricious fate has brought us together. With just a few changes of locale and family statistics, Berliner's film could as easily have been about my uncle Alberto. Joseph Cassuto and Alberto Pe/rera, who were evidently acquainted, were brothers under the skin.

After the showing I seek out Alan Berliner and shake his hand. He is nearly a generation younger than I am, but he has the seasoned melancholy of an old Jewish soul. His mother, Regina, is lovely in a wistful, *vieux monde* manner that reminds me of my great aunt Perla. (Unlike her son, she appears to be a full/blown romantic.)

"I counted Pereras among my friends in Alexandria," she tells me. She was too young to have known my grandfather, so I assume she meant some other Pereras.

Alan takes out the letter and birth certificate, which he has slipped inside a plastic sheet. The jolt of seeing the blue letterhead, and a signature not unlike mine, jogs my memory. Of course! Uncle Al/berto's "illegitimate" son. Only the year before, my cousin Penina asked me in Tel Aviv if I had ever met Uncle Alberto's son by his first wife, whom she calculated to be about my age. She had no idea what his name was.

That same evening I called my sister in California. She was not much help. "I don't think I have an uncle Alberto," she said. "And I know I don't have a cousin Victor Perera."

At our next meeting a month later, Becky dug into her memory and came up with the family story, although she herself had never met Uncle Alberto. She repeated to me the scandal of how Alberto had found his wife in bed with another man divorced her and disowned her son, saying the child wasn't his, and sent them back to Alexandria. They divorced years later.

Victor Perera obviously believed himself to be Alberto's son. If his claim held up, then my first cousin was the legitimate, firstborn Victor Perera, and I was the usurper. I doubted, however, that he was still alive.

Two months later I got a call from Alan Berliner. He told me his mother had been in London, and had met with my cousin Victor Perera. They had been playmates in Alexandria, where she had known him as Toto. That is why she had not made the connection when Alan introduced us.

The story was getting out of hand. I had met a number of other Victor Pereras over the years, none of whom were my relations: There was the Venezuelan physicist who fell in love with my girlfriend; the Sinhalese Victor Perera who ran a hotel in Sri Lanka; the two columns of Vitor Pereiras in the Lisbon phone book, none of whom I bothered to call. And the strangest of all, the Victor Perera I found in the Jerusalem phone book. He spoke no English and was immediately suspicious of my broken Hebrew. "Who are you, really?" he kept asking. "What is the real purpose of this call?" I concluded that my Jerusalem namesake was an agent of Mossad.

This Victor Perera, on the other hand, had a real claim on my name, and to some extent on my identity as well.

On the telephone, Regina told me about her childhood friend Toto. His mother, a family friend, had remarried in Cairo, and had been very protective of Toto. Now, after a thirty-year hiatus, a mutual friend had put them in touch, and Regina and Cousin Victor had met for dinner in London with his wife, Jean. Victor and his wife had no children of their own, because she was barren. They had two adopted sons.

What does my cousin Victor do? I ask her, wondering if he still worked in cotton.

"He is the London agent for Limoges, the French chinaware company. He does very well at it, and they are comfortably off."

I imagined Victor as corpulent and bald.

"Not at all," Regina corrects me. "He has kept in good trim and has all his hair, which has only begun to gray. Toto—I mean Victor— is quite healthy and robust."

"Did you tell him about me?"

"Not at the restaurant, because I had not made the connection. But I have written him a letter, and sent him your article on Alexandria.* I think he will appreciate it."

Regina offered to send me a photo taken by Victor's wife, of their dinner party at the London restaurant. I hesitated before asking her to send it to me.

This will decide it, I thought. If he looks like a Perera, he is the rightful first heir to my grandfather's name. If not, he is the usurper.

The photo arrived a week later. Victor Perera has the wide forehead and broad chin of a Perera. In fact, he strikingly resembles his father, the firstborn son of Aharon Haim Perera.

Regina called a week later to say that she had heard from Victor. He was not interested in hearing more *triste* family stories. But he left the door open a crack, and it was up to me to put a wedge in it or let it be.

I have much to talk about with my cousin Victor Perera. From my aunt Simha's memoirs, I know a good deal about his father—probably more than he does. And I know his half sister Esther, whom Victor has never met: another *triste* family story. We have some things to talk about, Victor and I. He is older, and probably has recollections that could shed light on my own early years in Guatemala, and on our grandfather's sojourn in Alexandria. And I imagine he has his own version of the scandal that caused Uncle Alberto to disown Victor and send him and his mother back to Egypt. Victor is, after all, a successful man of business (unlike his father), and a man of the world. We are both survivors, Victor and I.

I will begin by sending him this book.

---

*"Looking for My Grandfather in Alexandria," *Present Tense*, Winter 1983, Vol. 10, No. 2.

BIBLIOGRAPHY

The two works that started me on this journey of discovery were Cecil Roth's classic *History of the Marranos* (1932) and Isaäc da Costa's *Noble Families Among the Sephardic Jews* (1936). Da Costa's landmark study traces the Pere(i)ras to the ancient Abendana lineage of Toledo. The earliest reference I found to my ancestral name was 1373, when Meir Abendanno, son of Abraham, was mentioned in Pilar León Tello's *Judíos de Toledo* (1979), a compilation of transactions and legal activities by the Jews of Toledo published by the Arias Montano Institute. Other evidence may turn up that extends my ancestors' residence in Spain decades and possibly centuries earlier, but they are not likely to contribute much of substance to the biographical record.

For the Pere(i)ras' beginnings in Spain and Portugal I drew, among other older and still useful sources, from Yitzhak Baer (1978), Edmond S. Malka (1977), Meyer Kayserling (1971), Cecil Roth (1932), H. Graetz (1899), H. H. Ben Sasson (1976) and E. H. Lindo (1970). For the fourteenthcentury persecution and mass conversions, the Inquisition and the Expulsion of Jews from Spain and Portugal, I found no more trustworthy and painstaking guide than Henry Charles Lea and his elegant *History of the Spanish Inquisition* (1906). Among contemporary historians, I drew from Henry Kamen (1985), Yosef Yerushalmi (1976), Netanyahu (1966), Américo Castro (1948), Haim Beinart (1967, 1992) and numerous studies published or collected by the Arias Montano Institute in Madrid. Other archives I turned to repeatedly were the Judaica division of the New York Public Library, Hebrew University at Giv'at Ram, Yeshiva University and the Jewish Theological Seminary in New York City; and, of course, the Inquisition files in the Torre de Tombo in Lisbon.

Of the recent general histories of Iberian Jews, I consulted Jane Gerber (1992) on Jews and Visigoths and the Sephardic Golden Age. Howard Sachar's thorough *Farewell España* (1994) is particularly help-ful on the Jewish Golden Age in Spain, the plight of Sephardic Jews in World War II and the recent history of Marranos in Portugal. Sing-erman's (1975) is the most thorough bibliography up to the early 1970s. On Ladino ballads and *romanzas,* my best sources were José Mair Benardete (1981) and Armistead and Silverman (1986). I consulted Saporta y Bejas (1957) and a number of other published collections for the Ladino proverbs and apothegms. *Aki Yerushalaim,* a quarterly ed-ited in Jerusalem by Moshe Shaul, was most helpful on the living Ladino, as spoken in Israel and Turkey. Arias Montano's excellent scholarly journal *Sefarad* and the publications and tapes of conferences by Sephardic House in New York were also useful.

On the Dutch Pereiras I found everything I needed in the Uni-versity of Amsterdam's superb Bibliotheka Rosenthaliana and in the special collection of the Grand Spanish and Portugese Synagogue. Par-ticularly helpful on the Pereiras in Holland were the works of Professors Jonathan I. Israel, Henry Méchoulan (1987), Yosef Kaplan, and Wil-helmina Pieterse on the poet Daniel Levi de Barrios (1968). Professor Yovel Yirmiyahu (1989) was indispensable on the Marrano dissidents Uriel da Costa and Juan del Prado and their role in Spinoza's apostasy and excommunication.

On the baron d'Aguilar, the *Universal Jewish Encyclopedia,* Henry Wilson (1821), Malka and Elkan Adler (1930) all contain substantial biographies that contradict one another on key dates and provenances, as well as on d'Aguilar's place of birth and the origin of his barony. The conflicting accounts perhaps enhance d'Aguilar's mystique more than they detract from a credible biography. Maria Nunes and the baron d'Aguilar (less so his elder son) remain the most elusive of the Pereiras, and almost impossible to pin down historically.

On Jacob Rodrigues Pereira and the Pereire brothers, apart from Jean Autin (1984), I drew from Robert Fynne (1924), Edouard Sé-guin (1847) and the encyclopedias. New revelations on the Rothschild-Pereire imbroglios await the decoding and release of the Rothschild family papers, currently under way.

Joseph Nehama's monumental seven-volume *Histoire des Israél-ites de Salonique (1935–36)* is the most complete history on the Jews of Salonika but not necessarily the liveliest. Michael Molho (1950) proved invaluable on Jewish life in Salonika in the late nineteenth and early twentieth centuries, up to the arrival of the Nazis. Molho's study and his heroic rescue of the tombstones from the Salonika Jewish cemetery (1949) have never been accorded the recognition they deserve.

SELECTED WORKS

Abendana, Isaac. *Discourses of the Ecclesiastical and Civil Polity of the Jews*. London: S. Ballard, 1709.

Adler, Elkan. *History of the Jews of London*. Philadelphia: Jewish Publication Society of America, 1930.

—————. *Jews in Many Lands*. Philadelphia: Jewish Publication Society of America, 1905.

Akí Yerushalayim, Ladino biennial publication by *Sefarad*, Moshe Shaul, ed. Jerusalem.

Alcalay, Ammiel. *After Jews and Arabs*. Minneapolis: University of Minnesota, 1993.

Altibe, David F. "The Holocaust in Salonika," from *Sephardim and the Holocaust*, Solomon Gaon, editor (1987).

Amador De Los Ríos, José. *Historia Social, Política y Religiosa de los Judíos de España y Portugal*, 3 vols. Madrid: Aguilar, 1875–6; rev. ed. 1960.

Angel, Marc D. "The Sephardim of the United States: An Exploratory Study," *American Jewish Year Book*. Philadelphia and New York: Jewish Publication Society of America, 1973.

Armistead, Samuel and Joseph Silverman. *Judeo-Spanish Ballads from the Oral Tradition*. Berkeley: University of California, 1986.

Autin, Jean. *Les frères Pereire: la bonheur d'entreprendre*. Paris: Perrin, 1984.

Avni, Haim. *Spain, the Jews and Franco*. Philadelphia: The Jewish Publication Society of America, 1982.

Baer, Yitzhak. *A History of the Jews in Christian Spain*, 2 vols. Philadelphia: The Jewish Publication Society of America, 1978.

Barnett, R. D., and W. M. Schwab, eds. *The Sephardic Heritage: Essays on the History and Cultural Contribution of the Jews of Spain and Portugal*. 2 vols. London, 1971; Grendon, 1989.

Baron, Salo W. *A Social and Religious History of the Jews*, 2nd ed. New York and Philadelphia: Jewish Historical Society, 1957–58.

Beinart, Haim. *Conversos on Trial: The Inquisition in Ciudad Real*. Jerusalem: Hebrew University, 1981.

—————. *The Records of the Inquisition: A Source of Jewish and Converso History*. Jerusalem: Israel Academy of Sciences and Humanities, 1967.

————. *The Sephardi Legacy.* 2 vols. Jerusalem: Hebrew University, 1992.

Benardete, Mair José. *The Hispanic Culture and Character of Sephardic Jews.* New York: Sepher-Hermon Press, 1982.

————. *Judeo-Spanish Ballads from New York.* Berkeley: University of California, 1981.

Benbassa, Esther. *Une diaspora sepharade en transition: Istanbul, XIXe–XXe siècle.* Paris: Cerf, 1993.

Ben Sasson, Hillel H., ed. *A History of the Jewish People.* Cambridge, Mass.: Harvard University, 1976.

Ben-Zvi, Itzhak. *Eretz Yisrael ve-Yehudeha Tachat ha-Shilton ha-Otomani.* [The Land of Israel and Its Jews Under Ottoman Rule.] Jerusalem: Yad Yitzhak Ben-Tsevi, 727 (1966 or 1967).

————. *The Exiled and the Redeemed.* Philadelphia: Jewish Publication Society, 1957.

Berg, Philip S., ed. and trans. *The Zohar: Parashat Pinhas.* Jerusalem, New York: Research Center of Kabbalah, 1986.

Bernáldez, Andrés. *Memorias del Reinado de los Reyes Católicos.* Madrid edition: Real Academia de la Historia, 1962.

Carmi, T., *Penguin Book of Hebrew Verse.* New York: Penguin, 1981.

Castro, Américo. *España en su historia: Cristianos, Moros y Judíos.* Buenos Aires: Losada, 1948.

————. *The Structure of Spanish History.* Princeton: Princeton University, 1954.

Cohen, Gerson D., ed. and trans. *Sefer ha-Qabbalah: The Book of Tradition.* Philadelphia: Jewish Publication Society of America, 1967.

Cohen, Martin. *Martyr: The Story of a Secret Jew and the Mexican Inquisition in the Sixteenth Century.* Philadelphia: Jewish Publication Society of America, 1973.

Cohen, Robert. "Memorias para os Siglos Futuros: Myth and Memory on the Beginnings of the Amsterdam Sephardi Community." From *Jewish History,* Vol. 2, No. 1, Spring 1987.

Cutler, Allan Harris. *The Jew as Ally to the Muslim: Medieval Roots of Anti-Semitism.* Notre Dame, Indiana: Notre Dame University, 1986.

Da Costa, Isaäc. *Noble Families Among the Sephardic Jews.* London: Oxford University, 1936.

Dias Mas, Paloma. *Los sefardíes: historia, lengua y cultura.* Barcelona: Riopiedras, 1986.

Elazar, Daniel. *The Other Jews: The Sephardim Today.* New York: Basic Books, 1989.

Eliachar, Eliyahu. *Lihyot im Palestinim.* [Living with Palestinians.] Jerusalem: Va'ed 'adat ha⁄Sefardim bi⁄Yerushalayim, 735, 1975.

————. *Living with Jews.* London: Weidenfeld⁄Nicolson, 1983.

———— "The Sephardi Non ⁄Presence." *New Outlook,* January February 1977.

Emmanuel, I. S., and S. A. Emmanuel. *A History of the Jews of the Netherlands Antilles,* 2 vols. Cincinnati: American Jewish Archives, 1970.

Friedenreich, Harriet Pass. *The Jews of Yugoslavia.* Philadelphia, Jewish Pub⁄ lication Society of America, 1979.

Fynne, Robert. *Montessori and Her Inspirers.* London, New York: Longhans, Green and Co., 1924.

Galanté, Abraham. *Histoire des Juifs de Turquie,* 9 vols. (repr.) Istanbul: Isis, 1985.

Gerber, Jane S. *The Jews of Spain: A History of the Sephardi Experience.* New York: Free Press, 1992.

Goitein, S. D. *A Mediterranean Society,* 5 vols. Berkeley and Los Angeles: University of California, 1967–88.

Graetz, H. *History of the Jews.* Philadelphia: Jewish Publication Society of America, 1894.

H. P. Salomon, "A Copy of Uriel da Costa's *Examen dos Tradiçoes Phariseas* located in the Royal Library of Copenhagen," in *Studia Rosenthaliana, Jour⁄ nal for Jewish Literature and History of the Netherlands* xxiv (1990), pp. 153–68.

Halevi, Judah. *Book of the Kuzari.* Fifteenth⁄century Ladino translation. Moshe Lazar, ed. Culver City, Calif.: Labyrinthos, 1990.

————. *Kuzari: The Book of Proof and Argument.* Oxford: East and West Li⁄ brary, 1947.

————. *El Cuzari: Diálogo filosófico de Yehuda Halevi.* Traducido del Arabe al Hebreo por Yehuda Abantibon y del Hebreo al Castellano por Jacob Abendana [1663]. Buenos Aires, 1943.

Hyamson, Albert M. *The Sephardim of England: A History of the Spanish and Portuguese Jewish Community, 1492–1951.* London: Methuen and Co., 1951.

Israel, Jonathan I. *Empires and Entrepôts: The Dutch, the Spanish Monarchy and the Jews, 1585–1713.* London: Roncevert, 1990.

————. *European Jewry in the Age of Mercantilism, 1550–1750.* New York: Ox⁄ ford University, 1975.

————, and Harm den Boer. "William III and the Glorious Revolution in the Eyes of the Amsterdam Sephardi Writers," in *The Anglo⁄Dutch Mo⁄ ment: Essays on the Glorious Revolution and Its World Impact.* Jonathan I. Is⁄ rael, ed. Cambridge: Cambridge University, 1991.

Itshac, Emmanuel, "Los Jidios de Salonique," in David Recanati, ed., *Zikh-ron Saloniki*, 2 vols. Tel Aviv: 1972–86.

Kamen, Henry. *Inquisition and Society in Spain in the Sixteenth and Seventeenth Centuries*. Bloomington: Indiana University, 1985.

Kaplan, Yosef. *From Christianity to Judaism: The Story of Isaac Orobio de Castro*. New York: Oxford University, 1989.

————, ed. *Jews and Conversos, Studies in Society and Inquisition*. Jerusalem: Magnes Press, 1985.

Katz, D. S. "The Abendana Brothers and the Christian Hebraists of Seven-teenth Century England." *Journal of Ecclesiastical History* 40 (1989): pp. 28–52.

————, and J. I. Israel, eds. *Sceptics, Millenarians and Jews*. New York: E. J. Brill, 1990.

Katz, Solomon. *The Jews in the Visigothic and Frankish Kingdoms of Spain and Gaul*. Cambridge, Mass.: Medieval Academy of America, 1937.

Kayserling, Meyer. *Historia dos Judeus em Portugal*. Gabriele Borchardt, trans. São Paulo: Livraria Pioneira, 1971.

Kedourie, Elie, ed. *Spain and the Jews: The Sephardi Experience 1492 and After*. New York: Thames and Hudson, 1992.

La Rochelle, Ernest. *Jacob Rodrigues Pereire: Premier Instituteur des sourds-muets en France: Sa vie et ses travaux*. Paris: Paul Dupont, 1882.

Lea, Henry Charles. *A History of the Inquisition in Spain*, 4 vols. New York: MacMillan Co., 1906.

León Tello, Pilar. *Judíos de Toledo*, 2 vols. Madrid: Arias Montano, 1979.

Levi de Barrios, Daniel. *Triumpho del Govierno Popular y de la Antiguedad Ho-landesa*. 1683. Wilhelmina Pieterse, ed. Amsterdam: Bibiotheka Rosen-thaliana, 1968.

Lewis, Bernard. *The Jews of Islam*. Princeton: Princeton University, 1985.

————, and Benjamin Braude, eds. *Christians and Jews in the Ottoman Empire*, 2 vols. New York: Holmes & Meier, 1982.

Liebman, Seymour B. *Los judíos en Mexico y América Central: Fe, llamas, inquisi-ción*. Mexico: Siglo XXI, 1971.

Lindo, E. H. *The History of the Jews of Spain and Portugal*. London: Longman, Brown, Green and Longman, 1848, reprinted 1970.

Malino, Frances. *The Sephardic Jews of Bordeaux: Assimilation and Emancipation in Revolutionary and Napoleonic France*. Alabama: University of Alabama, 1978.

Malka, Edmond S. *Fiéis Portugueses: Judeus na peninsula Iberica*. Damaia, Portu-gal: Ediçoes Acropole, 1977.

Marin, Edgar. *Vidal et les Siens.* Paris: Seuil, 1989.

Me'am Loez: el gran comentario bíblico sefardí. Maseo, David Gonzalo. Madrid: Editorial Gredos, 1964.

Méchoulan, Henry. *Amsterdam au temps de Spinoza: argent et liberté.* Paris: Presses universitaires de France, 1990.

————. *Hispanidad y Judaismo en Tiempo de Espinoza. Edición de 'La Certeza del Camino' de Abraham Pereyra,* Amsterdam 1666. Salamanca: Universidad de Salamanca, 1987.

————, Yosef Kaplan and Richard H. Popkin, eds. *Menasseh ben Israel and His World.* New York: E. J. Brill, 1989.

Memmi, Albert. *The Pillar of Salt,* trans. by Edouard Roditi. New York: Orion, 1962.

Menéndez Pidal, Ramon. *El Idioma Español en sus Primeros Tiempos.* Madrid: Editorial Voluntad S.A., 1927.

————. *Los españoles en su historia.* Madrid: Espasa-Calpe, 1982.

Menéndez y Pelayo, Marcelino. *Historia de los heterodoxos españoles.* Mexico: Porrúa, 1983.

Michman, Jozeph, ed. *Dutch Jewish History.* 2 vols. Proceedings of the Symposium on the History of the Jews in the Netherlands, 1982. Jerusalem: Tel Aviv University, 1984–1989.

Molho, Michael. "El Cementerio Judío de Salonika." *Sefarad,* IX, 1949. Madrid: Instituto Arias Montano, 1949.

————. *Usos y Costumbres de los Sefardies de Salónica.* Madrid: Arias Montano, 1950.

Nahon, Gérard. "The Sephardim in France," from *The Sephardi Heritage: The Western Sephardim,* Vol. 2, ed. Richard D. Barnett and W. M. Schwab. London, 1989, pp. 46–74.

Nehama, Joseph. *Histoire des Israélites de Salonique,* 7 vols. Salonique: Librairie Molho, 1935–78.

————, and Michael Molho, eds. *In Memoriam: Hommage aux Victimes Juives des Nazis en Grèce.* Part 3. Thessalonique: Communauté Israélite, 1973.

Netanyahu, B. *The Marranos of Spain from Late Fourteenth to Early Fifteenth Centuries,* 2nd ed. New York: American Academy of Jewish Research, 1966.

Papo, Rabbi M. "The Sephardi Community of Vienna," from Josef Fraenkl, ed. *The Jews of Austria.* London: Valentine Mitchell, 1967.

Pereira, Aaron Raphael Haim, with Yitzhak Moshe Pereira. *Sefer Meil kodesh u-vigde yesha: hagahot u-veurim al Etz Hayim ve-Shaar ha-kavanot; Sefer Toledot Aharon u-Moshe.* [A Book Inspiring Sanctity and Salvation: Harvesting the

Light of the Tree of Life and the Gate of Will; a Book of the Generations of Aaron and Moses.] Includes *Efer Yitzhak* by Aaron Pereira. Jerusalem: Ahavot Shalom, 1977.

Pereire, Isaac. *La question religieuse.* Paris: C. Motteroz, 1878.

Pereire, Jacob Rodrigues. *Observations sur les Sourds et Muets, etc.* Published in *Mémoires de Mathematique et du Physique, presentés à l'Académie Royale des Sciences,* 1778.

Perera, Victor. "Encounter: A Visit with an Aged Sheik." *The New York Times,* March 2, 1975.

———. "Columbus and the Jews: A Personal View," *Tikkun,* September/October 1992.

———. *The Conversion* (a novel). Boston: Little, Brown, 1970.

———. "The Conversion," a story. *Commentary.* August 1968.

———. *Last Lords of Palenque: The Lacandon Mayas of the Mexican Rain Forest* (with Robert D. Bruce). Boston: Little, Brown, 1982. Berkeley: University of California, 1986.

———. "Letter from Israel," *New York Times Magazine,* May 5, 1974.

———. *Rites: A Guatemalan Boyhood.* New York: Harcourt, Brace Jovanovich, 1985. Mercury House, 1994.

———. "Uzi Diplomacy: How Israel Makes Friends and Enemies Around the World," *Mother Jones,* July 1985.

Petropoulos, Elias. *Les Juifs de Salonique: In Memoriam.* Paris: Atelier Merat, 1983.

Raphael, David, ed. *The Expulsion 1492 Chronicles.* North Hollywood: Carmi House, 1991.

Rejwan, Nissim. "The Myth of the Black Panthers." *New Middle East,* October 1971.

Rodrigue, Aron. *De l'instruction à l'émancipation: Les enseignants de l'Alliance Israélite Universelle et les Juifs d'Orient, 1860–1939.* Paris: Calmann Levy, 1989.

———. *French Jews, Turkish Jews.* Bloomington: Indiana University, 1990.

Roth, Cecil. *A History of the Jews in England.* Oxford: Clarendon, 1949.

———. *History of the Marranos,* Philadelphia: Jewish Publication Society of America, 1932.

———. *A Short History of the Jewish People.* London: East and West Library, 1969.

Sachar, Howard M. *Farewell España: The World of the Sephardim Remembered.* New York: Alfred A. Knopf, 1994.

Sale, Kirkpatrick. *The Conquest of Paradise.* New York: Alfred Knopf, 1990.

Saporta y Beja, Enrique. *Refranero Sefardí.* Madrid: Arias Montano, 1957.

————. *Salonique et ses Judeo-Espagnols.* 1957

Scholem, Gershon. *Major Trends in Jewish Mysticism.* New York: Schocken, 1961.

————. *Sabbetai Sevi: The Mystical Messiah* Princeton: Princeton University, 1973.

Séguin, Edouard. *J. R. Pereire, Premier Instituteur, etc. Notice sur sa vie et ses travaux: Analyse Raisonnée de sa Méthode.* Paris, 1847.

The Sephardic Journey, 1492–1992. New York: Yeshiva University Museum, 1992.

Sephiha, Vidal. *L'agonie des judeo-espagnols.* Paris: Editions Entente, 1977.

Septimus, Bernard. *Hispano-Jewish Culture in Transition: The Career and Controversies of Ramah.* Cambridge, Mass.: Harvard University, 1982.

Singerman, Robert. *The Jews in Spain and Portugal, A Bibliography.* New York: Garland, 1975.

Stillman, Norman. *The Jews of Arab Lands in Modern Times.* Philadelphia: Jewish Publication Society of America, 1992.

Twersky, Isadore, ed. *A Maimonides Reader.* New York: Behrman House, 1972.

Wilson, Henry. *Wonderful Characters,* Vol. 2, pp. 92–97. London: J. Robins, 1821–1830.

Yehoshua, A. B. *Mr. Mani* (a novel). New York: Doubleday, 1992.

Yehoshua, Jacob. *Ben masorat le-havai be-mishkenot ha-Sefardim bi-Yerushalayim.* [Spiritual Traditions Among the Sephardic Communities in Jerusalem.] Jerusalem: Va'ed 'adat ha-Sefardim bi-Yerushalayim, 1979–1982.

Yerushalmi, Yosef Hayim. *From Spanish Court to Italian Ghetto: Isaac Cardo. A Study in Seventeenth-Century Marranism and Jewish Apologetics.* New York: Columbia University, 1971.

————. *The Lisbon Massacre of 1506 and the Royal Image in the Shebet Yehudah.* Cincinnati: Hebrew-Union College, 1976.

————. *Zakhor: Jewish History and Jewish Memory.* Seattle: University of Washington, 1982.

Yirmiyahu, Yovel. *Spinoza and Other Heretics: The Marrano of Reason.* Princeton: Princeton University, 1989.

INDEX

Italicized page numbers refer to illustrations.

A NOTE ABOUT THE AUTHOR

Victor Perera was born in Guatemala City of Sephardic parents from Jerusalem and has traveled widely in Latin America, Europe, the Middle East and India. He is the author of a novel set in Spain, *The Conversion*, and three books on southern Mexico and Guatemala, *The Last Lords of Palenque* (with Robert D. Bruce), *Rites: A Guatemalan Boyhood* and *Unfinished Conquest: The Guatemalan Tragedy*. Mr. Perera, who teaches journalism at the University of California at Berkeley, has contributed articles and essays to *The New Yorker*, *The Atlantic*, *Harper's*, the *New York Times Magazine*, the *Los Angeles Times* Sunday Opinion page, *The Nation* and other newspapers and journals. He is the recipient of a National Endowment of the Arts writing fellowship, and a Lila Wallace–Reader's Digest Fund writing award.

A NOTE ON THE TYPE

The text of this book has been set in a typeface called Poliphilus. This face is a copy of a roman type that Francesco Griffo cut for the Venetian printer Aldus Manutius in 1499. It was cut by the Monotype Corporation of London in 1923, six years earlier than Bembo, the celebrated and widely used revival of the Aldine type used for Pietro Cardinal Bembo's 1495 treatise *De Aetna*. Thus it appears that before Bembo was cut, the Monotype Corporation had already designed a roman based on another Aldine type—that of *Hypnerotomachia Poliphili*—which was actually Griffo's second version of his roman.

The italic of Poliphilus is called Blado. The italic was cut especially to accompany Poliphilus and was based on a formal italic of the calligrapher and printer Lodovico degli Arrighi—the formal italic having been known as Vincentino. It is named after the Roman printer Antonio Blado, who printed many books in this font, using it as an individual type and not as a subsidiary to the roman.

Composed by ComCom, a division of Haddon Craftsmen,
Allentown, Pennsylvania
Printed and bound by Quebecor Printing, Martinsburg, West Virginia
Designed by Robert Olsson